Phil

The Death of Intimacy:
Barriers to Meaningful Interpersonal Relationships

Pre-publication
REVIEWS,
COMMENTARIES,
EVALUATIONS . . .

"**B**rown's book is must reading for anyone involved in counseling either couples or individuals who are dealing with issues related to their intimate relationships. The book will also be valuable for those who want to learn more about their own intimate relationships. Brown blends valuable theoretical information with relevant practice wisdom to shed new light on such significant issues as the role of differences in male and female socialization on the ability to form and sustain intimate relationships, the implications of sex and sexuality for intimate relationships, and how couples become 'coupled' and 'uncoupled.'"

Richard L. Edwards, PhD
Dean and Professor,
The University of North Carolina
at Chapel Hill School of Social Work

"**P**hil Brown takes a scholarly and yet impassioned look at the loss of intimacy in our society. His ability to integrate biological, psychological, interactional, and social theories helps us to understand couples in context. The book speaks to us as counselors, but also to that personal part of us that longs for our own authentic emotional experiences."

Lawrence Shulman, MSW, EdD
Professor, School of Social Work,
Boston University

"**D**r. Brown captures the very essence of today's relational disease, the decaying of human intimacy. His book reads clearly with the aides of pertinent case illustrations and excellent quotations as fertilizers to deepen our understanding of many interrelated, complex issues. *The Death of Intimacy* is a definite source of reading for professionals in the field of marriage and family therapy. The book can benefit many college-aged people in finding pathways to more enduring intimate relations. It will also provide many clients with the lenses needed to examine the relational patterns that are dysfunctional to their growth and healing processes. A book worthy to be considered as the year's best on the subject."

Daniel B. Lee, PhD
Professor of Family Therapy
and Clinical Social Work,
Loyola University of Chicago

"**A**t last this long-neglected but important subject has been given the thoughtful, well-researched, and well-documented attention it deserves. As Dr. Brown and his collaborators inform us in this warm and witty book, healthy intimacy has the potential to alleviate a myriad of emotional and relationship problems, while the growing cultural barriers to its expression contribute significantly to these problems. Dr. Brown has accomplished a monumental task in the way he has presented this serious subject in a scholarly yet accessible style."

Dr. Robert L. Barker
The Catholic University of America,
Washington, DC

The Death of Intimacy
Barriers to Meaningful Interpersonal Relationships

HAWORTH Marriage & the Family
Terry S. Trepper, PhD
Senior Editor

New, Recent, and Forthcoming Titles:

The Death of Intimacy
Barriers to Meaningful Interpersonal Relationships

Philip M. Brown, LCSW, PhD

The Haworth Press
New York • London • Norwood (Australia)

The Haworth Press, Inc., 10 Alice Street, Binghamton, NY 13904-1580

Library of Congress Cataloging-in-Publication Data

Brown, Philip M., LCSW, PhD.
    The death of intimacy : barriers to meaningful interpersonal relationships / Philip M. Brown.
      p. cm.
    Includes bibliographical references and index.
    ISBN 1-56024-926-9 (acid free paper).
    1. Man-woman relationships. 2. Intimacy (Psychology) 3. Sex. 4. Family. I. Title
HQ801.B866 1994
306.7–dc20   94-20593
                                                                       CIP

To my parents,
Maurice L. and Louella G. Brown,
who taught me my earliest lessons
about what it means to love and be loved.

ABOUT THE AUTHOR

Philip M. Brown, LCSW, PhD, a marital and family therapist for over 12 years, is Associate Professor at the Tulane University School of Social Work in New Orleans, Louisiana, where he teaches graduate courses in family therapy. He is the author of numerous professional articles and has presented numerous papers and workshops on couples therapy, family systems, and interpersonal relationships.

CONTENTS

Acknowledgements

No one can complete a project like this without the help of a great many people. I am deeply grateful for the assistance of my family, friends, students, and colleagues who have all encouraged and supported me throughout the two years that were required to complete this project.

Special thanks are due my wife, Beth Stinson-Brown, MSW, BCSW, who read and reviewed not only each chapter, but numerous drafts as well. Her unfailing love, support, and faith sustained me during those times when I began to feel overwhelmed by the immensity of this undertaking.

I also appreciate the excellent contributions of my research assistant, Angie Rice, BCSW, for gathering innumerable articles and books as well as for extensive reading and editing. Her dedication throughout the course of this project, not to mention co-authoring Chapter 2, was exemplary.

Thanks also to my co-author of Chapter 7, Lynn Finnegan, ACSW, who provided invaluable case material that exemplified so many of the theoretical issues discussed throughout the book. I will long remember our discussions and am glad that she "hung in there" when the going got tough.

Particular thanks to my brother and ace editor, Dennis Brown, who stayed up late many nights to review and edit eight of my nine chapters and gave generously of his time and energy without complaint.

Thanks to my good friend and colleague, Dr. Robert L. Barker for his honest and insightful editorial input as well as unflagging support. (I really cannot imagine repeating this process sixteen more times.)

Kudos to the graduate students at Tulane University School of Social Work who have given me extensive feedback about this work during its various stages, and to Dean Margaret Campbell for her financial support.

I would also like to thank my special friends and colleagues Peter Schmidt, Bob Webster, Jean White, Cindy Gagnier, Georgeanna Tryban, Lynn Keeton, and Hilary Weaver for their critical feedback and support during the various stages of this book's unfolding.

I am also grateful to The Howard Tilton Library at Tulane and the Chebeague Island Library, Chebeague Island, Maine.

And last, but certainly not least, I wish to thank the children, teachers, principals, and staff of Jack Elementary School in Portland, Maine who provided me with vivid memories of young children's developmental stages as discussed in Chapter 3.

Philip M. Brown
New Orleans, LA

Introduction

The need to form and sustain an emotionally intimate relationship is an essential developmental task which completes our personal identity as well as mitigates our larger sense of existential loneliness. However, within our rapidly changing social context, complex social barriers increasingly interfere with this coupling process.

Many theorists believe that the extent and nature of our ability to form healthy interpersonal relationships rests largely on our early developmental experiences. They argue that these primordial attachments potentially shape subsequent relationships with both sexes in terms of dependencies, emotional proximity, interpersonal style, perceived needs, etc. From a family systems perspective, how do the dynamics of the family system affect the individual's ability to initiate and sustain healthy interpersonal relationships? From a macro-perspective, how does the socio-cultural context of our society shape and influence individuals' ability to initiate and sustain meaningful interpersonal relationships?

Historically, social convention has dictated that certain rites of passage be observed prior to having and raising children. Since the family unit is the primary socialization agent in most cultures, this unit must necessarily be grounded in the values and worldview of that particular culture. However, social roles and values appear to be shifting in the 1990s. Today, having children out of wedlock not only lacks social stigma in many circles, it has even achieved a level of social acceptability. What are the implications of these changing social mores?

In virtually every culture known to humankind, courting rituals are an integral precursor to becoming a couple. Examples range from primitive tribal rituals which involve symbols and behaviors unique to that tribe (and thereby differentiate it from other tribes) to the complex social rituals characteristic of American society in the post-industrial age. However, in each case, the central purpose of such rituals is to affirm cultural values through the use of social protocols. Such rituals also act as rites of passage from one status to another and further establish that couples' place within the culture. Moreover, it is the ultimate intention of virtually every culture to sustain its existence by systematically reproducing itself both literally and figuratively.

Individuals come together for a complex variety of reasons: physical and emotional attraction, mutually unmet needs, perceived similarities/differences, relative status and values, cultural/familial expectations, etc. What is the underlying significance of these motives? However, to suggest that "coupling" is motivated solely by "romantic love" would be at once shortsighted and inaccurate. How have dating and courtship changed in the 1990s?

Christopher Lasch (1979) observed that the widespread acceptance of the birth control pill was revolutionary in that it freed women from their fear of pregnancy and liberated sex from its former constraints. Consequently, male-female relationships could focus on the purely narcissistic pleasures of sex without worrying about responsibility or emotional attachment. Unfortunately, the notion of sex without commitment effectively trivialized physical intimacy and further dissociated it from emotion. Has this shift in the nature and purpose of sexuality contributed to an increasing incidence of sexual dysfunction? What is the current relationship between sex and intimacy?

Given the dramatically altered social context of pairing in today's society coupled with widespread developmental traumas (physical and sexual abuse, neglect, psychological abuse, etc.), the stage is set for a myriad of pathological pairings. The spiraling incidences of psycho-emotional disorders such as depression, anorexia-bulimia, and borderline personalities are having a potentially devastating impact on healthy coupling. Well-functioning marriages require not only well-balanced individuals, but also well-balanced relationships.

Why is marital intimacy more elusive today than ever before? Where do these couples go when their relationship is not working? Often, nowhere. The human ability to deny that a serious problem actually exists appears to be substantial indeed. Some partners turn to friends for assistance. However, with a growing scarcity of close friendships, many couples are seeking professional help. Chapter 7 looks at issues anad conflicts faced by couples in therapy. Case examples which illustrate prominent conflicts and issues are analyzed to shed additional light on the struggle for intimacy among couples today.

Nevertheless, despite their best efforts, there are times when couples necessarily part. At times, this is a healthier choice for both partners. However, parting has its price. Disengagement from any significant emotional attachment is a traumatic experience (even if, and sometimes especially if, the relationship was a dysfunctional one such as a co-dependent with an alcoholic spouse). What is the process that individuals and couples must undergo during marital separation and divorce? How many marriages terminate in a healthy, or even amicable manner? How does one cope with the persistence of emotional attachment when the relationship is no longer a viable reality?

As work and career assume an increasingly important role in people's lives, what is the changing nature and significance of interpersonal relationships in the workplace? What else do individuals need to know in order to better understand the larger search for identity, relatedness, and meaning? Finally, based on past and current trends, what is the future of intimate relationships?

This book focuses on heterosexual couples. For the purposes of this analysis, a couple refers to an intimate pairing of two individuals who:

1. experience a mutual emotional interest and bonding;
2. have some sort of history together;
3. are mutually interdependent;
4. have a distinct sense of identity as a dyad;
5. hold a shared commitment to a continued relationship;
6. share hopes/dreams for a common future.

Written from a multi-systems/ecological perspective, this analysis of intimate relationships examines the dynamic interplay between individuals and the larger systems of which they are a part (e.g., couple, family, culture, and society). In contrast to the numerous self-help books which offer formulas for achieving the "perfect relationship," *The Death of Intimacy* instead seeks to challenge the reader's underlying beliefs and conceptualizations about intimate relationships within the ever-changing social context.

Philip M. Brown
New Orleans, LA

REFERENCE

Lasch, C. 1979. *The culture of narcissism.* New York: W. W. Norton & Company, Inc.

Chapter 1

Identity and Intimacy

Change is perhaps the single most salient characteristic in most of our lives. The ever-accelerating pace and overwhelming complexity of modern life frequently engenders a vast array of stressors and stress-related illnesses. Life sometimes seems like a runaway train roaring down the tracks along a mountainside uncertain where, when, and how it will finally stop. As in this metaphor, pervasive feelings of danger and lack of control characterize what many people experience when thinking about their own lives and the lives of those most dear to them. How can this train be stopped? What is its final destination? Is it moving too fast to safely jump off even if one should? What are the relationships among the train's passengers? In a very real sense, this is a book about runaway trains and the ways in which that context affects the identities and interpersonal relationships of the passengers.

THE STRUGGLE FOR IDENTITY

How does our changing cultural landscape affect individual identity and our ability to form meaningful interpersonal relationships? To begin with, one needs to understand what is meant by identity. Identity is a conviction of self-sameness–a bridge over the discontinuities which invariably creep or crash into our lives. It is the link between the child of 7 and that same person at 17; between the 17-year-old and the 70-year-old self to come. In brief, it is our sense of personal history and anticipated future.

This sense of continuity (the belief that who we now are is directly related to who we once were and who we will someday become) is crucial to one's ongoing sense of personal identity. The presence of other people who have shared our past or who at least can affirm our memory of the past is essential. Individuals need others to bear witness to their personal history, others who are willing to take note of their passage through life's many transitions. Long-term relationships reassure us that our past did indeed take place and that those experiences helped create a context for the person we are today (Kilpatrick, 1975).

Identity is not a static achievement, but a dynamic and continuous process of consolidation and reorganization. It is an ongoing synthesis of many interests and choices which creates one's unique and distinctive style–but a synthesis that never stops. A healthy identity maintains a balance between continuity and change.

Noted anthropologist, Edward T. Hall (1976), further asserts that despite massive evidence to the contrary, Western society labors under a number of delusions, two of which are that people are sane and that life makes sense. Having been taught to think linearly rather than comprehensively, people do this not through conscious design or because they are unintelligent or incapable, but because of the way deep cultural undercurrents structure life in subtle yet highly consistent ways that are not consciously formulated. Individuals live fragmented, compartmentalized lives in which contradictions are carefully sealed off from each other.

These factors are further complicated by the accelerated nature of modern life. Toffler (1970) addressed this issue when he observed that individuals' relationships with people, places, and things are increasingly fragile and impermanent. Individuals' relationships with the organizational/institutional environment, like their relationships with ideas or information are also increasingly short-lived. Over time, these relationships weave the fabric of social experience.

"Transience" is the rate at which these relationships turn over in one's life. If "identity integrity" is based upon one's choices and commitments and ability to stick to them and if one's individual relationships with these five central aspects (things, places, people, organizations, and ideas) is increasingly brief, then the task of constructing and maintaining a stable sense of identity becomes vastly more difficult.

The rate at which change now occurs is staggering. For example, Americans now relocate their households more than twenty times during the course of their lifetime. Many of these moves represent major transitions across the country and throughout the world. The problem is that much of one's identity is rooted in a particular regional context in which ongoing relationships have been formed with particular places, people, things, and organizations. As a result, these transitions also uproot psychic and emotional moorings. Individuals' accustomed and ongoing sense of who they are is often severely disrupted.

In many cases, individuals carefully pack their treasured personal belongings only to have them stuffed into bins on large moving trucks and dragged halfway across the country by total strangers. For most people, the reason these belongings are so important frequently has more to do with sentimental than monetary or utilitarian value. These are the visible links to one's past. They are associated with the people, places, and things long since gone from one's life. These personal belongings help individuals affirm that who they are is directly connected to the person they once were.

Even more than material belongings, long-term relationships with significant others affirm one's identity and experiences in ways that nothing else can. Toffler (1970) describes spouses as "portable friends" who carry essential aspects of their spouse's personal identity with them. Consequently, it is readily apparent why the loss of a spouse or significant other is so emotionally traumatic. Beyond just losing an intimate emotional attachment, individuals are literally losing a part of themselves, a part of their past, as well as a part of their anticipated future (including their personal hopes and dreams).

Erik Erikson (1968) asserts that identity requires a threefold continuity; a continuity of significant others; a continuity with one's past self; and a continuity with one's anticipated future. With such rapid turnover in our significant interpersonal relationships, it is no wonder that many people are left with a vague feeling of belonging nowhere and to no one. The nomadic features of modern life loosen our sense of identification with particular places, people, organizations, and things. Moreover, the transient nature of these relationships has a profound impact on our individual and collective existence.

Erikson (1963) also believes that identity precedes intimacy. He feels that the requisite self-abandon necessary for a meaningful relationship with another requires a fairly well-developed sense of self. Intimacy requires identity, but identity is in turn strengthened by intimacy. Until a person risks a relationship, identity remains tentative and ill-defined. Each new relationship forces us to define ourselves a little more clearly. The risk lies in making the wrong choices. It is this fear of wrong choices that often shapes the ways in which one approaches potentially significant interpersonal relationships.

LONELINESS

A predictable adjunct to this pervasive sense of rootlessness is the widespread social and emotional isolation Robert Weiss (1980) explores in his insightful book, *Loneliness*. Why is it that loneliness is a condition that virtually all have experienced but very few understand? To paraphrase Webster, loneliness refers to being solitary and/or isolated; it means unfrequented or uninhabited; it denotes longing for friends, company, or companionship; it is associated with unhappiness.

The identity associated with one's lonely self is quite different from one's normal self. This is because other people (especially significant others) carry a part of our identity with them, which reaffirms who and what we are. This social identity is a crucial part of our definition of self and in times of social anonymity, accompanied by a metaphysical loss of home, it is no wonder that our individual and collective senses of who we are remain uncertain.

Yet, the response of loneliness to just the right kind of relationship is remarkable. Given the establishment of the needed relationships, loneliness will vanish almost instantly and without a trace. One was lonely but suddenly one is lonely no more (Weiss, 1980).

Loneliness implies a sense of separateness, but has also come to imply a way of rediscovering and reconnecting with oneself. Out of the inescapable pain of social and emotional isolation have emerged some of the most significant insights into one's truer self. At times, these insights born of painful introspection reframe our sense of who we are as well as our place in this world. Unfortunately, while we recognize the merits of such an existential journey, most of us will do almost anything to avoid the excruciating pain of our own loneliness.

Sullivan once described loneliness as "the exceedingly unpleasant and driving experience connected to the inadequate discharge of human intimacy" (1953:290). In loneliness, there is a drive to rid oneself of distress by integrating a new relationship or regaining a past relationship; whereas in depression, there is instead a surrender to it. However, loneliness can be distinguished from grief, which refers to that syndrome of shock, anger, protest, sadness, and despair resulting from traumatic loss. Grief will subside with time, but loneliness, in contrast, will be compounded by time unless the needed intimate or social relationships are acquired.

Loneliness appears to be a response to the absence of some particular type of needed relationship (as well as what that relationship provides). In many instances, it is a response to the absence of an intimate emotional attachment. It may also be a response to the absence of meaningful friendships or other linkages to a coherent community. There are other forms of loneliness as well, such as the loneliness of parents whose children have left home. Moreover, at Christmastime or other important holidays many of those who are unable to join with kin or other loved ones feel distressed because they are not able to reaffirm their fundamental commitment and connection with one another. These examples support the presumption that loneliness is a response to a relational deficit (Weiss, 1980).

Weiss further suggests that many of the symptoms associated with loneliness stem from a re-experiencing of the anxiety produced by childhood abandonment. The complex of symptoms associated with the loneliness of emotional isolation is strongly reminiscent of the distress experienced by small children who fear being abandoned by their parents. Moreover, the accompanying feelings of vulnerability and powerlessness are also apparent in this analogy. In times of great loneliness, one's adult coping capacities are dramatically reduced. Loneliness is, by definition, regressive in that it reduces one's psychic ability to find a way out of it. Or, to put it psychoanalytically, loneliness potentially overwhelms the coping capacities of the ego.

Lonely individuals are constantly searching, appraising others for their potential to fill relational deficits. Whether in social situations, at work, or walking down a crowded street, this compulsive unconscious search occurs. As Weiss (1980:21) explains, "the lonely individual's perpetual and motivational energies are likely to become organized in the service of finding remedies for his or her loneliness. . . . Occasionally, the hyperalertness of the individual suffering from the loneliness of emotional isolation produces an over-sensitivity to minimal cues and a tendency to misinterpret or to exaggerate the hostile or affectionate intent of others."

Is loneliness more prevalent in men or women? Interestingly, women sometimes assume that loneliness is a women's affliction. Based on traditional male-female roles, women have sometimes been envious of what is perceived as men's increased ability to get out of the house; get involved in the workaday world; go out alone to the theater, bars, sporting events, etc. However, although certain vestiges of this thinking remain, women's roles relative to work, play, and family have now shifted dramatically.

According to Freud, Bowlby, and numerous others, a great many psychiatric disorders can be understood as resulting from the malfunctioning of a person's capacity to initiate and sustain affectional bonds with particular others. Moreover, this ability to form and maintain healthy object relationships in adult life is determined to a significant degree by the kinds of relationships formed by the child within his/her family of origin. While traditional psychoanalysis focused upon the mother-child attachment as primary, later systemic work not only emphasizes the importance of father-child and sibling relationships, but also the developmentally significant events of the family system and that system's relationship to and interaction with the surrounding environment. (See for example, Carter and McGoldrick, 1989 or Boyd-Franklin, 1989).

Within the family, the growing child establishes emotional and affectional bonds with a few significant others, which, under normal circumstances contribute to healthy growth and development. However, when these bonds are either skewed or broken by involuntary separation or death, the child becomes anxious and distressed. A growing body of literature now exists which addresses the impacts of traumatic loss on children either through marital separation/divorce or death. In order to develop fully in an atmosphere of safety, young children need consistent, predictable nurturance accompanied by expectable limits against which they can test and further themselves. Persistent bonds between individuals are the rule in most species.

"ERNESTO AND ERNESTINE"

I am reminded of a beautiful pair of cardinals who lived in the yard of a house we rented some years ago. (They were affectionately nicknamed "Ernesto" and "Ernestine" by my wife, Beth.) Cardinals mate for life and their behavior was illustrative of this pairbonding. To see one was to know that the other was not far away. When one approached the bird feeder the other would be nearby, keeping a lookout. Their awareness, communication, and connection with one another was readily apparent. If one moved, the other would react in some corresponding and complementary fashion. For example, if potential danger approached in the person of our resident gray squirrel, then one mate would warn the other.

Since it was Beth who more often fed them than I did, they both seemed to be particularly aware and possibly even attached to her. At one point, she had occasion to travel out of the country for several weeks and I was left with strict instructions to fill the bird feeder regularly–which I did. However, during her absence the cardinal's behavior appeared to change. They would fly up to the window, sit on the sill, look in as if they were searching for something, and sing in rather agitated tones. They appeared to be upset. This unusual behavior continued until Beth returned, at which point it ceased. Was it possible that Ernesto and Ernestine were attached to Beth and were upset by her prolonged absence?

In any event, the behavior of this pair of cardinals is illustrative for human pairs as well. According to Bowlby (1980), bonded partners tend to remain in close emotional (if not physical) proximity to one another. Should they for any reason be parted, each will sooner or later seek out the other to renew proximity. Moreover, any attempt by a third party to separate a bonded pair is strenuously resisted. In addition, many of the most intense of human emotions arise during the formation, maintenance, disruption, and renewal of affectional bonds. Subjectively, individuals describe the formation of affectional bonds as falling in love; maintaining a bond as loving someone; and losing a partner as grieving over someone. Similarly, the threat of loss immediately arouses anxiety, whereas the actual loss produces sorrow. However, each of these situations is likely to arouse anger. Finally, security could be seen as the unchallenged maintenance of a bond, whereas the renewal of a bond is a source of joy (Weiss, 1980).

What is the difference between attachment and dependency? Weiss (1980) points out that passengers are dependent on an airline pilot to bring them down safely, but they are not attached to him. Conversely, an adult may be very attached to elderly parents but be in no way dependent on them. Many Americans have been raised to believe that dependency is somewhat childish and immature. However, an inverse value is placed on attachment. Someone who makes strong attachments is respected, while someone who remains unattached or detached is frequently seen as aimless or unstable. So despite the fact that many people confuse attachment and dependency, they are, in fact, quite different.

CONCLUSIONS

The ways in which attachment behavior becomes organized during a person's childhood set the pattern for subsequent caretaking and sexual behavior. These patterns are not only central to individual identity, but also to one's adult capacities to form and maintain intimate relationships. It is for these reasons that individuals' early intimate relationships within their family of origin are so critical. Because the structures, values, and roles are changing so rapidly, it will be helpful to analyze the developmental influences on intimate relationships in today's families.

REFERENCES

Bowlby, J. 1980. Affectional bonds: Their nature and origin. In R. Weiss, *Loneliness*. Cambridge, MA: MIT Press, 38-52.

Boyd-Franklin, N. 1989. *Black families in therapy.* New York: Guilford Press.
Carter, B. and McGoldrick, M. (Eds.) 1989. *The changing family life-cycle.* Boston: Allyn and Bacon.
Erikson, E. 1963. *Childhood and society.* New York: Norton.
Erikson, E. 1968. *Identity: Youth and crisis.* New York: Norton.
Hall, E. 1976. *Beyond culture.* New York: Doubleday.
Kilpatrick, W. 1975. *Identity and intimacy.* New York: Dell Publishing Co.
Sullivan, H. S. 1953. *The interpersonal theory of psychiatry.* New York: Norton.
Toffler, A. 1970. *Future Shock.* New York: Bantam Books.
Weiss, R. 1980. *Loneliness.* Cambridge: The MIT Press.

Chapter 2

Intimacy Within the Family: Developmental Perspectives

Angie H. Rice
Philip M. Brown

Skolnick and Skolnick (1986) refer to a family as an intimate environment in which two or more people live together in a committed relationship and share close emotional ties and functions. By fostering the growth and development of children, society replenishes itself. As the primary socialization agent of the culture, individuals receive their first taste of limit setting, the basic rules of living, and the civilizing force of the culture within their families of origin. Ideally, families provide safety and emotional refuge and engender a sense of personal and familial identity by providing a sense of belonging and relatedness. The sense of basic trust which develops within the family during early childhood is revisited and reworked within the context of later relationships.

Family constellations have changed dramatically in the 1990s. However, despite the particular type of family, the intimate environment of the family provides the building blocks for one's subsequent capacity for intimate relationships. Moreover, since the family is a microcosm of the broader culture in which it exists, many of the interpersonal dynamics closely parallel those which the individual must later confront in the larger society. Hence the microanalysis of the development of intimacy within the family says much about the culture in which individuals reside.

SEPARATION-INDIVIDUATION

The notion that a person must achieve separation-individuation prior to the development of intimate emotional relationships is a pervasive theme in the human development literature. Entire theories have been constructed around the importance of separation and individuation, as evidenced in Margaret Mahler's work (1968) as well as Murray Bowen's family of origin theory (1985). The ideas of separation and connection, maintenance of "space," a balance of consciousness of self and connection to the world have been termed the life project of the individual. This is the struggle between fusion and isolation. Mahler believes that the process of separation and individuation was the fundamental task of human bio-psycho-social growth. The innate endowment of the individual is shaped by the experiential world and relationships. However, it was up to the child to extract those elements necessary for adaptation from the environment. Mahler saw development as proceeding in three stages from birth to approximately age four, ending with successful separation/ individuation and the achievement of object constancy. An optimal balance of need gratification and frustration is necessary to promote growth and differentiation. Only with a preponderance of positive interpersonal experiences between the self and significant other can separation-individuation be achieved.

The seeds of ambivalence, are sowed in the separation/individuation stage, particularly in the subphase called rapprochement. This phase occurs around sixteen to twenty-five months, a time when the child begins to actively explore the environment, but returns to the parent or caretaker from time to time for reassurance and security. The restrictions which the caretakers and the environment place on the child and the ways in which reassurance and security are offered (or not offered), give rise to feelings of frustration, anger, and even hate which are coupled with feelings of dependency, need, and love. The issues of power and control in relationships also have their origins in these early stages of development and are shaped by subsequent interactions in the family and socialization experiences. It is a complex interplay of individual temperament, endowment, and learning within the context of familial and cultural influences which sets the stage for the subsequent handling of ambivalence as well as issues of power and control in intimate relationships.

The terms differentiation and fusion are used to describe the processes of separation and connection, both in individuals and families. Bowen (1985) linked these concepts to what he termed natural forces toward individuality and autonomy, or togetherness and fusion. Differentiation of self referred to the ability to separate intellectual and emotional functioning with higher levels of functioning associated with the ability to maintain an autonomous sense of self in relationships. Indeed, the "health" of both individuals and families has been described in the terms of fusion, enmeshment, or lack of differentiation.

OBJECT RELATIONS PERSPECTIVES

Object relations theory, an outgrowth of early psychoanalytic thought, stresses the importance of early developmental history and relationships on the development of personality and future intimate relationships. However, it differs from classical Freudian theory by its emphasis on the early years of life (before the age of four), rather than the Oedipal conflict stage, and its emphasis on relationships rather than impulse gratification. The term object refers not to things, but to people, or more specifically, to the internal representations of our experiences with people. Such representations invariably include an affective component as well.

Melanie Klein (1986) holds that personality development begins at birth, and that the early experiences with the mother are of utmost importance. She also states that our relationship with the world is mediated by images or internal object representations, also called introjects. Introjection is the earliest and most primitive level of internalization processes and organizes memory and perception of interactions with the environment. These introjects or images do not necessarily result from things done by the external object, but by what is perceived in the infant mind. These images are reacted to as though they were the objects themselves, and form the basis of the child's relationship to reality. If these images, with the associated feeling content, are too frightening due to disturbed relationships, the child's connection to the outer world may be weakened, and internal objects become fragments of experiences which are split-off and polarized. "Good" and "bad" objects are separated. Love and hate cannot be experienced together. Split-off or projected feelings preclude experiencing self and others as whole, separate identities. Erikson (1963) asserted that identity precedes intimacy. However, in more feminist terms, there is a lack of more complex continuation and interrelatedness. Projection makes the development of close emotional relationships more difficult, and in some cases almost impossible.

Building on the idea of empathic reflection of the child, the notion of the "holding" or facilitating environment which contains the feelings of the child, providing safety and trust, was developed. This leads to the growth of the "true self" which is capable of experiencing its own feelings, and consequently the feelings of others. If the holding environment is impaired in some way, the child may try to accommodate more to the state and mood of others and will fail to distinguish its own desire. A "false" or caretaker self emerges, in which the child is the emotional caretaker of the parent. Difficulties in authentically relating to others develop. It was believed that negative object experiences, those which were painful or unpleasant, resulted in dissociation–a fading of the personality, which made intimate relations impossible (Kwawer, 1982).

Object relations theory says all of us form internal versions of others. Children possess both maternal and paternal introjects as well as introjects of the parental relationship. If the maternal introject has somehow been "degraded" or "injured," then children grow up with the part they associate with mother (usually the loving and nurturing parts) less than whole. If the paternal introject is one of shadow, indifference, or harshness, the child also grows up with isolated and distant parts of the self (Luepnitz, 1988). Ultimately, degradation and distancing of the parents is degradation and distancing of the self for both sexes.

Attachment and Intimacy

An individual's capacity for intimacy begins to develop during childhood, via the holding and responsiveness of caregivers, in what Bowlby has termed attachment behavior. Attachment theory provides a conceptual framework for understanding the human need to forge strong affectional bonds with others. Attachment not only implies emotional or affectional bonds but proximity and physical contact. Attachment behavior refers to any behavior or pattern of behavior which results in attaining or maintaining proximity and contact with a significant other over time. These attachments will be influenced by age, sex, and environmental circumstance (Bowlby, 1979). Attachment is an adaptation that supports species survival because it promotes infant care and survival, and facilitates development that leads to later pairing and successful rearing of children (Morris, 1982).

The quality of attachment directly impacts the development of the capacity for intimacy. Impairment in the level of attachment can impair emotional development and one's ability to form and maintain intimate relationships. On the other hand, securely attached infants and children have internalized a secure base from which to explore and interact with the environment allowing for a growing sense of competence and self-esteem. These children can engage in cooperative effort, compromise, and do not lose a sense of self-definition in interactions with others. However, the child with more anxious attachment is left with a never-ending search for a "secure base." Due to feelings of isolation, insecurity, and dependency, an individual may develop a protective shell to defend against feelings of vulnerability which may cause difficulty successfully negotiating later interpersonal crises, especially intimacy. Anxiously attached children may continue to experience considerable emotional hunger and grow to seek out relationships as a format for reworking issues of basic trust (Morris, 1982).

Bowlby (1979) asserts that there is a strong relationship between parental/child attachment and later dysfunctional marital relations and problems with children. The most important variable in attachment is the extent to which the parents recognize and respect the child's need for a secure base and encourage exploration from it. A sense of secure attachment helps develop the internalized representation of a self worthy of love. A sense of connection to others also lends purpose and direction while providing clearer self-definition. Anxious attachment in children holds particular implications in the rapprochement subphase of Mahler's developmental schema which emphasizes exploratory behavior of the child from a secure base. If the child does not successfully negotiate this phase, there can be impairment of object constancy, leading to a predisposition to depression and setting the stage for possible borderline functioning.

Living Systems: A Biological Basis for Intimacy

The issues of separation and attachment have been seen as universal developmental and existential struggles for all individuals, families, and groups. Psychotherapeutic treatment often involves work related to separation and attachment. Although theoretical perspectives and interventive approaches vary considerably, the human experience of identity and existence emerge from the dynamic interplay between two basic elements–a sense of belonging, and a sense of separateness. The existential condition of being "alone" is ultimately rooted in a person's biological condition. Individuals are born separate entities, with what Chilean biologist Humberto Maturano (1978) has termed "structural determinism." Maturano's work on cognition and perception in living systems has been used as a basis for constructing a "living systems" model for family systems. He noted that all living systems are circularly organized and can be considered closed and autonomous. However, closed does not mean static or unchanging, as the structure of living systems changes in interactions with the environment. That is, they have plasticity or malleability (Dell, 1985). This biologically determined structural organization specifies how a system will behave in interaction with the environment. This structure gives meaning to interactions and information coming from the environment. There is no such thing as objective information, since all information is perception of our own self-determined, or autopoietic (self-producing) system (Maturano, 1980). The relationship between a structurally determined system and its environment has been called structural coupling. This is the building block of all human and animal interactional systems. Structural coupling is synonymous with existence or "knowing how to exist," and comes from the fit of living systems with each other and with the environment. As long as a structurally plastic system survives, it will automatically become coupled to its environment. If an environment consists of other structurally plastic living systems, these systems will become richly coupled to one another (Dell, 1985). The very human desire for belonging and relatedness is derived from the biologically determined desire for perceiving, a validation of self, confirming that the person really exists. This desire for perception leads to structural coupling. As a result of this structural coupling, individuals automatically lose some of their fit with the environment, and thus, must change. This loss of some of one's individual identity leads to the constant pull of separation and individuation, or what some feminist writers have termed the self-in-relation.

Feminist Perspectives

Ideas, just like persons, have histories and cultures and do not exist without connection to these. Modern feminist writers have pointed out that most theories and perceptions about development in this country have arisen from a male-oriented system. The theories and/or pre-suppositions to which one subscribes color the interpretation of events and shape what is considered important. Typically, theories of human development have been biased toward the male experience (especially white and middle class), which leave the distinctive differences of women and ethnic minorities largely unaddressed. Developmental theories have stressed autonomous, independent functioning (where one operates without the need for others) as the hallmark of maturity. Our culture equates healthy adulthood with qualities that are associated with maleness–the rugged individual, the rational thinking man whose decision making is ruled by ambitious, goal-directed activity. These ideas emphasize separation and individuation, but neglect the impact of connection to others, affiliation, and continuity. Qualities historically defined as more feminine, such as emotional expressiveness, warmth, and caring, have been systematically devalued. These are qualities which are necessary for nurturance and intimacy in families. Unfortunately, what is commonly thought of as healthy adult functioning stands in direct contrast with those qualities essential for healthy family functioning, especially with respect to nurturing of children. This creates a double bind for both men and women within the family. If, on the one hand, they behave like "mature adults," they are not behaving in ways which benefit the emotional well-being of the family. The notion that the more one pulls away and separates, the more one can be intimate with others is inherently paradoxical.

In Erikson's (1963) eight stages of man, only the first stage, basic trust, is focused on relationship. Until one reaches adulthood, most of development is directed to pulling away or separating. Having spent most of the time developing the capacity to be separate, one arrives at the stage of intimacy vs. isolation in young adulthood supposedly possessing the capacity for intimacy. It seems contradictory to emphasize separation within the family when individuals live in intimate connection in both time and space. Must persons continually distance themselves in order to develop, or is this how it has been interpreted by our male-oriented culture?

Jean Baker Miller (1991) suggests that the ideas of separation and differentiation may not be an adequate description for what happens in the human family. Infants and children do not really distance themselves as they grow in competence and skill their relationships become more complex. As cognitive and experiential capacities increase, the ability to understand others also develops. There is a growing tolerance for ambiguity and contradiction, and a more complex engagement with others, rather than a growing distance. Miller calls this the "increasing complexity of the self-in-relation" or relational self. This construct implies that our identities do not develop in isolation from others; indeed, the only way to truly know our "selves" is through relations with others, in how we affect them and they us. Thus, it might be better to examine the dynamics of being close, of interrelatedness and mutual interdependence. It is in the interactions with others, first in our families and later with the wider world, that we come to have a picture of who we are, and who we are not, and this depends on contact and closeness, not separation.

Feminist writers have posited that current theories of development based on a male world view, may not be valid for females or even wholly for males. Nancy Chodorow (1978, 1989) states that the selves of men and women tend to be constructed differently, due to the fact that they are parented primarily by women. The women's self is more grounded in relations and connection, rather than difference, and the men are more grounded in separation and denial of connection, and recognition of difference. She states that this causes men and women to experience intimacy differently, with men more afraid of commitment and less afraid of discontinuity than women. Carol Gilligan (1982) also addressed this difference in development in her book *In a Different Voice*. In a study of the images of violence in men and women's stories, it was found that men see danger more often in close personal affiliation than in achievement, and construe danger to arise from intimacy. Women perceive danger in impersonal achievement situations resulting from competitive success. The danger of intimacy men describe in their stories is entrapment or betrayal, being caught in a smothering relationship, or being humiliated by rejection and deceit. In contrast, women portray danger in achievement as danger of isolation, a fear that in standing out or being set apart by success, they will be left alone (Gilligan, 1982). Unfortunately, this fear is not without basis in our society. Girls and women have experienced feelings of rejection by others when they have pursued their own desires and achievements. A recent survey (Basow, 1991) reported that 50 percent of college women have admitted "playing dumb" and hiding their abilities at least once for fear that they would not be found attractive to men.

FINDING OUR FATHERS

In her book, *The Family Interpreted*, Deborah Luepnitz (1988) analyzes the issues of emotional and physical absence of fathers, and the control they exert in families. She characterizes the modern family as patriarchal, but with father either emotionally or physically absent. Nevertheless, she maintains, he still wields tremendous influence in the family despite his absence or exclusion. Dinnerstein (1976) suggests that because every person is first cared for by women, it is she who becomes associated with infantile projections of love and rage, with needs met or ungratified. These "massive orienting passions" are associated with the female and not the male in the family. These infantile projections are what fuels the transcultural phenomena of ambivalence toward women. Such ambivalence is more profoundly experienced by males because they are "other than mother." Luepnitz and Dinnerstein both claim that while other types of change may influence the family, nothing would more profoundly affect the family and our "deepest experience of self and other" than men also becoming the objects of early infantile projections.

In his book *Finding Our Fathers* (1986), psychologist Sam Osherson suggests that a boy may experience a sense of loss or fear of abandonment because he recognizes he is different from mother, and worries about his ability to exist without her or as different from her. Yet, he finds it difficult to identify with an absent or amorphous father. Having no strong source of identification of sameness for himself, he may turn to devaluing that which seems feminine as a way of establishing identity. He does not learn how to get nurturance and intimacy from men, starting with father, and values that come from women, leading to later problems in intimacy. Whenever a part of our experience is devalued, that part of ourselves associated with that experience will also be devalued, eroding our relational capacity and capacity for intimacy.

Osherson based his book on interviews with 370 men in the Adult Development Project at Harvard University, clinical interviews with men in their 30s and 40s, and other recent research on male development. This work led him to state that men grow with a "wounded father" inside, a conflicted inner sense of masculinity arising from their experience of their fathers as rejecting, incompetent, or absent (Osherson, 1986). He states that men's early and ongoing relationships with their fathers shape the issues of intimacy and work that men face. He became convinced that the absence of fathers, psychologically or physically, from their families is a great underestimated tragedy of our times (Osherson, 1986). A recent clinical example may better illustrate the preceding points.

Case Example: James

James, a large, attractive man, aged 48, had recently been divorced from his second wife, and was suffering from depression and feelings of loss over the failure of his marriages. He had begun to have a vague sense that "maybe something was wrong" with him since both his marriages had failed, and his partners had complained of his lack of closeness and sharing with them and his stepchildren. As therapy progressed, a picture of a lonely, isolated childhood unfolded. James and his younger sister had been parented primarily by their mother, described as a quiet, unassuming homemaker, who liked to keep the peace and seldom made demands of any kind on her husband. His father, a traveling salesman, had difficulty making ends meet and was seldom home. When he was home, primarily on weekends, he often drank heavily.

While not abusive, he was not available to his children emotionally or physically. He seldom talked to them and when he did so, it was usually about superficial topics, such as school grades or to tell them not to make too much noise. With a trace of longing tinged with bitterness, James recounted how he had never played ball with his father, and was embarrassed as a child because he could not play well.

Due to financial difficulties and his father's frequent job changes, James's family moved so many times that he could not remember them all. He said that he could sometimes remember houses and places, but there were never any people or feelings associated with these. His parents never seemed to discuss the moves with each other or with the children. James's father would walk in one day and announce that the family was moving, usually within the week. He never had any friends because his family moved so often that he figured it was useless to invest in relationships that were just going to end anyway. He remembered how his father had said that friends were just a waste of time anyway, with people always wanting to "nose in on your business."

Case Analysis

James learned powerful lessons in his family about what it meant to be in relationship to others. Fathers were mainly seen as removed from day-to-day family life, sharing little of themselves and the outside world of which they were a part. The role of a man which James learned from his father was to keep to oneself, share little with family and friends, and to put work first (which James subsequently did in both his marriages, much to the detriment of all involved). James had not only a "wounded father" inside, but a wounded man who had no tools with which to work on healing himself or his relationships. While not uncaring, he had no way to share this caring with others except by bringing home a regular paycheck and providing a stable roof. This was something that his father had been hard pressed to do, but at which James felt successful. For many years James felt that this was enough and could not understand why his wife and stepchildren frequently asked for more. In therapy, James gradually came to see how his experiences and lack of closeness in his family had ill-prepared him for marriage, parenthood, or intimate relationships of any kind.

FATHERS AND DAUGHTERS

The psychological and/or actual absence of the father shapes daughters no less than sons. In fact, the influence of the father in the family may be heightened by virtue of his "novelty" (Lamb, 1981). Recent writings and research have pointed to the profound influence fathers have on their daughters' subsequent development, not only in theories of intimate relationships, but in the areas of achievement and mastery (which for women are interrelated issues). Clinical experience has long pointed to the effect, often detrimental, that women's relationships with their fathers has had on subsequent relationships with men. In her book, *The Cinderella Complex*, Collette Dowling (1981), traces women's deep-seated sense of inadequacy and resultant fear of independence directly to a woman's relationship with her father. Studies of teenage girls and women have showed that those who are seen as successful and better adjusted have fathers who have encouraged their abilities and sense of mastery (Hamilton, 1977).

Recent writings and research on infant development have pointed to the importance of the sense of mastery as a motivation for development and sense of self-esteem (Zenah et al., 1989; Stern, 1985). Environments and contexts that encourage and reinforce mastery efforts promote positive feelings of self-efficacy and internal perceptions of control (Zenah et al., 1989). The sense of self-efficacy, or an effective self-in-relation, where one has an internal sense of control rather than a need to "fuse" with another person for control, has implications for the development of true intimate relations, not only for women but also for men. For women, a sense of mastery is not only a sense of control of the environment and ability to achieve or produce (a more male view of mastery), but it is also a sense of being an effective self-in-relation, a sense of mastery and competency in relation, the ability to positively affect others in our environment. People wish to feel competent in relationships, and matter to the other. Intimacy has been called a "dialogue emerging with differentiation between equals" (Carter and McGoldrick, 1989).

However, it would be difficult to achieve true intimacy in a relationship if a woman suffers from a basic sense of inadequacy and low self-esteem as there would be no sense of equality. A sense of mastery, of effective self-in-relation, fosters the capacity for intimacy and allows for a comfortable level of connection between equals.

Intimacy is often confused with closeness and fusion. A search for a sense of control and completeness in self can lead to attempts to "fuse" with another person for this sense of completion and control. This may be part of the reason that men fear what they perceive as draining or suffocating relationships (i.e., they fear this sense of completion and control). When a person attempts to fuse with another in a marriage, there is a distortion of communication. Projection can run rampant, with each projecting desires, wishes, and perceptions onto the other. Women are especially prone to tell their partners what they want to hear rather than what they themselves think and feel. Rather than being nurturing, this is draining for each, and makes it difficult to sustain an intimate relationship which successfully embodies differences. The case of Amy may help exemplify the previous discussion.

Case Example: Amy

Amy was an attractive young woman in her middle thirties, married, with a teenage son. A series of job-related and personal crises brought her to therapy. Her marriage was on the brink of dissolution and she was suffering from a stress-related illness. While she described her family of origin as average, it soon became clear that she came from a family in which feelings, particularly anger, were never really expressed or shared, and people were not emotionally close.

Amy's father was described as very authoritarian and cold with both his wife and his children. She remembered that she was never allowed to express anger and that her father never said he was sorry or wrong about anything. Amy's mother assumed the role of peacemaker and tried to downplay any negative interaction in the home. There had always been a struggle between what she and her father each wanted and deemed appropriate. Amy remembered that she was pushed to excel, but only within certain prescribed limits.

When younger, if she pursued what she wished to do, such as building scooters as a grade school child or working as a candy-striper as a teenager, her father often discouraged her or would not allow the activity, saying that it was too much trouble, too difficult, or not appropriate for her. She was not encouraged to pursue things that she liked, but only those things that her father thought were appropriate. She felt that she never quite lived up to his expectations, and particularly disappointed him in her teenage years when she ran away once.

In therapy, Amy traced her deep feelings of inadequacy, which were affecting her job performance and marital relationship, to her relationship with her father. She felt that his lack of validation as well as his lack of warmth and closeness had left her needy and hungry inside. Yet, she was afraid of being overwhelmed by these needs. She subsequently married a man to whom she was not able to relate intimately as an equal. He too had ideas, engendered by his upbringing and socialization, about how she should be and act as a wife and as a woman. She felt that she had to continually "dampen down" parts of herself because it was threatening not only to her but to the relationship. She felt powerless to effect change in the relationship as she had felt powerless to effect her father's view of herself.

Case Analysis

Amy was a bright and talented young woman who had a deep sense of personal inadequacy despite her obvious achievements. She had been conditioned to believe that some aspects of the world were just too much for her to deal with. As a result, her sense of achievement and mastery were not fostered (particularly in directions she desired). Because there was little room allowed for discussion or negotiation of these issues, Amy felt powerless in this relationship. She could find no effective and acceptable way to make a meaningful difference in her relationship or alter her role vis-à-vis her father and family. In later years, this carried over into her relationship with her husband. After a time, she began to realize that there were few, if any, effective and acceptable ways of negotiating issues with him. When she did try to negotiate she was consistently made to feel guilty and wrong for trying to do so. At work she also found it difficult to advocate for things that would make her job easier, more satisfying, and ultimately more effective. In many ways, she acquiesced to the needs of others, just as she had so often in her family of origin and present family. Her differences from others were not seen as important and worthy of recognition even though they were. Amy had no sense of competency or being an effective self-in-relation.

COMPARING "DIFFERENTIATION" TO "GROWTH THROUGH CONNECTION"

The failure to appreciate or allow for differences in self and others comes from never really having become emotionally independent of these issues with one's parents (Carter and McGoldrick, 1989). There is a tendency to repeat the patterns evident in one's family of origin in an attempt to resolve these relationships. Bowen's family systems theory (1985) relates this incomplete differentiation from the family's "undifferentiated ego mass" to the tendency to fusion. In this view, poorly differentiated parents produce poorly differentiated children, and people tend to marry those at the same level of differentiation as their family of origin. These patterns of relating and functioning are transmitted generationally through the family projection process of emotional triangulation. Bowen believed that the smallest stable unit of relationship was a three-person unit. Moreover, under stress a two-person relationship would "triangulate" a third person in order to stabilize the relationship. This process could continue within the family until the ultimate level of fusion or undifferentiation, namely schizophrenia, was reached. Feminist critics of this theory have pointed out that the qualities which are valued in the differentiated person are those for which males are more socialized. The differentiated person is described as autonomous, goal-directed, intellectual, and being-for-self, while the poorly differentiated person is described as seeking love and approval, relatedness, and being-for-others. Luepnitz (1989) points out the differentiated person is not described as having "the ability to integrate thought and feeling . . . the ability to tolerate conflict and avoid cut offs," and the "capacity to both compete and collaborate." All these are surely qualities of mature functioning, a sense of balance and completeness necessary for intimacy. Luepnitz (1988) further states that it would be most difficult for women, due to the expectations of primary responsibility for nurturing children, to be able to "be-for-self" as much as a man can, given his different training and socialization. Societal expectations may actually foster lack of differentiation by teaching females to always put other's needs first.

CHANGING FAMILY CONTEXTS: SINGLE-PARENT FAMILIES

Time for sharing in an unhurried, unstructured fashion for parents and children is necessary for the development of intimacy. Quality time is a myth. There has to be a certain quantity of time before one can get to the point of quality. Time for sharing is very hard to come by in our society, where people have to work hard to survive or where the stress of poverty, divorce, and single parenthood leaves little time or energy for much else but surviving.

However, a poor or single-parent family is not automatically a dysfunctional family. One study showed that the majority of families, when not plagued by poverty, had children with as good as emotional adjustment and self-esteem as their counterparts in two-parent families (Howard and Johnson, 1985). Those families who managed a functional existence were those that maintained access to sources of social, emotional, and environmental support through extended families, community agencies, and institutions (Carter and McGoldrick, 1989). There are changes in family functioning in single-parent families but the long-term effects on children are still being studied. One report of several studies seemed to indicate that girls raised without fathers may have more difficulty in establishing relationships with men later in life, and boys may exhibit extreme masculine behaviors, such as excessive fighting and risk taking (Romer, 1981). Girls from father-absent homes were less skilled in interaction with males and seemed to have more negative attitudes toward males, especially if the absence was due to separation, abandonment, or divorce. The boys' masculine behaviors were believed to be due to overcompensation by some mothers who heavily encouraged masculine behaviors in their sons.

Judith Wallerstein's longitudinal study of the children of divorce points to the long-term effect on children's emotional and mental well-being. One of the most important findings for continued emotional development and the capacity for intimate relations later in life, was the continued involvement of both parents in the life of the child. As most children live with their mothers after divorce, the mother's mental health and quality of parenting is the crucial factor in a child's psychological development and well-being over the years. However, while contact with the father is important, the nature of the father-child relationship heavily influences the child's psychological development (Wallerstein and Blakeslee, 1990). Children raised with their mothers may experience more collaborative, democratic relationships during childhood (Carter and McGoldrick, 1989). Shifts in decision making and authority structure within the family increase communication among family members, and thereby may increase the amount of intimacy single parents and their children experience beyond what parents and children in two-parent families experience (Howard and Johnson, 1985).

In separation and divorce, issues of power, authority, and decision making can cause problems in families, with parents triangulating children and others into the struggles. Difficulty in maintaining generational boundaries may result in enmeshment or symbiosis with parent-child relationships. Children may overfunction to fill in gaps or rebel because of emotional difficulties. Dysfunctional alliances in any family undermine everyone's ability to function more adequately. Communication suffers and problems are not resolved. Appropriate levels of intimacy within the family may not be maintained. Children cannot fulfill a parent's need for adult closeness and communication, and trying to do so may interfere with childhood growth and development.

Borderline Personality Development

Many families contain members who have failed to develop a sound sense of self, including the capacity for initiating and sustaining intimate relationships. Increasingly, many of the individuals seen by mental health professionals exhibit behaviors and emotional difficulties associated with what is termed borderline personality organization. Dr. Otto Kernberg (1990), a foremost authority on the subject, estimates that 7 percent to 15 percent of the population of the United States has borderline personality organization. Historically, the term was introduced to describe personalities that lay between psychoses and neuroses. There was, and still is, some disagreement and confusion about the term as a diagnostic entity and its main characteristics (Goldstein, 1984). However, with advancing developments in ego psychology and child development research, borderline personality organization has come to identify those individuals who are seen as having severe ego deficits and chronic personal and social difficulties caused by early developmental difficulties and disturbed object relations.

A developmental view of borderline pathology was set forth by Margaret Mahler, arising out of her observations of mother/child interaction. She outlined phases of symbiosis, and separation and individuation which a child must successfully negotiate in order to achieve mature personality organization. Mahler felt that borderline pathology related to difficulties in the particular subphase of separation/individuation called "rapprochement," occurring between sixteen and twenty-five months of age (Edward, Ruskin, and Turrini, 1981). The mother is seen as libidinally unavailable, and lacks sensitivity to the child's unique characteristics and phase-appropriate needs in the separation/individuation process (Goldstein, 1984). Having separated, the child returns to the mother for support. However, the mother's withdrawal has punished the child for separating and left it vulnerable to feelings of abandonment and anxiety (Eisendarth, 1980). Failure to master the rapprochement crisis impairs the individual's ability to achieve object constancy. Hence, a sense of self and realistic view of others does not solidify. This sets the stage for the development of borderline pathology.

Kernberg (1986) views borderline personality organization as a type of internal structural organization linked to developmental failure during the period after self-object differentiation, but before the development of object constancy. He places this at the third stage of development of normal internalized object relations, which occurs from approximately the fourth month to the end of the first year of life. This is even earlier than Mahler's formulations. Kernberg (1990) attributes excess aggression at this stage, either due to a very strong inborn aggressive drive (nature or secondary to excessive frustration (nurture), to the development of the child's inability to integrate good and bad self and object representations, which leads to splitting and other primitive defenses. While reality testing and ego boundaries are firm, identity does not coalesce–the id, ego, and superego do not consolidate into a mature intrapsychic structure (Goldstein, 1984).

Drawing on the writings of Mahler and Kernberg, Masterson and Costello (1980) state that the cause of the developmental arrest of the borderline patient was the mother's emotional unavailability at the child's efforts to separate and individuate. This unavailability could have a number of causes–the most common being the presence of borderline pathology or a more serious disorder in the mother, which caused her to reward regressive behavior and withdraw from efforts at separation/individuation in order to maintain her own emotional stability. Other possible causes are long physical separation from the mother, emotional and actual parental absence, parental depression, psychosis, or death. This parental withdrawal at rapprochement is experienced as an abandonment threat which prevents the child from moving ahead.

Borderline persons often exhibit phenomena referred to as difficulties with the self–poor self-regulation, low self-esteem, and inhibition of self-expression (false self). All are aspects of developmental arrest and failure to individuate. Feminist views would point to a failure in developmental progression to more complex interrelatedness and mutual interdependence rather than arrest or failure to individuate. The relational self would be impaired because connections to others were distorted or absent. These failures of self-expression and feelings of abandonment depression can be reactivated later in life when more complex functioning is needed, and make intimate relationships threatening and impossible.

Borderline Development and the "Disintegrating Culture"

A theory of stage-specific trauma may not entirely explain borderline pathology, because there are always influences (both corrective and destructive) from other stages of development. It is also important to examine sustained traumatic situations existing in family and interpersonal relationships, and include all family members, their shared defenses, and family group dynamics (Berkowitz, 1981). It seems that many families with borderline members exhibit behaviors and attitudes which are detrimental to the successful completion of developmental tasks and further reinforce maturational failure that characterizes borderline functioning. As previously noted, societal pressures and changes impact family functioning and one cannot separate the family from the environment in which it exists. Individuals are socialized in families to what has been termed our "disintegrating culture." An increase in the pathology may be tied to changing social patterns of family structure and parent-child interaction. Childrearing patterns, stability of home life, and child abuse and neglect, are all issues worthy of examination. If one subscribes to the theory of multigenerational transmission of emotional and mental illness, then it is easy to see how borderline symptomatology is spreading. Borderline functioning can be seen partially as a response to social stresses and strains and exacerbated by these same forces.

Other writers have highlighted the pattern of a passive, or emotionally distant father, who by his actions, or inaction, reinforces the restrictive mother-child bond (Kreisman and Strauss, 1989). Perhaps the distant, absent, or cold father is what causes a maternal-child bond to develop that does not allow for mutual interdependence. The violence that can exist in families distorts and destroys relationships, and unfortunately, studies show that most cases of incest, sexual abuse, and child murders are committed by males (Finklehor and Browne, 1985). Luepnitz (1988) uses feminist theory to interpret the modern family as patriarchal but father-absent, with the father's position in the family restricting the lives of women and children. She calls for a father who is not viewed as a tired nightly visitor, only serving to periodically separate mothers and children, but for one who is an authentic presence, a tender, engaged parent, reinforcing the bonds between all family members. One cannot help but feel that such a parent would lessen the possibility of the development of borderline symptomatology and other interpersonal difficulties.

INTIMACY AS A DYNAMIC SYSTEM

Intimacy can be conceptualized as a dynamic system with a variety of interactive levels, including individual, couple, family and societal. On the individual level, the development of a sense of self is crucial. One needs to be aware of one's own thoughts, feelings, and perceptions and integrate these with one's experience. Feminist writers assert that one's individual thoughts, feelings, and perceptions all evolve in relationship with others. This connection is first experienced in the cradles of our families, with each family developing its own emotional climate through the expression of emotions. A balance of tension and harmony results from this emotional expression. A supportive family climate is one in which criticisms and punishments are not levied by family members for the expression of feelings. Such a climate is not out of balance from too much tension and allows for self-disclosure, not only of feelings, but also thoughts and ideas. Self-disclosure may be instrumental in achieving a sense of identity because two of its major functions are self-clarification and social validation. (Derlega and Grzelak, 1979). Individuals develop in connection with others in families through appropriate disclosure of feelings, thoughts, and ideas. This also teaches them ways of relating to others in the larger society. In his book, *Intimate Behavior*, zoologist Desmond Morris (1971) states that the closeness of modern society, especially in urban settings, forces curtailment of "public intimacies," causing more heavy reliance on "private intimacies." However, these intimacies often fail to develop, even in families. Public restraint spills over into private life, and persons engage in the secondhand intimacies of video touchings, love songs, and romance novels (Morris, 1971). There is no supportive climate in either the society or the family for the sharing of thoughts, ideas, and feelings and definition of self in relation to others. Thus, the circle of intimacy is broken.

Morris further asserts that there is a cycle of close pairing, independence, and autonomy, which he termed the intimacy sequence. This primary sequence of changing intimacies, "hold me tight/put me down/leave me alone" is initiated in the family and repeated throughout life. There are forms of bodily contact, caring, and intimacy between parents and children that are appropriate at each developmental phase, and if these are too advanced or retarded, trouble may ensue (Morris, 1971). Just as there are appropriate levels of physical intimacy, there are appropriate levels of emotional intimacy and self-disclosure. If the level of self-disclosure changes, then the level of intimacy changes. If a parent over-discloses to a child, the levels of intimacy may change, thus triangulating or enmeshing the child and disrupting parental/child boundaries. As a result, the family cannot engage in appropriate interactions that foster relatedness and the development of the capacity for initiating and sustaining intimate relationships.

CONCLUSIONS

A vast array of forces influence the individual's developing capacity for intimacy (i.e., biological, environmental, familial, and societal). However, the family provides the essential initial context in which these multiple forces are made manifest. These early experiences shape our subsequent ability to express and experience both physical and emotional intimacy. Modeling is a powerful teaching tool. Parents model behavioral, emotional, and attitudinal modes in intimate relationships and reinforce these through their behavioral and interactive patterns. Individuals repeat what they know and attempt to achieve a sense of mastery over their childhood experiences and relationships. Yet, these relationships do not take place within a vacuum. The socio-cultural context lying beyond the boundary of the family's intimate environment is also critical in shaping the ever-changing constellation of male and female role. What are the differences in the childhood socialization of males and females? How does this male-female socialization affect subsequent gender identity, social role, and expectations for relationships? How has the women's movement and feminist consciousness impacted female and male identity and interactions?

REFERENCES

Basow, S. 1991. Gender stereotypes. Lecture, Newcomb College Women's Forum. Tulane University, October 30.

Berkowitz, D. 1981. The borderline adolescent and the family. In Lansky, R. (Ed.) *Family therapy and major psychopathology.* New York: Grune and Stratton, 183-201.

Bowen, M. 1985. *Family therapy in clinical practice.* Northvale, NJ: Jason Aronson, Inc.

Bowlby, J. 1979. *The making and breaking of affectional bonds.* London: Tavistock Publications.

Carter, B. and McGoldrick, M. (Eds.) 1989. *The changing family life-cycle.* Needham Heights, MA: Allyn and Bacon.

Chodorow, N. 1978. *The reproduction of mothering.* Berkeley, CA: University of California Press.

_____ 1989. *Feminism and psychoanalytic thought.* New Haven: Yale University Press.

Dell, P. 1985. Understanding Bateson and Maturana: Toward a biological foundation for the social sciences. *Journal of Marital and Family Therapy,* 11(1):1-20.

Derlega, V. and Grzelak, J. 1979. Appropriateness of self-disclosure. In: Chelune, G. (Ed.) *Self-disclosure.* San Francisco: Jossey-Bass, 151-176.

Dinnerstein, D. 1976. *The mermaid and the minotaur.* New York: Harper & Row.

Dowling, C. 1981. *The Cinderella complex.* New York: Simon and Schuster, Inc.

Edward, J., Ruskin, N., and Turrini, P. 1981. *Separation-individuation: Theory and application.* New York: Gardener Press.

Eisendarth, R. 1980. The borderline patient: Individual therapy from a family point of view. In: Pearce, J. and Friedman, L. (Eds.) *Family therapy: Combining psychodynamics and family systems approaches.* New York: Grune and Stratton.

Erikson, E. 1963. *Childhood and society.* New York: Norton.

Finkelhor, D. and Browne, A. 1985. The traumatic effect of child sexual abuse: A conceptualization. *American Journal of Ortho-Psychiatry,* 55(4):530-541.

Gilligan, C. 1982. *In a different voice.* Cambridge, MA: Harvard University Press.

Goldstein, E. 1984. *Ego psychology and social work practice.* New York: The Free Press.

Hamilton, M. 1977. *The father's influence on children.* Chicago: Nelson-Hall.

Howard, T. and Johnson, F. 1985. An ecological approach to practice with single-parent families. *Social Casework,* 66(8):482-489.

Kernberg, O. 1986. Structural derivatives of relationships. In: Buckley, P. (Ed.) *Essential papers on object relations.* New York: New York University Press.

Kernberg, O. 1990. The borderline personality. Workshop, Touro Infirmary, New Orleans, LA. April 6.

Klein, M. 1986. A contribution to the psychogenesis of manic-depressive states. In: Buckley, P. (Ed.) *Essential papers on object relations,* New York: New York University Press.

Kreisman, J. and Strauss, H. 1989. *I hate you–don't leave me.* New York: Avon Books.

Kwawer, J. 1982. Object relations theory and intimacy. In: Fisher, M. and Stricher, G. (Eds.) *Intimacy.* New York: Plenum, 53-64.

Lamb, M. (Ed.) 1981. *The role of the father in child development.* (2nd ed.) New York: John E. Wiley & Sons.

Luepnitz, D. 1988. *The family interpreted.* New York: Basic Books.

Mahler, M. 1968. *On human symbiosis and the vicissitudes of individuation.* New York: International Universities Press.

Mahler, M., Pine, F., and Bergman, A. 1975. *The psychological birth of the human infant.* New York: Basic Books.

Masterson, J. and Costello, J. 1980. *From borderline adolescent to functioning adult: The test of time.* New York: Brunner/Mazel.

Maturano, H. 1978. *Psychology and biology of language and thought.* New York: Academic Press.

_____ 1980. Autopoiesis: Reproduction, heredity and evolution. In: Zelleny, M. (Ed.) *Autopoiesis, disadaptive structures and spontaneous social orders.* Boulder, Colorado: Westview Press.

Miller, J. 1991. The development of womens' sense of self. In: Jordan, J. Kaplan, A., Miller, J., Stiver, I., and Surrey, J. *Women's growth in connection.* New York: Guilford Press, 11-26.

Morris, D. 1982. Attachment and intimacy. In: Fisher, M. and Stricker, G. (Eds.) *Intimacy.* New York: Plenum.

Morris, D. 1971. *Intimate behavior.* New York: Random House.

Osherson, S. 1986. *Finding our fathers.* New York: The Free Press.

Romer, N. 1981. *The sex-role cycle: Socialization from infancy to old age.* New York: McGraw-Hill, Inc.

Skolnick, A. and Skolnick, J. 1986. Family in transition (5th ed.). Boston: Little, Brown, and Co.

Stern, D. 1985. *The interpersonal world of the infant.* New York: Basic Books.

Wallerstein, J. and Blakeslee, S. 1990. *Second chances.* New York: Ticknor and Fields.

Winnicott, D. 1965. *Maturational processes and the facilitating environment. Studies in the theory of emotional development.* New York: International Universities Press.

Zenah, C., Anders, T., Seifer, R. and Stern, N. 1989. Implications of research on infant development for psychodynamic theory and practice. *Journal of the American Academy of Child and Adolescent Psychiatry.* 28(5):657-668.

Chapter 3

Different Voices, Different Songs
(Male-Female Socialization)

It is difficult to sort out the effects of social structural changes on the individual and the family. A fragmented sense of self may reflect the fragmentation of modern society. The industrialization and increasing urbanization of the late eighteenth and early nineteenth centuries may have set the stage for the peripheral father leaving more responsibility for childcare to the mother. Accelerating social change has disrupted what once had been "normal family life." Today, individuals marry later, more often and have fewer children. This has created a break in the individual-family-society continuum which is basic to establishing and maintaining meaningful intimate relationships.

One occupies many statuses in a lifetime. However, the ascribed status of male or female is possibly the most significant in affecting the remainder of one's social roles. These roles are defined and structured around the various privileges and responsibilities which gender status is seen to possess. When expected role behavior is rigidly defined, individual freedom and choice are severely hampered. Moreover, the social institutions constructed around established social protocol are held together by ideologies or belief systems which assure us that the explanations of life that they symbolize are valid. As a result, commonly held beliefs evolve regarding those who are perceived to belong to the same category. These stereotypes are integral to the creation of racism and sexism. False generalizations based upon widely held stereotypes are elevated to a belief system which is then codified within social institutions and sanctified by the law of the land. This process leads inexorably to various forms of institutional discrimination. For example, Joseph Feagin (1989) defines racism as an ideology which considers a group's unchangeable physical characteristics to be linked in a direct causal way to psychological or intellectual traits and which, on that basis, distinguishes between superior and inferior groups. Although this is a definition of racism, it convincingly defines sexism as well.

Lindsay (1990) states that the term sex refers to the biological aspects of a person, involving characteristics which differentiate females from males by chromosomal, anatomical, reproductive, hormonal and other physiological characteristics. Gender, on the other hand, implies those social, cultural, and/or psychological features linked to males and females through particular social contexts. In other words, sex is an ascribed status while gender is an achieved status.

CHILDHOOD SOCIALIZATION

In Kohlberg's view (1966) one of the earliest ways a child organizes reality is through the self, which becomes an essential component of his or her existence. That which is associated with the self is likewise valued. As early as age three, children begin to identify themselves by sex and accurately apply the proper labels to themselves and others. This is true even though they are too young to understand that these categorizations are widely applicable and more or less invariant. This is the foundation of gender identity (Lindsay, 1990).

Once gender identity has developed, behavior is organized around it. Children then actively seek models which are labeled as "boy" or "girl" to reinforce their newly discovered identity. Identification with the same-sex parent often increases at this developmental stage. Once children acquire this rudimentary understanding of their own sex, much of their behavior will be consistent with the understanding of that label (Lindsay, 1990). From birth onward girls enter the "pink world" and are handled more gently than males, despite the fact that no substantial evidence of greater fragility exists (Lipman-Blumen, 1984).

Recent trends toward dressing little girls in overalls rather than dresses have inevitably widened their socially acceptable range of physical activity. Graduating into blue jeans rather than skirts has already enabled teenage girls to shed certain physical limitations tied solely to restrictive clothing. Clothes that allow females to move easily ultimately influence their self-confidence and independence (Lipman-Blumen, 1984).

Although girls and boys are about equal in learned aggressiveness, boys are more likely to act out this learned behavior than are girls (Bandura, 1973). The biological explanation for this rests on the association between testosterone and aggression in males. Androgens (of which testosterone is one) are partly responsible for modifying the brain as it is being developed, making neural circuits more susceptible to testosterone. When newborn female mice were treated with testosterone, they reacted similarly to males with aggression increasing (Edwards, 1968). When young female monkeys were given testosterone aggression also increased. However, lest one conclude that testosterone is the sole variable in explaining aggression, one should remember that these differences are also highly correlated with male and female socialization.

Male children have a four- to eight-times greater incidence than females of infantile autism, hyperactivity, and conduct disorders. These disorders may be interpreted as extreme developments of normal and valued masculine traits. That is, autism may be interpreted as a pathological resistance to human attachment and emotional connection, often accompanied by a fixation on mechanical objects. Goldberg (1983) points out that this is not unlike the obsession some grown men have with their automobiles, television sets, and gadgets. These are often men who are uncomfortable in a person-to-person environment.

For many males, the importance of team play is learned early through boys' childhood games. For example, young boys learn to play cooperatively with teammates whom they may not like personally but who are essential to completing the team task. Team sports enable boys to develop skills that later assist them in working effectively with colleagues whom they may dislike personally. Lessons are also learned about the importance of leadership and winning. Team captains control players by devising strategies and calling plays. Team members are taught to work together to follow the captain's directives. Such training enables boys to assume the captain's role with subtlety and skill when their turn comes (Lipman-Blumen, 1984).

In contrast to boys, little girls infrequently play in large groups or teams. Typically, they play in small two- or three-person groups, (a pattern which carries over into the teenage years). Until relatively recently, competitive team sports were the exception rather than the rule for girls. When expanding female awareness began to recognize the importance of these games for adult skills, overt physical competition was more actively encouraged among females (Lipman-Blumen, 1984).

Not surprisingly, the will to win at competitive games remains less evident among girls. Girls are still taught that over-competition in general is unfeminine (especially against friends). In the female world friendship and relationships are more important than winning. Girls learn to select valued friends as playmates, even if the friend is less skilled at that particular game than a nonfriend. On occasion, elementary-age girls will deliberately allow their friends to win at competitive games simply in the name of friendship. This sharply contrasts the boys who are socialized to compete overtly (even against friends); to play to win, and to tolerate unliked teammates for the sake of the game. One long-term outcome of this childhood socialization is that women are less prepared for the realities of American organizational and political life which require competition, team play, and a winning orientation (Lipman-Blumen, 1984). Since friendship and relationships are so highly valued in female socialization, it is not surprising that female achievement is measured within the context of relationships. Lipman-Blumen further suggests that girls are groomed to helplessness and dependence by fathers who, in the name of love, pretend to have their daughters best interests at heart. Girls are socialized to first trust their fathers and later their boyfriends, husbands, and lovers. This pattern is reiterated when women are later asked to entrust their political fate to society's male leaders. Daughters learn to respect their father's "better judgment" because he has historically been regarded as the head of the house. This differs dramatically from the mother-daughter relationship. "Daddy's little girl" then learns the subtle yet invaluable lesson of controlling the powerful through demonstrated helplessness. But this learned helplessness simultaneously entraps women.

While self-esteem for boys and girls is fairly equal during elementary and middle school, there is a dramatic drop for females during the teen-age years. The gender scripting which emphasizes attractiveness as a primary goal for females contrasts with the primary goals of achievement and success for males (Basow, 1991). Women frequently conceal their actual abilities so as not to alienate males. Many females who experience success often shrug it off or minimize it whereas males tend to tend to do the opposite.

Even as small children, males are trained for a world of independent, aggressive action. In this "blue world," boys are groomed to confront problems "head on" and to take the world by storm. Boys soon learn that goals are most effectively reached by being active rather than passive and by controlling rather than being controlled. Determination, power, and skill pave the road to successful achievement. Achievement and success become ends in themselves. Boys are taught to enjoy the very pursuit of success and are given the message that their sense of self-worth, personal happiness, and self-satisfaction are garnered from successfully competing–by overcoming one's opponent or overcoming obstacles. In addition, the more skilled one's opponent or the larger the obstacle, the greater one's sense of success. Losing is failure. Failure is unacceptable. Males are taught that success is measured in terms of productivity, resources, and control–all the result of direct action. In our society the importance of self-reliant, individual action is systematically inculcated in males. To be masculine requires not only self-reliance and self-control, but control over other people and external resources.

Boys are encouraged to explore and investigate their environment. Although males and females do not differ in their exploratory behavior before age 3, between the ages of 3 and 6 boys begin to outdistance girls in their willingness to explore new environments (Lipman-Blumen, 1984). Endemic to this male training, boys are encouraged to deny and suppress fear.

In childhood games, boys test their strength and agility and are encouraged to take risks. Relatively speaking, girls are generally more protected. Childhood play is strongly related to gender roles and becomes an important aspect of socialization. During sibling play when Jane talks Dick into playing house, she is inevitably the mommy while he is the daddy. Or sometimes she convinces him to be the pupil while she as teacher eagerly anticipates the prospect of scolding him for his disruptive classroom behavior. Games such as these are typically short-lived and dissolve into conflict. Often, they are dependent upon the relative availability of same-sex peers with whom siblings would rather play (Lindsay, 1990).

Peer play socializes children in other ways as well. Boys games are frequently more complex, competitive, rule-governed, and allow for more role differentiation and a larger number of participants than games played by girls. As such, they may be seen as preparatory for roles to be assumed later in life. More often, girls play ordered games like hopscotch or jump-rope, in groups of two or three, with a minimum of competitiveness (Lindsay, 1990).

Girls are most often disciplined by the parents' withdrawal of their love. Withdrawing love encourages girls to depend on others' good will and affection. In contrast, young boys are socialized to a life of autonomy and self-reliance, undistracted by strong needs for external approval and affection. Girls' love-and-affection upbringing seems appropriately linked to the maternal role females have been trained to expect and seek in adulthood (Lipman-Blumen, 1984).

Both social and cognitive development are closely related to these socialization processes. Preadolescent girls have fewer, more intensive peer relationships while boys have numerous, less intensive ones. After children acquire a pattern of same-sex relationships, these are reinforced through a same-sex pattern of trust. A lesser degree of trust could then inhibit later cross-sex friendships. This leaves the respective worlds of male and female further divided (Lindsay, 1990).

THE EFFECTS OF TELEVISION
ON CHILDHOOD SOCIALIZATION

Television is a powerful source of socialization, especially for young children. It sets standards of behavior, offers role models and communicates behavioral and attitudinal expectations at a variety of levels based upon explicit and implicit messages. These images are further reinforced by other mass media, including movies, magazines, and popular music.

Television teaches. According to Miller and Reeves (1976) children, especially boys, identify with same-sex characters. Frequently, boys identify with characters possessing physical strength while girls identify with those who are physically attractive. Television is also gender stereotyped. Even those shows typically deemed acceptable for children commonly portray stereotyped female roles (Lindsay, 1990). Gradually, these images are beginning to improve. As more women become writers, directors, and producers, a slow but noticeable shift in gender stereotyping is occurring. Male consciousness about the deleterious effects of such female stereotyping is also changing (thanks in large part to the women's movement). In both commercial and cable TV a wide variety of viewing options, cultural orientations, and points of view have begun to broaden the range of available female role models.

That being said, the research is conclusive that children's television remains generally sexist and gender stereotyped. Contrary to reality, American children are being presented with a steady stream of stereotypic portrayals of males and females. Children see more males in significant roles with females constituting only 22 percent of all characters (usually in minor or supporting roles). Relatively few female characters work outside the home. Men, on the other hand, can be found in a variety of professional occupations such as attorney, physician, and scientist (Lindsay, 1990).

Television themes can also be categorized according to how the sexes are portrayed. Females pursue goals related to altruism, home, and family. Self-preservation is typically an important female goal because female characters are likely to be the targets of threats or violence. Male goals are characterized by self-indulgence, wealth, revenge, and expressions of hatred. Interestingly, women are more likely to achieve their goals when compared to men. However, these female goals are invariably traditional and therefore socially acceptable. For those television women who venture into a "man's world" the outcome is not as successful (Lindsay, 1990). Moreover, female characters are frequently portrayed as helpless victims who must be rescued by stronger, more competent male characters.

Saturday morning TV is replete with commercials aimed at selling toys and sugared cereal. Younger children, heavy viewers, and boys from low income homes are most susceptible to these commercials. So advertisers exploit these young impressionable minds by leading them to believe that doing without their product would be an intolerable hardship. Furthermore, they remind children that these products are readily available and waiting to be purchased at nearby stores. Unfortunately, such commercials are blatant in creating desires for toys encouraging domesticity in girls and high activity in boys (Lindsay, 1990).

Even more disturbing is the research which reveals that television may actually encourage antisocial behavior. A 1983 National Institute of Mental Health (NIMH) study reported that by age 15 a child has witnessed over 13,000 television killings.

The Male Machine

Much may be gleaned about a particular culture based upon its heroes, for its heroes symbolically depict deeply held cultural values, aspirations, and ideals. These are the role models to which both young and old aspire. In American culture, these heroes are often athletes, entertainers, or politicians. Typically, they are strong, independent males who are emotionally self-contained. Their arsenal of abilities may range from the ability to throw a football to the creative savvy to write a top-ten song. Thanks to an insatiable media, these intimate strangers are sometimes better known to us than members of our own extended family. The male hero is reflected in those men who constitute our fantasy identification figures. According to Goldberg (1976), they share certain specific characteristics: emotional muteness, an extremely independent style, and a lack of transparency or apparent emotional vulnerability, and in general, a very narrow band of outward expressiveness.

Despite substantial social and cultural changes over the last three decades the independent strong achiever who can be counted on to always be in control is still essentially the preferred male image. Success in the working world is still predicated on the repression of the vulnerable emotional self and the display of a controlled, deliberate, and calculated persona. From a traditional male point of view, effective leadership dictates that one be totally goal-oriented, undistracted by personal factors, and able to tune out extraneous unrelated "noise," human or otherwise, so that forward motion will not be impeded. The man who "feels" is inefficient and ineffective because he is emotionally involved and distracted from the business at hand. Under such circumstances his more dehumanized competitor will then surely pass him.

Herein lies one of the many double binds of traditional male socialization. In order to achieve success he must compete and alienate himself from others (i.e., "Nice guys finish last!") However, the price he must pay is the lack of satisfying emotional connections to other people. Or, as Goldberg (1976) put it, incompetence in personal relationships is the inevitable result of belief in the masculine ideal, the degree of incompetence is directly proportional to the degree of belief.

When American men speak personally about themselves to other men, they are often seen as individuals whose problems have gotten the better of them and who simply cannot help it. Men not driven to despair do not talk about themselves. Self-disclosure and expressiveness are associated with weakness. This is part of the reason that many men have such resistance to seeking professional help for their personal problems.

Obsessive competitiveness also severely inhibits male communication and friendships. Competition is the principal mode through which men relate to each other–at one level because they do not know how else to make contact, but more basically because it is the way to demonstrate to themselves and others the key masculine qualities of unwavering toughness and the ability to dominate and control. As a result, males constantly inject competition into situations which do not call for it (Fasteau, 1975).

This competitiveness substantially interferes with openness between men because of their inability to admit to, let alone reveal, vulnerabilities. "Real men" are not supposed to have doubts about achieving their goals. Though such feelings and concerns are part of everyone's inner life, "real men" must keep quiet about them. If others know how you really feel, you can be hurt, and that in itself is incompatible with traditional manhood. The inhibiting effect of this imperative is not limited to disclosures of major personal problems. Frequently, men do not even share day-to-day uncertainties and half-formulated plans of daily life with their friends (Fasteau, 1975).

One major source of these inhibitions among heterosexual men is homophobia. Although this is beginning to change within the younger generation, nothing is more frightening to traditional heterosexual males. It threatens, at one stroke, to take away every vestige of their claim to a masculine identity–something like knocking out the foundations of a building–and to expose them to ostracism, ranging from polite tolerance to violent revulsion, of their friends and colleagues. In many parts of the United States today a man can still be labeled as homosexual not just because of overt sexual acts but because of almost any sign of behavior which does not fit the masculine stereotype. In mainstream American society, the touching of another man, other than shaking hands or, under extreme emotional stress, like an arm around the shoulder, is taboo. Women, on the other hand, may kiss each other when they meet; men are uncomfortable when hugged even by close friends.

According to Goldberg, (1983) the contemporary male is a machine, driven by the unending need to prove himself. He lives by acquiring symbols that validate him, rather than experiencing the process of life. He is motivated by how things make him look as a man, not how they actually feel. As a result he diminishes his capacity for human intimacy.

For men, the fear of submission translates into a competitive compulsion to win and creates a grim seriousness, even when men play. Therefore, there is no relief from tension and competition in men's games. Everything becomes a variation on war. Men are conditioned to thrive on it. They are resentful when they lose and resented when they win. The man hates losers and he hates himself when he loses. Since losing becomes more likely as he gets older, feelings of self-hate and failure are built into his life experience. In the final analysis, it ends up being easier to socially isolate oneself rather than engage in never-ending hand-to-hand combat and symbolically re-enact some primordial struggle. (Goldberg, 1983).

Sex, Violence, and Sports

For men, sports provide a kind of state religion, something they can care about and share in a way that reaffirms fundamental components of their identity (Sabo and Runfola, 1980). Early on, males are taught to view their "natural aggression" as a resource to move them toward targeted goals in the public sphere. They are conditioned to act with unabashed competitiveness acting both for themselves and others in life's major arenas. They also learn that teamwork is both an approved of and effective strategy for success, one that is consistent with the ideology of large-scale institutions within which they must succeed (Lipman-Blumen, 1984).

The masculine mystique is based on toughness and domination. Though these qualities may once have been necessary in a time when men felled trees and slew wild animals, they are seriously outdated in contemporary society. These archaic and destructive values have no legitimate place in our world but continue to exist as idealized standards for some lofty state of masculinity. According to Komisar (1980) the ultimate proof of manhood is sexual violence. Even the language of sex is a lexicon that describes the power of men over women. Men are "aggressive" as they "take" or "make" women, showing their potency (power) in the conquest. Women, on the other hand, "submit" or "surrender," allowing themselves to be "violated" and "possessed."

For cultural feminists, male sexuality is not only compulsive, but, as Dworkin (1987) describes "the stuff of murder, not love." Thus for men, Dworkin asserts, sexuality and violence are closely intertwined and find their cultural expression in pornography. Cultural feminists are so convinced that male sexuality is, at its core, lethal that they reduce it to its most alienated and violent expressions. The actions of the Marquis de Sade or Son of Sam come to symbolize the murderousness of male sexuality, and sexual intercourse becomes a mere euphemism for rape (Echols, 1989). What happens when such damaging assumptions about men and male sexuality are actually put into practice in intimate male-female relationships?

If aggression is linked to the fracture of the human connection, then caretaking activities make the social world safe, by avoiding isolation and preventing aggression. From this view, aggression no longer appears as a dangerous impulse that must be repressed but rather as signifying a fractured connection or failed relationship. Hence, the prevalence of violence in men's fantasies, denotes a world where danger is ever-present. Moreover, it signifies a problem in making interpersonal connections, causing relationships to dissolve and turning separation into a dangerous isolation (Gilligan, 1982).

By exploiting the anti-pornography movement, cultural feminism has succeeded in mobilizing feminists regardless of sexual preference. Unfortunately, anti-pornography activists have united feminists by manipulating women's traditional sexual conservatism and appealing to widely held stereotypes regarding male and female sexuality. In advocating a return to a female sexual standard, cultural feminists ignore the extent to which femaleness functions as the complement to maleness and therefore reflects dominant cultural assumptions.

Echols (1989) suggests that by treating femaleness as an pure force for good, cultural feminists have tried to associate capitalism and sexual repression. Ultimately, cultural feminism degenerates into the view, so eloquently articulated by cultural feminist entrepreneur Laura Brown, that "feminism is anything we say it is."

In his disturbing book, *Sexual Suicide*, George Guilder discussed the correlation between sex and violence. While his polemic arguments were largely reactionary propaganda he did note that men commit over 90 percent of the major violent crimes: 100 percent of the rapes, 95 percent of the burglaries; comprise 94 percent of our drunken drivers, 70 percent of suicides and 91 percent of offenses against families and children. More specifically, the chief perpetrators are single men. Single men comprise between 80-90 percent of most of the categories of social pathology (Guilder, 1975).

While one might argue with the accuracy of the statistics Guilder cites, the basic fact remains that most of the violent crimes today are committed by men and a great many of the victims are women and children. The haunting question is what is it that predisposes men toward violence? Across urban America, violence has become a painful daily reality, including black-on-black violence and cross-racial violence originating from both sides of the color line.

Recently in uptown New Orleans a young white couple had parked their car and were walking up to their home one evening when out of nowhere three black youths ranging in age from 13 to 15 years old rode up to them on their bicycles and threatened them, demanding their money. The frightened couple then tried to escape and bolted toward their house. The youths immediately took aim and killed the young man. Then the terrified young woman fled for her life back to their car, somehow managed to unlock the passenger door, then closed and locked the door in the nick of time. At that point, one of the youths rode his bicycle up to the car, promptly pulled out a gun and fatally shot the young woman in cold blood.

This real-life tragedy is deeply disturbing in so many ways. The fact that the youths were black and the victims were white fuels the deepest racial fears and hatreds already so rampant throughout this country. The fact that the perpetrators were so young undermines peoples' collective hopes for a better world. This was wanton and senseless violence. Tragically, this isolated incident is increasingly typical in urban America. However, within the context of this book, the burning question is how and why did these three males learn to behave this way and what kind of men will they become?

Gender and Power

Power refers to the process whereby individuals or groups obtain and/or maintain the capacity to impose their will upon others, despite implicit or explicit opposition, through invoking or threatening punishment, as well as offering or withholding rewards. Once power is firmly established, the explicit use of punishments and rewards is unnecessary. The mutual realization that one controls such resources is usually sufficient to evoke compliance from the less powerful (Lipman-Blumen, 1984).

Gender roles provide the blueprint for all other power relationships including power relationships between generations, socioeconomic classes, religious, racial, and ethnic groups as well as between imperial powers and their colonies (Lipman-Blumen, 1984). Generally, both the powerful and powerless take the social structure for granted without recognizing the degree to which laws, customs, and institutional practices perpetuate differential power based on gender. A cultural mythology is concocted to explain and justify the status quo and those in charge pretend to bear the burden of protecting the interests of the less powerful when in fact they are merely consolidating their privileged social standing. Since power is the infrastructure of the sex-gender system these gender roles are carefully preserved lest changes in this primal power relationship spread to all other established power relationships.

Historically, Western culture has viewed the relationship between men and women as the earthly replica of that between God and humans. This religious metaphor attempts to sanctify male patriarchy. Moreover, so long as gender roles maintain their "proper power balance," all other power relationships based on this model were safe. Because it is such a complex and ongoing dialectic, attempts to redefine this balance of power are strenuously resisted due to social and institutional inertia.

Men and women are locked in an endless power struggle which involves the interface of the public and private spheres. However, decisions made in the public sphere, commonly called "public policy" have a clear impact on private lives. In other words, male-controlled public institutions (as well as the laws which regulate them) exert a direct influence over all men's and women's private lives. In our increasingly bureaucratic society institutions have a tremendous ability to reward and/or punish individuals. Consequently, public decisions have enormous potential for widespread personal impact. These public decisions, typically made by men, can alter the very direction and nature of individuals' personal lives.

Major societal decisions (macrodecisions) and private interpersonal decisions (microdecisions) are inextricably intertwined with the gender power struggle. Not surprisingly, when men engage in macromanipulation women often react with micromanipulation. Although growing numbers of women are participating in the larger public arena, this is often around micro-related issues directly connected to the family (private) sphere. (Lipman-Blumen, 1984). At present, men still monopolize the authority to define, evaluate, and reward women.

Restricted to micromanipulation, women become well versed in interpreting the meta messages and body language of men. Lipman-Blumen explains that "by employing various interpersonal strategies of micromanipulation, women have learned to sway, circumvent, and subvert the decisions of the powerful to which they seemingly have agreed" (Lipman-Blumen, 1984:30).

Power is neither an attribute of the powerful nor a commodity. Rather, power is a process characterized by ongoing negotiation and renegotiation between the more and the less powerful. Each interchange defines and redefines the relationship by decisions about who and what can and will prevail. The cultivation, protection, and poaching of power between men and women continues in earnest at a wide variety of public and private levels. The male-female power relationship is at the core of our social fabric. Once it begins to unravel so do all other power relationships (Lipman-Blumen, 1984).

THE FAILED PROMISE OF ANDROGYNY

The term androgyny has two commonly confused meanings: (1) monoandrogynism where both feminine and masculine characteristics exist together in every individual; and (2) polyandrogynism, whereby persons could develop any set or sets of traits regardless of their biological sex. Most psychologists when using the term androgyny are referring to the first definition, monoandrogynism. Many writers have argued, however, that the concept of monoandrogynism could become as restrictive as traditional sex roles if everyone must develop both agenetic and expressive characteristics. In this sense, polyandrogynism, or "sex role transcendence" allows individuals greater freedom. Another conceptual problem with androgyny as a theoretical construct lies in precisely defining two distinct sets of personality characteristics, namely, masculine and feminine (Basow, 1986).

Judith Lorber (1989) contends that if gender is a social construction and that if the relations between men and women are essentially social relations, then what is socially constructed can be reconstructed and social relationships can be rearranged. Thus a social order without gender as an organizing principle is possible. The construct of gender rests on the biological dichotomy of the sexes which is then extended to other social realms.

To Lindsay (1990) androgyny refers to the integration of "masculine and feminine" characteristics. Through this integration, a

new model for male and female roles would emerge based upon the belief that it is both possible and desirable for individuals to possess and express both masculine and feminine qualities. Ideally, androgyny would eliminate unnecessary restrictions imposed by rigid gender roles, thereby increasing our range of available options. The new androgynous ideal combines masculine autonomy with feminine affection. Emotional expression has become increasingly acceptable for both sexes and intimate relationships in the private sphere have become the major arena for developing one's unique self. In contrast, the ideal masculine self that accompanied the rise of capitalism praised independence, emotional control, and success in the public sphere. Conceptions of love also became increasingly androgynous after feminized love was superseded by new ideals of husband-wife companionship and open communication. Ideals of intimacy and androgyny did not become powerful, although these ideals were visible much earlier, during the transition to capitalism (Cancian, 1989).

Human relationships were increasingly analyzed in economic terms governed by the rules of the free market due to the growth of a market economy and wage labor, coupled with other trends such as urbanization and geographical mobility.

Glorifying womanliness consolidates female unity and power, but when pushed to extremes it comes dangerously close to reviving the cult of true womanhood and the ideology of separate spheres. Cancian posits that the long-term goal of feminism must be no less than the eradication of gender as an organizing principle of post-industrial society. Male and female are strictly socially constructed roles because the basic biological nature of the human species is hermaphroditic (Cancian, 1989).

As children pass through physical and biochemical changes associated with puberty, their behavior is further dichotomized and organized around gender-appropriate sexual scripts. These scripts vary from society to society, and within societies depending upon class, race, religion, and ethnic group. Anatomical secondary sex characteristics are less important in signifying gender than the extensive display signals which Birdwhistle calls "tertiary sexual characteristics" (Lorber, 1989).

Socialist feminism envisages a society in which maleness and femaleness are socially irrelevant, in which men and women as we know them, will no longer exist. The impact of this "genderlessness" is put into a different perspective by Alice Echols (1989) in The New Feminism of Yin and Yang. She believes that it is tempting for any oppressed group to seek solace in the reclamation and rehabilitation of that identity which the larger culture has systematically denigrated. This approach is especially compelling when the prospects for radical structural change seem remote, and the only alternative seems to be the liberal solution of token representation and assimilation into an oppressive and inegalitarian system. Unfortunately, as post-modern feminism has become synonymous with the reclamation and establishment of a so-called "female principle," it has come to reflect and reproduce dominant cultural assumptions about women.

Cultural feminists have now made gender an absolute rather than a relative category. Thus, cultural feminism has equated women's liberation with the development and preservation of a distinct female counterculture.

Cultural feminists hold that if the source of the world's many problems can be traced to the dominance of the male principle, its solution can be found in the reassertion of the female principle. However, this explanation reduces men and women to mere caricatures of themselves. As Echols (1989) puts it, such failed logic is most apparent in their characterization of male sexuality as compulsive and violent and female sexuality as muted and ethereal.

It is ironic that cultural feminists advance biological explanations of gender given the energy that radical feminists devoted to refuting biological justifications of gender hierarchy. Such arguments generally attribute patriarchy to the rapaciousness or barrenness of male biology. Thus Susan Brownmiller writes in *Against Our Will* that rape is a function of male biology based on the inescapable construction of male genitalia just as the human male is predator and the human female is his natural prey (Brownmiller, 1975).

While radical feminists perceived female biology as a liability and thus mirrored the culture's devaluation of the female body, cultural feminists have overreacted by arguing that female biology is in fact a powerful resource. Cultural feminists distinguish between patriarchal conditioned femininity, which they characterize as passive and submissive, and femininity which they define as nurturant, loving, open, and egalitarian. According to their logic, female passivity is only a conditioned response whereas male violence is a reflection of the basic character of men. By interpreting masculinity as immutable, the cultural feminist analysis assumes that men are the enemy by virtue of their maleness rather than the power that the patriarchal system lends them (Echols, 1989).

Cultural feminists vilify the "political left" because its analysis so completely contravenes their belief system, especially their faith that truly radical change will be achieved only when the culture returns to female values and that race and class are merely ancillary to the gender hierarchy. In fact, cultural feminists treat race and class oppression like patriarchal fallout that will be swept away by a women's revolution. They make feminism synonymous with female bonding and contend that the rehabilitation of the mother-daughter relationship is central to feminism (Echols, 1989).

Christopher Lasch (1979) believed that once women began to question the inevitability of subordination and to reject those conventions formerly associated with it, they could no longer retreat into the safety of those conventions. Yet today, women have retreated. Despite the fact that most women today believe in the benefits and value of the women's movement, only 16 percent of college-age women and 33 percent of middle-age women consider themselves feminists (Basow, 1991). This is not to minimize the impact of the feminist movement. What it does is highlight the enormous confusion about what feminism means. Considering the prior discussion in this chapter it is apparent that an array of very different feminist perspectives continue in earnest.

WOMEN'S CHANGING ROLE IN THE FAMILY

In recent years women have been marrying later and less often, having fewer children, and divorcing more. Those with the most education and income are the most likely to divorce and least likely to remarry. In contrast, the wealthiest and best-educated men are the most likely to stay married or to remarry quickly. If the couple divorces, the woman is far more likely to suffer economically.

Women experience an average drop in income of 30 percent during the first year following divorce, whereas the man's income rises an average of 17 percent. Today, 75 percent of the poor are women or children, mostly living in single-parent households. After divorce men have an ever-larger pool of marriageable spouses from which to choose. In first marriages, the average wife is three years younger than her husband; for second marriages the wife is, on average, six years younger than her husband (Carter and McGoldrick, 1989).

Traditionally, women have been held responsible for the maintenance of family relationships as well as caretaking; for their husbands, children, parents, their husbands' parents, and any other sick or dependent family members. Today, almost one-fifth of women aged 55-59 are providing in-home care to an elderly relative. Usually one daughter or a daughter-in-law has the primary care of an elderly mother. Clearly, caregiving for the very old (who are mostly women) is primarily a women's issue. Increasingly, however, younger women have joined the labor force, and thus are unavailable for caretaking without extreme hardship. More than half of all women aged 45-64 are working outside the home, and most of them full-time. With an ever-increasing trend toward four-generation families, the caregivers are more apt to be elderly themselves, and struggling with their own declining functioning. Consequently, today's middle-aged women are caught in a "dependency squeeze" between their parents and their children (Carter and McGoldrick, 1989).

Betty Friedan (1981) entreated the women's movement to enter its "second stage" and take on the problems of restructuring work and home, or else a new generation of women would be vulnerable to backlash. Yet, the women's movement has not moved into that necessary second stage, so the women struggling with these new problems view them as purely personal, not political, and no longer look to the women's movement for solutions. Friedan is urging us to free a new generation of women from its new double burden of guilt and isolation. The guilt of less-than-perfect motherhood and less-than-perfect professional career performance is real because it is not possible to have it all when jobs are still structured for women whose only responsibility is running their families. Friedan implores women to tackle the formidable political tasks of restructur-

ing home and work so that women who are married and have
children can also earn and have their own voice in the decision
making at the public policy level.

For men the relationship of family and work is seen as mutually
supportive and complementary, but for women work and family
have historically presented conflicting demands (Carter and
McGoldrick, 1989). The cultural contradiction is that although
women are increasingly participating in the nation's labor force, the
dominant cultural value suggests that women remain in the home.
The "superwomen myth" of the 1980s claimed that "women could
have it all"–spouse, family, career, and home. Unfortunately, this
turned out to be a cruel hoax because the many women who tried to
have it frequently ended up overloaded, overstressed, and over-
wrought. Rather than feeling that they are doing any single job well,
women commonly end up feeling as if they are letting everybody
down. Coupled with persistent female socialization about the need
to please others this has a particularly damaging effect of women's
self-esteem. Unfortunately, this self-destructive cycle shows no sign
of abating.

Even though the majority of women work, the sharing of family
responsibilities to balance the work load is not occurring. While
husbands and children participate slightly in housework, the vast
majority of household labor is done by wives–between 74-92 percent of the major tasks. Employed women continue to do 4.8 hours
a day of housework, compared with 1.6 hours for their husbands.
As so many women put it, "If I don't do it, it doesn't get done."
Husbands performed between 12 percent and 26 percent of tasks
with the exception of outside errands, where they did 54 percent
and their wives 74 percent (the overlap represents work done together or alternated). Children did between 7 percent and 13 percent
of the tasks. Respondents made it clear that the household remained
the wife's responsibility although other family members sometimes
helped her (Carter and McGoldrick, 1989).

WOMEN AND MEN: AN OVERVIEW

The role prescriptions for men and women vary substantially,
based upon the prevailing cultural mores of one's particular genera-

tion. For today's senior citizens the traditional role models still apply even though these models are out of step with our post-industrial society. However, the "baby boomers" (i.e., those born between 1945 and 1960) are a transitional generation. Though raised with traditional bedrock American values the baby boomers have been forever transformed by the social upheaval of the 1960s and 1970s. The women's movement continues to enjoy its greatest numerical, spiritual, and political strength from among this generation. Interestingly, today's youth are not nearly so politically inclined as supported by the fact that only 16 percent of college-age women consider themselves feminists (Basow, 1991). In some ways today's youth are a throwback to the 1950s generation. Establishment oriented, they grew up in the Reagan-Bush era, believing in the prevailing neo-conservative ideology so widely propagated in this age of conservatism. It is a peculiar combination and in some sense a generation lacking a clear-cut identity. The resurgence and continued popularity of sixties music and musicians has been made possible by a younger generation who have not yet found their souls and perhaps never will.

The ever-increasing feminization of poverty over the next several years means that by the year 2000 the vast majority of the poor will be women and children (Carter and McGoldrick, 1989). A 1988 study showed that 46 percent of all women earned less than $10,000 annually and that 90 percent of all single-parent families were headed by women (Basow, 1991). In addition, almost one-half of all single parent families live below the poverty level.

How will these changes affect the ways in which children are raised and nurtured? The chronic stress of unemployment, poverty, and discrimination makes it very difficult to sustain relationships and leaves little time to learn the skills necessary for intimate relating (Carter and McGoldrick, 1989).

This is the first generation in which most young women today expect to have a career and family. In a recent national survey of high school students only 5 percent expected to be full-time homemakers. However, 20 percent of high school females still believe in traditional marital roles, (wife at home raising a family) while 46 percent of high school males believe in it. For college-age women the percentage remains at 20 percent, but drops to 31 percent for college-age males (Basow, 1991).

Despite the more entrenched attitudes of the older generation, women are participating in greater numbers in the workplace. Between 1970 and 1990 the rate of working women between 25 and 34 years old increased from 45 percent to 73 percent. Today, 58 percent of all women and 77 percent of all men are in the labor force (Basow, 1991). However, occupational segregation continues in earnest. Basow also observes that the top 10 jobs for women in 1990 are not unlike 1960:

1. Secretary
2. Cashier
3. Bookkeeper
4. Registered Nurse
5. Nurse's Aide/Orderly
6. Teacher
7. Waitress
8. Salesperson
9. Child Care Worker
10. Cook

Fewer than 3 percent of top executive positions in this country are held by women. Nearly half of all women earned less than $10,000 annually in 1980. In 1990 white women earn 68 percent of male wages, while black women earn 61 percent, and Hispanic women earn 54 percent (Basow, 1991).

Basow further estimates that at the current rate of change, full equality for women will take somewhere between 400 and 500 years (Basow, 1991). Despite modest gains in the most recent election, women still hold fewer than 20 percent of elected offices in the United States (and most of these are lower status such as local school board, etc.). It is therefore apparent that women have not come as far as many would like to believe. One of the harbingers as well as shapers of prevailing attitudes, the commercial media, has ever so gradually begun to alter its stereotypic portrayals of women. However, portraying women as strong and independent merely to sell more perfume, blue jeans, or athletic shoes is a dubious improvement at best. The meta-message that "if you buy our product you will be more powerful, in control, and/or independent" ultimately exploits female anger and discontent for the sake of monetary gain.

Nonetheless, the available role options for both men and women have broadened substantially. In fact, part of the difficulty in analyzing contemporary male and female roles is that there is no longer any single viable cultural prototype which readily applies to either. Traditional stereotypes of the strong, independent male and weak, dependent female are no longer appropriate, but what are our alternatives? We are bombarded with a dizzying array of male and female role models, most of whom have little to do with the day-to-day challenges of post-industrial life. Nevertheless, the mass media still offers up the perfect images of models and supermodels whose flawless appearance not only projects sex appeal in order to sell products, but also sets the standard for gender role ideals. The end result is that men and women are confused (and hence more susceptible to external influence). Unfortunately, this role and identity confusion translate directly into our diminishing ability to form and maintain intimate relationships. Given the impossible standard to which men and women are encouraged to aspire, the level of personal and social expectations has increased dramatically. Consequently, the probability for failure in interpersonal relationships far outweighs the possibility for success.

During the last three decades, the women's movement has substantially altered the landscape of men's lives in four different areas. First, the feminist revolution has made gender roles visible. Women have demonstrated the centrality of gender in social life. Gender has joined race and class as one of three primary axes around which social life is organized. Second, women are in the workplace to stay. The rapidly increasing numbers of women in the workplace has unalterably shifted the prevailing definitions of male and female roles and responsibilities. Third, the efforts to balance work and family life have substantially redrawn the boundaries of private and public spheres and women's participation in each. Finally, women have redefined the sexual landscape. It is women, (as well as gay men) who have been the real sexual revolutionaries over the last two decades. Women now feel empowered to claim sexual desire as a natural aspect of their being (Kimmel, 1991).

Men, on the other hand, have not undergone a comparable revolution. While women's consciousness and roles have shifted dramatically, men have been left in the starting blocks. Heretofore, men have not felt empowered to change their dysfunctional role patterns in any substantive ways. The conflict between traditional male roles and ever changing female roles is creating a widening gap in social and personal expectations. In other words, men aren't doing worse; women's expectations have simply risen to the point where the two are vastly out of sync.

At present, there is no ceremony by which adolescent males can achieve a secure manhood. Consequently, proving one's masculinity turns into a relentless struggle which is never completely won. Society has constructed definitions of masculinity around wealth, power, and status–whoever has the most toys when he dies, wins–but few men are ever wealthy, powerful, or respected enough to feel secure. There is always someone more successful, and males secretly covet their success. As a result, most men feel like failures not only professionally, but as men (Kimmel, 1991).

During adolescence, when sexual awakening is coupled with the craving for a secure gender identity, sexuality and gender identity merge. Robert Bly (1992) talks about finding the "warrior within" as a means of uncovering one's truer masculine self. He also speaks of healing primordial wounds inflicted by the loss or absence of one's father. His fascinating masculine and feminine archetypes offer men provocative new perspectives about the deeper mystical roots of male and female.

Kimmel (1991) further believes that we, as a culture, must confront adolescent males' need for developing a secure, confident, inner sense of themselves as men, which he believes can only be accomplished by changing what it means to be a real man. Otherwise, we shall continue to face the dangerous consequences that come from our twisted efforts to prove ourselves.

More and more men are finding that their relationships with other men and with their children are impoverished by precisely the things that they thought would make them real men. Sexism and homophobia continue to distort men's relationships with other men as well as with their children, making them uneasy around other men and as well as fearful of the feminization of children (Kimmel,

1991). But the emotional impoverishment of men's own lives, coupled with the demands of women that men participate in child-care–as well as their own desires to do so–will make it imperative that men raise these issues.

According to Kimmel (1991) masculinity means always going for it, taking no prisoners, and living on the edge. Their relentless pursuit of sex is but the most concrete expression of men's obsessive drive to prove their own masculinity. However, two issues which directly stem from this obsessive pursuit are date rape and AIDS. Men's obsessive risk-taking makes them far more vulnerable to stress-related diseases, accidental death, and AIDS. Has AIDS become a man's disease? Over 90 percent of all AIDS patients are men; AIDS is now the leading cause of death for (white) men aged 33-45 nationwide (Kimmel, 1991).

Two surveys were conducted by the Roper organization in 1970 and 1990. In each, 3,000 American women and 1,000 American men were asked a set of questions about their perceptions of men. Findings indicated that in 1970, two-thirds of the respondents agreed that men were kind and considerate; in 1990, slightly less than half agreed. In 1970, 41 percent believed that the only thing men wanted from a date was sex; in 1990, 54 percent agreed. In 1970, 42 percent believed that men were basically selfish and interested only in their own opinions; in 1990, 58 percent agreed. In 1970, 49 percent believed that men's egos require that they put women down; in 1990, 55 percent agreed. In 1970, 39 percent believed that men were really only interested in their work, and not really interested in their families. By 1990, after two decades of a fatherhood revolution, 53 percent of those surveyed believed that men were only interested in their work, up 14 percent (Kimmel, 1991).

CONCLUSIONS

Male and female roles are caught in the vortex of a darkening social storm, which threatens the social and psychological underpinnings of each while promising an uncertain future. The potential for positive change is substantial but so is the potential for continued conflict. At present, precious few of these struggles have been successfully resolved. This leaves men and women locked in the throes of conflict, each struggling to cast off the shackles of their traditional roles, with neither very willing to concede to the other.

Confusion over the definitions, aims, and tactics of feminism has ended up alienating both men and women (but particularly men). The zero-sum nature of our current political system dictates that in order for women to make gains, men must give something up. Naturally, men and male-dominated institutions have used any number of means to resist losing any status, power, or privilege. It is one thing to agree in principle to equal rights for women and quite another to relinquish what are deemed by some men to be their inalienable birthright.

The ideal male and female roles are elusive concepts because each is the joint product of biology, socialization, family, social stratification, politics, and cultural conditioning. Ultimately, perhaps it is more helpful not to conceive of either role as a fixed ideal, but rather as an ongoing dialectical interchange between men and women. As this dialectical process continues to unfold in ways expected and unexpected, our respective abilities to listen, communicate, and adapt our attitudes and behavior to the needs of others are perhaps as important as the actual choices we make. Some three decades ago Alvin Toffler suggested that our abilities to form and maintain friendships would soon be more important than any of our actual friends. To extrapolate this notion to male and female role might suggest that our ability to flexibly integrate new attitudinal, behavioral, and role expectations into our gender identity might prove far more important than any fixed and enduring aspects of male or female. Encouraging men and women to incorporate a broader and more flexible role repertoire into one's existing male or female identity (Basow's sex role transcendence) is perhaps a more realistic goal.

While it is a noble-sounding goal, sex role transcendence is much easier to achieve in theory than actual practice. Given the excessive role strain and complex stresses engendered by rising expectations for both men and women, how have these factors affected dating and courtship in the 1990s? How do male and female communication patterns differ on the verbal, non-verbal, and contextual levels? Finally, given the complexity and excessive demands of modern life, how can any two people possibly find each other and come together in order to establish and maintain a meaningful intimate relationship?

REFERENCES

Bandura, A. 1973. *Aggression: A social learning analysis.* Englewood Cliffs, NJ: Prentice-Hall.

Basow, S. 1991. "Gender Role Stereotypes in the 1990s," Lecture presented at Tulane University, November 1991.

_____ 1986. *Gender alternatives.* Belmont, CA: Wadsworth, Inc.

Bly, R. 1992. *Iron John.* New York: Random House, Inc.

Brownmiller, S. 1975. *Against our will.* New York: Simon and Schuster.

Carter, B. and McGoldrick, M. (Eds.) 1989. *The changing family life cycle.* Needham Heights, MA: Allyn and Bacon.

Cancian, F. 1989. Love and the rise of capitalism. In: Risman, B. and Schwartz, P. (Eds.) *Gender in intimate relationships.* Belmont, CA: Wadsworth Publishing Co., Inc.

Dworkin, A. 1987. *Intercourse.* New York: The Free Press.

Echols, A. 1989. The new feminism of Yin and Yang. In Risman, B. and Schwartz, P. (Eds.) *Gender in intimate relationships.* Belmont, CA: Wadsworth Publishing Co., Inc.

Edwards, D.A. 1968. Mice: Fighting by neonatally androgenized females, *Science* 161:1027-28.

Fasteau, M.F. 1975. *The male machine.* New York: Dell Publishing Co.

Feagin, J. 1989. Racial and ethnic relations (3rd edition). Englewood Cliffs, NJ: Prentice-Hall, Inc.

Friedan, B. 1981. *The second stage.* New York: Summit Books.

Gilligan, C. 1982. *In a different voice.* Cambridge, MA: Harvard Press.

Goldberg, H. 1983. *The new male-female relationship.* New York: Signet.

_____ 1976. *The hazards of being male.* New York: Signet.

Guilder, G. 1975. *Sexual Suicide.* New York: Bantam Books.

Kimmel, M. 1991. Issues for men in the 1990s. *Changing Men,* 17(22):4-6/17.

Kohlberg, L. 1966. A Cognitive-Developmental Analysis of Children's Sex-Role Concepts and Attitudes. In: Macoby, E. (Ed.) *The development of sex differences.* Stanford, CA: Stanford University Press.

Komisar, L. 1980. Violence and the Masculine Mystique. In Sabo, D. and Runfola, R. (Eds.) *Jock: Sports and male identity.* Englewood Cliffs, NJ: Prentice-Hall, Inc.

Lasch, C. 1979. *The culture of narcissism.* New York: Warner Books.

Lindsay, L. 1990. *Gender roles/A sociological perspective.* Englewood Cliffs, NJ: Prentice-Hall.

Lipman-Blumen, J. 1984. *Gender roles and power.* Englewood Cliffs, NJ: Prentice-Hall.

Lorber, J. 1989. Dismantling Noah's Ark. In Risman, B. and Schwartz, P. (Eds.) *Gender in intimate relationships*. Belmont, CA: Wadsworth Publishing Co., Inc.

Miller, M.M. and Reeves, B. 1976. Dramatic TV content and children's sex-role stereotypes. *Journal of Broadcasting*, 20(1):35-50.

Sabo, D. and Runfola, R. 1980. *Jock: Sports and male identity.* Englewood Cliffs, NJ: Prentice-Hall Inc.

Chapter 4

Dating and Courtship

The changing social context has irrevocably altered the nature and structure of dating and courtship. Today the traditional notion of "courtship" is often deemed a quaint ritual of times past. However, in order to fully understand dating and "courtship" today it is necessary to explore the larger philosophical and historical contexts which constitute the basis for today's confusion about the rules, structure, and purposes of "coming together."

THE PSYCHOLOGICAL SIGNIFICANCE OF LOVE

Freud believed that we cloak our beloved in the clothes we wish for ourselves; that we project onto the person we love those characteristics which constitute our own ego ideal. Thus, for Freud, falling in love was, at its essence, a substitute for personal achievement.

Theodore Reik (1944) held that there are two stages in loving someone. The first stage, the desire and inclination to fall in love, grows out of a need to escape from internal discontent. In contrast, the second stage, in which we actually love another person in a committed, enduring fashion, requires personal courage and security about the self.

Fromm (1956) distinguished between immature and mature types of love. In immature love, the lover exploits the beloved in order to satisfy his/her lover's needs; while in mature love, the lover possesses a genuine concern for the beloved's welfare. Fromm further theorized that both sexual attraction and romantic love are motivated by the tension between opposing polarities. He maintained that just as sexual attraction is based on the need for psychological union with the opposite sexual pole, romantic love depends upon a need for psychological union with the opposite sex character type. To a large extent, these opposite character types correspond to traditional sex-role stereotypes. Fromm believed that the masculine character type is defined by qualities of activity, discipline, and adventurousness while the feminine type reflects receptiveness, protection, and motherliness.

Rollo May (1969) suggested that in the worldview of Christianity, equality referred to the paradoxical notion that as elements of a common humanity, we are all "one," though each person is also separate and unique. Fromm suggests that in modern society, equality has come to mean sameness rather than oneness, and he maintains that this change has affected erotic love. Women are equal because they are not different any more.

Reik (1957) further postulated that "falling in love" is an attempt through the possession of an admired love object, to obtain those personal qualities that one lacks. The linkage between falling in love and the presence of oppositional polarities between the partners was also made by Jung (1921) and by Roszak and Roszak (1969). However, more recent evidence (Critelli et al., 1986) links a similarity in values and personality to liking, while oppositions between partners are more likely to generate romantic love.

Maslow (1968) distinguished between "deficit love" and "being love." For Maslow, the type of love is closely intertwined with the type of individual who loves. Those who are more "self-actualized" (more personally secure and open to challenging experiences) are viewed as being more likely to engage in "being love" than those who are less secure.

Genuine love has been described as a rare expression of optimal functioning that involves active caring for a partner's needs and a desire to experience the other at an intimate level without masks and roles. On the other hand, "pseudo love" is much more passive (something one falls into) and denotes neurotic dependency. Romantic love is characterized by affiliative and dependency needs, feelings of exclusiveness and absorption, physical attraction, passion, and idealization. In contrast, conjugal love refers to love between mature adults and is composed of close friendship, trust, lack of criticalness, appreciation, respect, sharing, intimate knowledge of the other, loyalty, and a willingness to sacrifice for the partner (Critelli et al., 1986).

COURTSHIP THEN AND NOW

Throughout most of our country's history, coupling has typically been arranged by either the respective families or a third party whose job it was to make suitable matches. In colonial America there was minimal individual freedom and choice. Love was not nearly so important as social, economic, ethnic, and familial considerations. Ostensibly, sexual passion was expected to be contained. Yet, as Cate and Lloyd (1992) point out, the premarital conception rate in colonial America in the 1770s hit an all-time high of 30 percent. By the early 1800s the definition of love and affection became an emotional as well as an economic decision. Love was deemed to be more compelling than friendship, more lasting than passion, more serious than romance. Valued traits in a potential mate included openness, candor, and sincerity. However, romantic love was devalued, since it was viewed as immature and unreliable. During the mid-nineteenth century women were seen as morally superior to men. But this type of superiority was a double-edged sword. Because the women were of a higher moral character than the men of the household, it was felt that certain legal rights (e.g., the vote) were unnecessary for women (Rothman, 1984). Thus, social equality was not met with full legal or economic equality. Among the privileged classes during the late nineteenth century and early twentieth century an elaborate system of etiquette was established to enable young women to receive appropriate gentleman callers usually in their own home. Such regular visits by gentleman callers were intended as a suitable precursor to marriage. As the decades progressed, the system of informal controls loosened and courtship moved into the dance halls and cabarets. This change was significant in that it loosened family and kinship controls over who dated whom and in what context. Ironically, the movement of courtship from the home to the public sphere ended up affording less privacy and time to get to know one another (Cate and Lloyd, 1992). Moreover, while the cabaret allowed for more potential partners and greater sexual experimentation, it ended up inhibiting emotional openness and candor. At some levels, these social inter-actions among relative strangers fostered a tendency to more selec-tively self-disclose and adopt a somewhat more distant and self-pro-tective social posture.

By 1920 informal, unchaperoned, male-female interaction with no specific commitment had become the centerpiece of twentieth-century American courtship. The rules of dating were established by the peer group rather than the community at large. These new social protocols represented an almost revolutionary social change for that era. The rise of dating in the first part of the twentieth century was attributable to both the creation of adolescence as a distinct period of the life cycle and the emergence of mass culture. Adolescence enabled the selection of a mate to be delayed while the emergence of mass culture provided a uniform set of rules of eti-quette to be followed by all. Other scholars cite the shift from rural to urban society, the emancipation of women, the emphasis on companionship marriage, widespread ownership of cars, the emer-gence of motion pictures, and the resulting decrease in community control as forces which brought dating into prominence (Cate and Lloyd, 1992). It was dating–not baseball–that was to become this country's national pastime.

In addition, the rules of courtship were irrevocably changed. Dating and courtship were becoming increasingly separate, each with its own objectives. Dating was focused on increasing one's popularity without becoming emotionally involved, whereas court-ship focused on finding a mate who possessed those enduring traits deemed essential for successful family life (honesty, maturity, loy-alty, and trust–to name a few). Dating turned into courtship once a young couple began keeping "steady company." By the 1930s steady relationships had emerged as a distinct stage between casual dating and the commitment to marry.

During the late 1940s the much publicized "man shortage," the changing male and female roles during and after World War II, and the changing sociocultural attitudes fueled changes in dating, court-ship, and marriage. The widespread migration of women out of the private sphere (home) and into the public sector (paid employment) also created dramatic shifts in women's self-concepts and social roles vis-à-vis men. Women and men were forced to acknowledge that females could competently perform the work that was formerly the sole province of men. Women became more self-confident and independent and began to challenge the confines of their traditional roles both outside and inside the home.

Dating in the 1940s began tentatively in early adolescence and continued in earnest throughout high school. "Going steady" became both fashionable and desirable as an adolescent "rite of passage." Moreover, "going steady" brought a whole new set of rituals, including tokens of commitment (such as a class ring), a specified number of telephone calls and dates each week as well as the expectation of greater sexual intimacy (Cate and Lloyd, 1992). Although teens often went steady several times during their high school years, each time was expected to include strong affection and love for the partner. For college women, "landing a man" by senior year was not only an openly acknowledged goal, it was frequently one of the stated reasons why young women in that era were attending college in the first place.

The 1950s heralded women's return en masse to their prior unpaid jobs as wives and mothers. The men who had returned from World War II not only wanted their jobs back, they wanted things to return to the way they were before (including the women in their lives). However, the attempt to "return women to their rightful place" was motivated by men's need to control and dominate women. Men regained this dominance over women in part by artificially glamorizing the roles of wife and mother, but as anyone who has ever been a wife and mother will attest, the role is anything but glamorous. Nevertheless, women of that decade were invariably willing to return to the way "things had always been" since there was greater security and apparent nobility in conforming to prevailing social expectations. After all, these were women who had been strictly socialized to conform and "do what was expected of them" (particularly in relation to males).

Between 1960 and 1972 the proportion of women attending college increased threefold. T, this increase in college attendance for both men and women effectively extended adolescence and delayed transition to adulthood. Youth as a life stage was extended in both directions. These factors, coupled with the increased emphasis on careers for women combined to delay the age of one's first marriage. The youth culture was increasingly associated with liberal attitudes toward dating and sex.

THE RECENT ORIGINS OF MALE-FEMALE CONFLICT

During the 1960s and 1970s the separation of sex from procreation made it possible for men and women to value erotic life for its own sake. This dramatically shifted the very nature of intimate relationships and contributed to the emergence of the so-called "free-love generation." The number of children decreased and this left more time for men and women to respond to each other's emotional needs. Christopher Lasch (1979) believed that the marriage contract lost its binding character and couples found it possible to ground sexual relations in something more solid than legal compulsion. This growing predisposition to live for the moment, whatever it may have done to the relations between parents and children, established the preconditions of a new intimacy between men and women. Eventually, both men and women came to approach personal relations with a heightened appreciation of their emotional risks. Determined to manipulate the emotions of others while protecting themselves against emotional injury, both sexes sought to cultivate a protective shallowness and cynical detachment which embittered personal relations merely through its repeated profession.

The 1970s were a time when women's long-repressed anger toward men emerged in earnest. This simmering outrage originated not only in erotic disappointments, but also in females' growing awareness of their own oppression. Marriage was labeled the "ultimate trap," the ultimate routine in a routinized society, the ultimate expression of banality that pervades and suffocates modern life (Lasch, 1979).

Lasch believed that in theory, it should be possible for feminists to advance beyond the stage of sexual recriminations by regarding men simply as the class enemy, involuntarily caught up in the defense of masculine privilege and therefore exempt from personal blame. The symbiotic interdependence of men and women, however, made it hard to attain such intellectual detachment in everyday life.

Some militants revived discredited theories of matriarchal origins or myths of the moral superiority of women, thereby consoling themselves for their lack of power. They appealed to the illusory solidarity of sisterhood in order to avoid arguments about the proper goals of the feminist movement. By institutionalizing women's activities as alternatives to the male culture, they avoid challenging that culture and protect women from the need to compete with men for jobs, political power, and public attention. What began as a tactical realization (that women have to win their rights without waiting for men to grant them) degenerated into the fantasy of a world without men (Lasch, 1979).

Male-female relationships became increasingly risky. Men and women made extravagant demands on one another and experienced irrational rage when these demands were not met. Personal expectations were steadily increasing. Men and women sought escape from emotion not only because they had suffered too many wounds in the wars of love but because they experienced their own inner impulses as intolerably urgent and menacing (Lasch, 1979).

Based upon gender role conditioning, it was clear that neither men nor women possessed the capacity for genuine intimacy. Males' fear of it and females' desire for it were both distortions. Men feared losing control by getting too close because they were subconsciously aware that they would be engulfed by women's needs and the pressure to perform and take care of their partner. Furthermore, men felt guilty if they failed (Goldberg, 1983).

Goldberg added that what women traditionally wanted was not intimacy, but the fulfillment of the need to define their identity through men; to be taken care of and protected, and to have their sexuality legitimized by a "committed relationship." Female capacity for real intimacy was no greater than male, it simply appeared to be greater. Moreover, genuine intimacy was impossible in direct proportion to the degree that couples fit traditional models of masculinity and femininity.

Shifting Social Expectations

Lois Lane seeks Superman (35-50). Not necessary to own cape or leotard, work for *Daily Planet* or leap tall buildings–but it wouldn't hurt. Please, no Kryptonites!

Cleveland Classified Ads, February, 1984

The 1980s heralded a return to a more conservative system of courtship. In the early 1980s a controversial *Newsweek* cover story on the "man shortage" created a nationwide furor. Sensational claims that the odds of a woman finding a suitable mate after age 35 were "less likely than being struck by lightning" ignited deep-seated fears of loneliness and disillusionment in American women. Yet contrary to this infamous Harvard-Yale study featured on the June 2, 1986 cover of *Newsweek*, never-married college educated women at thirty have a 58-66 percent chance of marrying. Moreover, at thirty-five the statistical odds range between 32 and 41 percent while at forty the odds are 17 to 23 percent (Faludi, 1991). Another popular message was that women could have both a marriage and career. Unfortunately, this vision fed into the "superwoman" fantasies which contended that women could "have it all and do it all." This popular cultural myth ended up overloading women's lives to the point where they were "bursting at the seams."

> What is 31 years old, 5'7'' tall, has blue eyes, brown hair, and weighs 165 lbs.? Answer: THE MACHINE. Is what they say about him true? Find out for yourself. Seeking attractive, financially secure women for fun-filled dates.

Cleveland Classified Ads, February, 1984

The classic image of the male as predator (wolf) preying on innocent female victims (lambs) still persists in earnest today. Yet one should not assume by any means that this image is typical of all males. However, thanks in part to the persistence of traditional male and female socialization, women continue to be victimized far more often than men in intimate relationships as well as in society at large. Since men have historically enjoyed more power, money, and privilege many continue to exploit women for their own ends. Nevertheless, the question remains whether men and women can work out a more just and equitable relationship, or whether women in their justifiable anger at men will continue to blame them and seek merely to turn the tables. According to Lillian Rubin (1983) change outruns consciousness while changes in consciousness frequently lag well behind changing social norms or personal behaviors. No matter how revolutionary a period of change may seem on the surface, the old ways continue to haunt us. "Consciously derogated, unconsciously avoided and denied, they continue to speak with a power and persistence that will not be dismissed. Consequently, these two contradictory systems of ideals exist within us— the emerging one vying for dominance with the old one, new behaviors creating internal conflicts as they rub against obsolete but still living rules" (Rubin, 1983:3).

These internal conflicts are fundamentally reshaping the very nature of male-female interaction. There is a different tenor in the air. Today, there is a disquieting edge in social interactions between men and women, honed by submerged female anger which is liable to erupt at any time.

Basic Instinct

Basic Instinct–See the movie twice before responding; first for pleasure and enjoyment and second for depth and meaning. Add the qualities of a loving, compassionate, sharing, and giving individual to THAT woman and it equals me to a "T," MINUS THE MURDERS. I am sweet, kind, and generous but if you try to use and abuse me, I will nail you, MINUS THE ICE PICKS. We should all be in this game of life to win, and it is the thrill of the hunt not the kill. I am definitely looking for my counterpart. I have had the singer/night club owner and he has been history for a while. Perhaps the hot shot (shooter) cop is yet to come, although the field is open to any professions. It is the man both inward and outward that counts. I believe the "American Dream" still exists, but it exists in our BASIC INSTINCT. It is no longer the hubby off to work and the little woman sitting behind the white picket fence caring for 2.5 children and a dog. Women are sharing more with their men. The woman who has the ability to think like a man, when necessary, yet maintain her individuality, femininity, and sexuality, will obtain this new "American Dream." Get your hormones intact and if you are a determined man of power, who thinks he can handle me, IN EVERY ASPECT, not JUST SEXUALLY, send a note and a reasonably recent photo.

Gambit Personals, New Orleans, La. (9/92)

This recent personal ad has much to say not only about the individual woman who authored it, but about the dramatically shifting attitudes of an increasing number of women toward relationships with men. Movies like *Fatal Attraction* and *Basic Instinct* highlight the increasing emphasis on danger as well as emotional and physical violence. The risks in dating today are far greater than they were a generation ago. According to many singles, dating has become a form of Russian Roulette. It is hard to imagine ever returning to the idyllic fantasy of TV's *Wonder Years* in which Kevin is struggling to figure out if Winnie Cooper really wants to go steady or just likes him as a friend. ("Winnie, do you like, like me, or just like me?") Indeed, this is part of the show's appeal. It offers an irresistibly nostalgic journey back to the days when life was simpler and the normal problems of adolescence existed in idyllic white middle-class communities where life and relationships basically made sense. Prior to the sexual and political revolution and widespread impact of the Civil Rights Movement suburbia was a comfortable, if unrealistic cultural oasis to which many Americans long to return.

Concern over sexually transmitted diseases such as AIDS have also affected attitudes about dating and sex. Recurrent reports from the news media and World Health Organization rightfully depict the AIDS epidemic as the most virulent and horrifying plague of our time. Millions of people worldwide are currently infected and the threat is increasing most rapidly amongst America's heterosexual youth. On a purely emotional level, the threat of AIDS for ourselves and our children is terrifying.

However, despite the fact that today's singles are more aware and concerned about the threat of HIV and a host of other lesser-known sexually transmitted diseases such as chlamydia or genital warts, they are not substantially altering their sexual behavior.

Average Bear

I haven't read the classics since high school but I am working on it. I recently purchased a "Far Side Calendar." Most of my friends are on their 1st or 2nd marriages, have 2.2 kids & live in brick houses in the "burbs." And I love these poor unfortunate guys, (what does that say about me?). But the burbs? Never.

I am not a rocket scientist although I like to stare at the moon. I have been told that I am attractive. I am not bald. I have all my teeth and I am not overweight. But who knows? What I am is a thirty-something white male seeking a white female late 20s-early 30s. Can you meet these criteria: Must possess a general dislike for the New Kids on the Block; pizza with anchovies & gourmet cat food (yes, I know you have cats); must like to dance to rock & roll in your living room; must have a good relationship with ex-spouse/lover; please no angry people (I come with references, how about you?); must desire friendship, dating, walks, talks, dancing, merry-making and getting to know one another on many levels before romance can ensue. A picture would be great, a phone number a must. Please translate the phrase "Zoe Mous Zas Agapo" and write to your average bear."

Gambit Personals, New Orleans, La. (9/92)

So what happens when "average bear" runs into "basic instinct" on a date set up by two well-meaning friends who recognize the underlying loneliness within each of them? Is this formula for emotional disaster a recurring theme of dating in the 1990s? Clearly, each has expressed a very distinct and particular orientation toward coupling which appears to represent opposite ends of the dating continuum. However, in some ways, both these individuals are prototypes of the era in which we live.

As little as fifteen or twenty years ago these particular types did not yet exist per se. They are products and reflections of our time. Given the fact that personal ads were not yet in vogue in 1972, imagine how men and women of that era would have reacted to the movie *Basic Instinct*, let alone the flesh and blood personification. The movie itself, with its explicit sexual content and graphic violence, would have been seen as extreme and in poor taste.

Today, sensitive, caring men are offended by what sounds more like a barroom challenge than an invitation to intimacy. ". . . get your hormones intact and if you are a determined man of power who thinks he can handle me, IN EVERY ASPECT, not JUST

SEXUALLY, send a note and reasonably recent photo." Answering this ad would be tantamount to contemplating a date with the Glenn Close character in *Fatal Attraction*.

The male response to women in the 1990s has included generous amounts of confusion and dismay. Clearly, the average bear sounds like a fairly benign, well-meaning guy who has absolutely no desire to end up with an ice pick through his heart (either literally or figuratively). God only knows what "Zoe Mous Zas Agapo" means, but it is a good bet that it does not translate to "seeking woman with a history of violence."

Despite appearances to the contrary, "average bear" and "basic instinct" have several things in common. Each has foregone the usual means of social introductions and resorted to the personal ads. Each is expressing a personal view of him/herself and past painful relationships. Neither of them wants to be hurt again and they have each explicitly spelled out how *not* to treat them. At some deeper emotional level each is expressing a deeper need for meaningful contact and communication with a member of the opposite sex.

These two may be living in the same city, but they are worlds apart. Is it any wonder that meaningful interpersonal relationships are becoming harder and harder to come by?

While discussing contemporary male-female relationships, Rubin (1983) points out that increasingly, both sides have come to see that they made a bad bargain, if not an impossible one. Men and women have come to recognize that both have been feeling frustrated, confused, and fearful (feelings that often get acted out against each other under the cover of behaviors not easily recognized as rebellious: hostile withdrawals; critical, perfectionist demands of spouse and children; escapes into work, television, drinking, and sometimes even violence).

Perhaps never in history have we expected so much and so little at the same time: never before have we seen such an odd conjunction of heightened expectations about the possibilities in human relationships and disillusion, if not despair. (Rubin, 1983:8)

INTERPERSONAL ATTRACTION

Most theories of attraction suggest that people are attracted to individuals whose presence is rewarding to them. Two major categories of rewards influence attraction: (1) direct rewards–all the positive consequences we obtain from being with someone and (2) indirect rewards–when a partner provides us access to desired external rewards such as money, status, or opportunities.

Both direct and indirect rewards underscore the interactive nature of attraction. Brehm (1992:60) asserts that "attraction involves the needs, preferences and desires of the person who becomes attracted: the perceived characteristics of the person who is seen as attractive; and the situation in which these two find themselves." One's own emotional needs can substantially affect the perception of potential dating and mating partners. Does one fall in love with the person or one's image of that person? There is considerable evidence to support the latter contention. The impact of projection of desired characteristics onto potential partners should not be underestimated. The perceived characteristics of another person can likewise influence our desires and reactions to the situation. Moreover, the situation itself can reshape our preferences and our perceptions. The "love at first sight" phenomenon offers a case in point.

Throughout recorded history countless individuals have reported in effect that "I loved him/her from the very first moment I laid eyes on him/her." How can one love someone whom one does not know per se? This romantic phenomenon relies heavily on the projection of preconceived conscious and unconscious needs and desires onto another person who may or may not possess these hoped-for attributes. Attraction is based on rewarding experiences with another person, but those rewarding experiences are subjectively defined. Moreover, individuals often do not adequately discriminate between love and attraction.

Proximity is integral to the development of intimate relationships. Except in the case of fantasy relationships (such as those fans have with celebrities) one's meaningful interpersonal relationships grow out of daily interactions with those nearby. In Festinger's classic study (1951) the particular location of people's apartments had a dramatic effect on the particular friendships they formed. His study concluded that whenever individuals select the place where they will live, work, or attend school, they also take a major step toward determining who the significant others in their life will be. Hence, by selecting a place to live, one is simultaneously setting the stage for any potential friends, associates, and lovers.

However, while proximity does provide the opportunity for social interactions, it does not determine the quality of these interactions. Brehm (1992) points out that proximity is a spatial concept whereas familiarity refers to frequency of contact. Proximity is a necessary prerequisite for familiarity. Moreover, repeated contact with someone potentially increases our positive response to that person. However, extreme familiarity can also decrease attraction if a person strongly dislikes someone from the beginning. In that case repeated exposure is likely to increase one's hostility.

The Bias for Beauty

People are more rewarding to be with when one finds their appearance pleasing. Although the determination of beauty is highly subjective, many believe that the greater the physical attractiveness, the greater the aesthetic appeal. Beyond mere aesthetics another possible explanation of this "bias for beauty" is that people overgeneralize from appearance, assuming that those who are attractive on the outside are also nicer on the inside and have remarkably good future prospects (Brehm, 1992).

This stereotype potentially influences attraction in several ways. First, if someone is perceived as good as well as beautiful, then they offer two potential sources of rewards. In addition, if people respond more positively to beautiful people due to projected images of goodness, then physically attractive people may develop the expected "good" personal characteristics (Brehm, 1992). Is this to imply that on the whole the beautiful are better? No, but social reinforcement may encourage the expression of certain personality traits considered to be "desirable."

The third possible explanation of the bias for beauty is that the physically attractive are more socially skilled. And in fact, some studies have found that physically attractive individuals are more skillful in their verbal communications with others (Brehm, 1992). However, an alternative possibility is that since those deemed physically unappealing do not enjoy the same social advantages, they may develop better social skills to compensate for any superficial disadvantages.

The fourth possible explanation of the bias for beauty relates to the potential social profit that may be derived from associating with physically attractive individuals. Brehm (1992:67) suggests that "a person of average attractiveness is seen as more attractive in the presence of someone who is very good-looking and as less attractive in the presence of someone who is quite unattractive." And while men benefit from being seen with attractive women, women are not affected by the looks of their male partner. For women, only their own looks seem to matter.

The relative importance of physical attractiveness is closely correlated with gender. Men are much more likely than women to emphasize their interest in having a physically attractive romantic partner. Yet there is a substantial disparity between what men and women say and what they actually do. A 1989 study by Sprecher found that when male and female college students received information about a person of the opposite sex, this person's physical attractiveness was the primary determinant of attraction, and men and women did not differ in the degree to which they were influenced by physical attractiveness information. But when asked how much physical attractiveness had determined their ratings, men reported that it played a greater role in determining their feelings than did women (Feingold, 1990). Rubin et al. (1981) found that egalitarian males tended to look for intellectual and expressive qualities in women and were more likely than traditional males to date women their own age. Research on college campuses in the early 1970s also showed that men tend to fall in love faster and out of love harder than women.

Even though men often feel freer than women to acknowledge their preferences for a physically attractive partner, not all men place the same value on physical appearance. Some men are much more concerned than others about this characteristic, depending on their level of self-monitoring. Brehm explains that self-monitoring refers to people's tendency to regulate their social behavior to meet the demands of social situations. "High self-monitors are ready, willing, and able to tailor their behavior to make a good impression on others. In contrast, low self-monitors are more consistent across situations, as they strive to be true to their own beliefs and desires" (1992:69).

The prevailing social wisdom has long suggested that men can profit socially by being paired with an attractive woman. Thus high self-monitoring men who seek social success are particularly interested in having an attractive dating partner. Not surprisingly, when researchers presented male subjects with dating choices that pitted physical attractiveness against a good personality, high self-monitors chose on the basis of appearance while low self-monitors selected on the basis of personality. Self-monitoring can also affect other aspects of intimate relationships. Low self-monitoring men are more cautious about getting romantically involved than high self-monitors. Among both male and female undergraduates, the high self-monitors appeared less committed to their current dating partner than the low self-monitors. Overall, it appears that being a high self-monitor is associated with a more superficial approach to intimate relationships emphasizing the partner's appearance and a tendency for less commitment (Brehm, 1992).

People frequently form relationships based upon similarities along any number of demographic characteristics including family background, social class, age, religion, and education to name but a few. According to Brehm (1992) the effects of personal similarity on attraction may involve both cognitive and emotional components. Those people who are similar in the ways that they structure and organize their thoughts and perceptions (cognitive complexity) are more attracted to each other and more satisfied with their relationship than those who differ in cognitive complexity. Parallel mood states may also enhance attraction. That is, non-depressed individuals are more attracted to others who are non-depressed than to those who are depressed. Likewise, stronger attraction toward mood-similar others has sometimes been found for depressed individuals.

Research also indicates a clear relationship between similarity in physical attractiveness and progression of the relationship. The more similar partners were, the more their relationship progressed. Murstein (1972) reported a low but significant correlation between the degree of physical attractiveness, similarity, and courtship progress his sample of "going steady" and "engaged couples." The more similar partners were more likely to indicate that their relationship had gotten closer over the six months of the study.

Overall, these findings suggest that similarity in physical attractiveness may serve as a screening device. For initial encounters, it may foster attraction and later could strengthen attachment. However, among committed partners a match has already been achieved, and so physical attractiveness similarity does not continue to influence the progress of their relationship–unless, of course, that match were to fade away.

Female Mate Selection

In her provocative analysis of the ways in which females choose their mates in both the animal and human realms, Mary Batten (1992) suggests that female choice involves more than a female merely showing her preference for certain males based upon attraction or sex appeal. In evolutionary terms, for female choice to be meaningful, it must also be adaptive. A female's decision must enable her to produce more offspring that are better adapted to survive than if she had mated randomly.

Batten continues by saying that not all males (either human or non-human) are equally valuable to the enduring survival of the species–some are more vigorous, some in better health, some are better able to parent. She asserts that female choice functions to screen males and select those of highest mate value. (However, Batten's analysis fails to consider unwanted or unplanned pregnancies.)

The evolutionary function of courtship is to help females evaluate fitness differences among males. Some male traits displayed during courtship may have been selected by generations of females because they signal superior genes or resources that will contribute to the female's reproductive success (Batten, 1992).

The theme of food in exchange for sex is universal in human courtship as well as among birds, insects, and fishes. Among humans, both men and women use food in courtship. The old adage "The way to a man's heart is through his stomach" expresses the belief that a woman who cooks well will attract a man. At the same time, men routinely use wining and dining (including some men who have also taken to cooking) to seduce women. Today many men feel that buying a woman drinks and dinner entitles them to have sex with her. A few may even become violently angry if their after-dinner advances are refused (Batten, 1992).

> Female megachild bees exhibit the same behavior. Males of this species control clumps of flowers that produce the pollen and nectar on which females feed. In order to get food, the female visits several territories within fifteen to thirty minutes and may copulate on demand with each resident male. If she doesn't copulate, the male may attack her as he would any other poacher that does not contribute to his reproductive success. (Alcock, 1984:417)

In their study of 300 middle-class women in the Los Angeles area, psychologist Susan Essock-Vitale and biologist Michael McGuire found that a woman's social situation affects the way her biology expresses itself. That is, because American society is organized around an elaborate division of labor by sex and a strong reliance upon resource exchange, there exists a particularly large payoff for retaining a male as provider of resources for, and care-giver to, mutually conceived offspring (Essock-Vitale and McGuire, 1985). Hence, the production of offspring with a reliable provider may ensure that a woman maintains or improves her existing social and economic status.

In their cross-cultural study of traits that women find attractive, psychologists Ellis and Symons (1990) looked at three categories of dominance cues: (1) physical, such as height and body carriage; (2) social, including family; and (3) behavioral, including aggressiveness and assertiveness. Ellis consistently found that men who expressed dominance cues were more sexually attractive to women. For women the world over, male attractiveness is bound up with social status, strength, bravery, prowess, and/or similar qualities.

In addition to material wealth and relative status, a man's resources may include his education, skills, position in the community and his ability to father–to pass on values and skills that will enable his offspring to succeed in their particular society. Moreover, in societies in which women select their own mates, intangibles are also important including a male's ability to be considerate, tender, loving, kind, fair, and humane. But while individual women may focus on the secondary resources (intangibles) material wealth and status remain powerfully attractive (Batten, 1992).

Is it possible that the achievements that a society prizes most highly are precisely those that have enabled men to obtain wives and sire offspring? Batten suggests that cultural differences grew out of the reproductive strategies used to attract mates in different environments. If this is true, then female choice, whether individual or familial, played a major role not only in determining how males look and act, but also in influencing cultural value systems, social structures, and the laws and customs for governing and maintaining those structures.

According to Batten (1992), whether rich or poor, women prefer high-status males. Batten further concluded that the more money a women makes, the more she values the financial and professional status of a potential mate. Moreover, as women's power and status increase, their taste in men becomes more, rather than less, discriminatory.

Male-Female Communication

The differing cultures and contradictory communication styles of men and women also constitute an important barrier to initiating and sustaining emotionally intimate relationships. Nonetheless, communication is the primary means through which intimacy is achieved. Consequently, these differences significantly impact dating and courtship.

In her insightful book, *You Just Don't Understand*, Deborah Tannen analyzes male-female communication from a sociolinguistic perspective. Intimacy is key in the female world of connection where individuals negotiate complex networks of friendship, minimize differences, try to reach consensus, and avoid any appearance of superiority, which would highlight differences. Intimacy implies, "We're close and the same" whereas independence implies "We're separate and different" (Tannen, 1990). Thus it is readily apparent that intimacy and independence dovetail with connection and status. The essential element of connection is symmetry in which people are the same, feeling equally close to each other. The essential element of status is asymmetry in which people are not the same and are differently placed in a hierarchy. It is the asymmetry of status that creates competition. Two people cannot simultaneously have the upper hand. Therefore, negotiation for status is inherently adversarial.

Most communication occurs at the non-verbal (analogic) rather than the verbal (digital) level. A myriad of non-verbal messages are transmitted and received usually at a preconscious or unconscious level which amplify and contextualize the literal content of any conversation. These messages serve to define relative position, status, and power. When these non-verbal messages are not consistent with the verbal messages, this double-level communication creates confusion. Such incongruence is commonplace in male-female communication because each has been socialized into different symbolic language systems with differing values and interpretations of the same words, ideas, and events.

As Tannen (1990:42) puts it, "If women speak and hear a language of connection and intimacy while men speak and hear a language of status and independence, then communication between men and women can be like cross-cultural communication, prey to a clash of conversational styles. Instead of different dialects, it has been said they speak different genderlects."

Men and women also have very different styles of helping behavior. When women confront men's conversational styles they often judge them by their own (female) standards. Women express concern by following up someone else's statement by questioning her about it. When men change the subject, women think they are showing a lack of empathy–a failure of intimacy. Unless trained differently by profession or family of origin, most men do not possess active listening skills. Instead, men tend to offer advice or opinions. Men's help is instrumental as in "I'll fix it for you" or "I'll help you figure out a solution." In contrast, when women ask for help they are not necessarily asking to have the problem fixed or to figure out a solution. Frequently, women just need to ventilate, be heard, and understood by someone who cares.

Another important difference in male-female communication is between public speaking (male) and private speaking (female) or, as Tannen puts it, "report talk" and "rapport talk." To many men conversation is primarily a means to express thoughts and ideas, as well as to preserve independence and negotiate status in a hierarchical social order. Within the complex social world of work, every professional disagreement is an attempt to maintain or redefine one's status position in the social hierarchy. This is often done by informally exhibiting knowledge and skill, and by holding center stage through verbal performance such as storytelling, joking, or imparting information. From childhood on, men learn to use talking as a way to get and keep attention. Consequently, they are more comfortable speaking in larger groups made up of people they know less well (i.e., "public speaking"). Unfortunately, men often approach even the most private situations like a public speaking engagement (more like giving a report than establishing rapport). Men also have a distinct tendency to interject competition into situations where it does not belong. Socialized to compete and win at any cost, men frequently introduce competition into their dating and subsequent marital relationships. Many men honestly do not know what women want while women honestly do not know why men find what women want so hard to comprehend and deliver (Tannen, 1990).

Women tell details of their lives to friends. These details turn into gossip if the friend to whom they are told repeats them to someone else–presumably another friend. "Telling what's happening in your life and lives of those you talk to is a grown-up version of telling secrets, the essence of girls' and women's friendships" (Tannen, 1990:97). Small talk functions to maintain a sense of camaraderie when there is nothing special to say. "Women, friends and relatives keep their conversational mechanisms in working order by talking about small things as well as large. Knowing they will have such conversations later makes women feel they are not alone in life. If they do not have someone to tell their thoughts and impressions to, they do feel alone" (Tannen, 1990:102).

Men, on the other hand, frequently despise gossip which they consider petty and superficial. This is not to suggest that men do not talk behind one another's back–which of course they do–but this is frequently a different level of conversation and is often more task-focused, impersonal, factual, and/or technical (work, politics, women, ideas, etc.). It shows a minimum of self-disclosure and a maximum of one-upsmanship.

Tannen (1990) further believes that noticing details demonstrates caring and creates involvement. In most conversations, however, men find women's involvement in details annoying. Because women are concerned first and foremost with establishing intimacy, they value the telling of details. Moreover, if interest in details is a sign of intimacy, a woman will frequently resist such interest if it comes from someone she does not want to be intimate with. On the other hand, men are encouraged to speak more directly and succinctly which within the male hierarchical world connotes self-assurance and knowledgeability. Any male who "wastes" valuable staff meeting time with "chatty" conversation is either the boss, a close relative of the boss, or about to be censured by his peers.

Shyness

Research has shown that approximately 40 percent of all Americans consider themselves shy and more than half of that number regard shyness as a personal problem (Weaver, 1987). Shyness frequently reduces interpersonal rewards, limits social support systems, and can potentially contribute to feelings of social and emotional isolation, boredom, feelings of incompetence, and low self-esteem. The shy person may have difficulty feeling safe and secure enough to trust another person which in turn inhibits self-disclosure, a necessary precondition for establishing and maintaining intimate relationships (Sprecher and McKinney, 1987).

"Conversation, or the exchange of information, is the first step toward intimacy, and an avoidance of communication can dramatically inhibit an individual's ability to initiate or sustain intimate relationships" (Weaver, 1987:115). A next step is self-disclosure, defined as the exposure of layers of the self, involving feelings, thoughts, or even the body (Jourard, 1971). As a relationship reaches more intimate levels, people disclose more information, positive and negative, and at a more personal level (Derlega, 1984). Shy people tend to prefer to conceal their inner-identities because they often perceive themselves to be inferior.

The alternative to revealing one's identity is to attempt to control the presentation of self to others. The outcome of social relationships and others' impressions of self are manipulated by selectively revealing or withholding images and pieces of personal information. "Paradoxically, the harder the individual tries to control the presentation of self, the more difficult it is to achieve intimacy" (Weaver, 1987:115).

Love and Romance

The word "love" first appeared in the English language around A.D. 825. The ancient Greeks recognized two kinds of love—agape and eros. Agape represented brotherly or spiritual love, such as a God might have for humankind, and had no sexual implications. Eros referred to sensuous desire and was personified as the god of love (Batten, 1992). In the context of attachment between the sexes, love refers to an intense attraction between a man and a woman. In psychological parlance love means "pair-bondedness" (Batten, 1992).

The enthusiasm and acceptance of marrying for love is most pervasive in American culture. Perhaps this is due to the absence of an aristocratic class and the force of egalitarian ideas as well as the notion that individuals (not families) should choose marriage partners because of emotional attachment (not economic concerns). This has become the dominant operating principle in our society. This principle shows no sign of weakening. Indeed, it has intensified. When college undergraduates were asked in 1967 whether they would marry someone with whom they were not in love, 64.6 percent of the men and 24.3 percent of the women said no. By 1984, the verdict was overwhelming among both males and females: 85.6 percent of the men and 84.9 percent of the women said no. Among heterosexuals, one marries for love, and when in love, one marries (Brehm, 1992). What would novelists, playwrights, poets, and scriptwriters do without passionate love? In reality, however, passionate love is often fraught with anxiety and obsession. It is frequently all-consuming and constantly intrudes on one's thoughts and work. Paradoxically, this agony just seems to increase the ecstasy. Hatfield (1988) characterizes passionate love as consisting of: (1) physiological arousal and (2) the belief that this arousal is caused by a reaction to the beloved. Oftentimes, the connection between arousal and love is obvious. Sexually aroused men typically report more love for their romantic partners than do those who are not aroused. However, the two-factor theory of passionate love allows for an unexpected outcome. Arousal can also be attributed to the wrong source (i.e., misattributed). When feelings of arousal in the beloved's presence are explained solely by that presence, passionate love is produced or at least intensified. The actual arousing effects of other aspects of the situation are ignored. This process is referred to as "excitation transfer." Excitation caused by one stimulus is transferred and added to that elicited by a second stimulus. This combined arousal is then perceived as being caused by only the second stimulus (Brehm, 1992).

Some claim that it is not necessary to rely on complicated processes like misattribution and excitation transfer to explain why romance blossoms. The link between fear and love offers another example of the ways in which social rewards can create attraction and strengthen attachment. Fondness for those who are with us in a time of distress grows out of the comfort one takes from their presence. Their presence is rewarding because having them with us helps reduce our distress.

All the factors described thus far as potential contributors to the experience of passionate love seem to imply that this experience will be relatively short-lived. Since the natural course of arousal is to decline, an idealized view of the beloved is difficult to maintain once contact with the beloved is frequent and routine. Nevertheless, there are times when passionate love does endure for quite some time. One example suggests that the eventual limit on passionate love might be imposed, not by time, but by certainty. Brehm (1992) suggests that if hope is completely lost, passion dies, and if love is secure and taken for granted, passion fades. However, if the beloved's commitment remains uncertain, arousal is constantly recharged and idealization can flourish. Under these conditions, passionate love can last a lifetime.

For most people, companionate love is more enduring than passionate attachment. Companionate love, though less emotionally intense, is typically deeper and more stable. Companionate love can exist between friends as well as lovers. It is built on a foundation of respect, admiration, and trust. In fact, interpersonal trust may be its single best defining characteristic. Companionate love involves both kinds of interpersonal trust: trust in the other person's reliability (the likelihood that he or she will do what he or she promised) and emotional trust (the security that each person will act to protect the other's welfare).

The Introduction Industry

Historically, beautiful women have been expected to marry rich men. Elder examined the relationship between the physical attractiveness of female high school students and their subsequent socioeconomic position as adults. He found that, particularly among those who came from working-class families, young women who were highly attractive in high school were more likely than their peers to marry men who were financially and professionally successful. At first glance this may strike many as an anachronism in the 1990s. Actually, however, it appears to be alive and well in the "dating marketplace" as represented by the personal ads in the print media and commercial dating services. Most studies of this marketplace indicate that the primary resource offered by females and sought by males is physical attractiveness, while the primary resource offered by males and sought by females is economic status (Brehm, 1992).

The particular setting where men and women meet is likely to affect the process by which they become acquainted and move into the "couple stage." A myriad of settings have been specifically created for purposes of male-female encounters–parties, dances, singles bars, singles groups/organizations, etc. (Sprecher and McKinney, 1987). Research showed that approximately 33 percent of the men and 36 percent of the women met their dating partners based on introduction from friends (Sprecher and McKinney, 1987). As Marwell et al. (1982:5-6) pointed out, "an introduction from a third party helps to legitimize the relationship." They note that "the friend has the right to interact with each of the two partners and he/she essentially vouches for the fact that the other person is 'all right.'" The friend also makes it improbable that the other person will behave in a rudely rejecting manner, and may also imply with the introduction that the two partners are both "available and appropriate for one another."

During the past few decades the "mating trade" or "introduction industry" has grown "from an obscure fringe operation to a billion-dollar industry functioning within our social mainstream." Some might suggest that an industry founded on loneliness and thriving on isolation quite probably should not exist at all. Why in this age of instantaneous communication, does this world need a vast, intricate, and costly system of enterprises designed solely to get men and women in touch with each other? (Mullen, 1984).

As with any industry the primary terms are supply, demand, and profit. Yet unlike other industries, the "mating trade" is fueled by social and emotional isolation and fraught with social stigma. The very notion of purchasing social introductions is a source of embarrassment and even humiliation in a society which continues to insist that each and every person should be capable of finding and retaining a suitable mate.

In 1818 Lord Lucan of Great Britain placed the following ad:

> Count Sarsfield, Lord Lucan, descendant of the royal branches of Lorraine and Capet, and other sovereigns of Europe, wishes to contract an alliance with a lady capable from her rank and talents of supporting the dignity and titles which an alliance so honourable would confer on her. (from Mullen, 1984:163)

Today's personal ads cannot really compare with the eloquence of Lord Lucan any more than they usually offer such distinguished titles or bloodlines. Nevertheless, the prevalence of personal ads in newspapers, magazines, and other assorted print media has literally mushroomed during the last 20 years. Invariably they merely identify one's gender, race, and marital status for openers and then proceed on a brief (though frequently imaginative) literary journey which portrays the many and varied wonderful attributes of the author. If these were taken at face value by any curious visitor from a faraway culture one might assume that ours is a society brimming with highly attractive, intelligent, and desirable individuals who, through no fault of their own, have neither the time nor the inclination to avail themselves of the traditional methods of acquiring meaningful companionship. Anyone who has either placed or answered a personal ad knows exactly how misleading such glowing descriptions can sometimes prove upon a face-to-face meeting.

Single men far outnumber single women in dating services, match-making clubs, and personal ads. Research has demonstrated that their stated attitudes about commitment are contrary to prevailing cultural beliefs. Some 93 percent of the men wanted marriage or a monogamous commitment within one year and only 7 percent of the men were seeking multiple dating partners.

In contrast, a 1970 Virginia Slims poll found an increasing preference for singledom among single women in their twenties and thirties. Fully 90 percent of never-married women stated that "the major reason they haven't (married) is that they haven't wanted to yet." Clearly, their "wanting to" could depend upon any number of extraneous factors, but the finding is nonetheless provocative. A 1989 Louis Harris poll of women aged forty-five to sixty found that the majority of them did not want to get married. Part of the reason for this striking decline in females' desire not to marry may be attributable to the sharp increase in male-female cohabitation (Faludi, 1991).

In addition, the tenor of personal ads is changing. As apparent from the few examples contained in this chapter one can see that it is a long way from "Lois Lane" to "Basic Instinct" (just as it is a long way from "THE MACHINE" to "Average Bear.") At some levels it is unfair and overly simplistic to stereotype the changing roles of men and women by implying that women are becoming more aggressive while men are becoming more passive. However, there are disturbing elements of truth in such an observation. For by reversing the traditional roles, women would merely succeed in replicating the same dysfunctional relationship in reverse. Women oppressing men is no better than its converse.

American society is now at a very difficult juncture in the history of male-female relationships. Role confusion and the ever-shifting rules of dating have left men and women in a quandary with each frustrated and blaming the other for not understanding.

As a society, we have imagined ourselves to be changing and progressing because this is one of our culture's prevailing myths (i.e., that Americans are constantly growing and progressing–that we are, both individually and collectively, constantly getting smarter and more sophisticated). Such cultural arrogance is one of major flaws in the American psyche.

DATING IN THE 1990s

In a recent television commercial for a popular camera company, Andre Agassi offers the intriguing double-entendre that "image is everything." Probably more than any other this sentiment succinctly characterizes the nature of dating in the 1990s. The increased emphasis on appearance and de-emphasis on substance has been a boon to the "image management industry" including cosmetics, clothing, diet, health clubs, etc. Popularized in books like *Dress for Success* and *Finding the Colors that are Right for You* as well as various magazines for both women and men, Americans are living in an age which associates looking good with personal happiness. The unfortunate corollary to this enhanced emphasis on "image" as the "sine qua non" of social value is the rising tide of eating disorders such as anorexia and bulimia which have now reached epidemic proportions across our college campuses. The dating industry is booming and trendy television shows such as *STUDS* and *Love Connection* parody and exploit the very real difficulties that males and females have when trying to make a meaningful emotional connection. What is being sold is an updated version of the "American Dream." Making it in American society has always included meeting and marrying one's ideal mate. However, the minimum requirements for an acceptable marital partner have risen dramatically.

Due largely to the fact that children are exposed to so much more at a much earlier age than previous generations, Americans are dating and becoming sexually active at younger ages than ever before. The competition in the dating marketplace is very real. So, in addition to sheer physical beauty, Americans are demanding more and more from prospective dating partners. For openers, a clean bill of health certifying that one is HIV negative and free from any one of a host of other sexually transmitted diseases is mandatory. Next, one's family, educational, and financial background are all scrutinized in microscopic detail. Exchanging professional résumés is not uncommon. However, since more and more prospective dating partners are meeting on the job, something of one's professional background may already be known.

Several recent television programs have discussed the now flourishing dating industry in New York City. With loneliness and social anonymity so prevalent in the city, the dating industry is "big business in the Big Apple." Understandably cautious singles are routinely hiring private investigators to conduct extensive background checks which reveal detailed financial, social, and familial histories. The proliferation of singles' ads across this country exemplifies the meticulous care taken to project just the right personal image. Should anyone actually pass the initial screening, the actual dating itself is conducted much like a political campaign with certain maneuvers made only at prespecified junctures in order to create the desired outcome and protect one's personal vulnerabilities. Sadly, this social paranoia is a necessary self-protective mechanism during a time when so many emotionally damaged and potentially destructive men and women are out there disguised as "Average Bear" or "Lois Lane."

As with spouse abuse, abusive dating relationships generally exhibit a pattern of repeated violence that escalates and increases in severity the longer the relationship continues. Dating violence has been linked by many to an intergenerational cycle correlated with a turbulent and abusive childhood. "Partners in physically abusive courtships exhibit more negative affect, conflict, verbal aggression, ambivalence about continuing the relationship, indirect styles of negotiation (i.e., withdrawal or crying), confrontation, blaming the partner, and expressing anger. Partners in abusive courtships are also distinguished by their use of persistence as a negotiation strategy, high investment in the relationship, and the belief that the partner can be changed" (Cate and Lloyd, 1992:105).

Unfortunately, Americans are frequently mixing violence with sex in both the media and real life. Date rape is increasing at an alarming rate. And although the precise definition of "date rape" remains an ongoing source of contention between men and women, the fact remains that in order to commit an act of violence against another one must first objectify and dehumanize that person. This dehumanization process is most apparent in times of war such as when the Japanese people were characterized by American soldiers as "Japs" during WW II or when the Vietnamese people were characterized some years later as "Cong" or "VC." Sadly, a similar dehumanization process is occurring today in the war between men and women.

Caveat Emptor

When recently asked what the average length of time they dated a particular partner was, students at a leading university offered answers ranging from a few weeks to six months. Given that these students are not necessarily representative of all singles and are still in the developmental stage of experimenting with identity, relationships, sex, etc., their responses nonetheless raise an intriguing question: What is the average length of male-female dating relationships in the 1990s? While no hard data is available, anecdotal evidence strongly indicates that these relationships are becoming shorter and shorter. Potential partners are approached with a cavalier attitude about each other and the future. (e.g., "If this doesn't work out, then I can always find somebody else.") At no time in our country's history have we had so many options and choices of potential dating partners. The irony is that despite that fact, social and emotional isolation are on the rise. Generational and maturational differences seem to indicate that older, more stable individuals tend to have relationships of longer duration.

"Self-preservation" has become the "prime directive" for dating in the 1990s. Both men and women are pulling back on their levels of self-disclosure in order to protect their vulnerabilities. Due to the increasingly impersonal society in which Americans now reside, dating has become more and more depersonalized, objectified, and ultimately dehumanized. With our modern professional lives so compartmentalized, individual dating partners are often characterized and categorized more by their occupational roles than their individual personalities. Thus one no longer dates John Smith human being, one dates his classification: student, lawyer, plumber, teacher, bricklayer, etc. With men and women spending more and more time outside the home involved in emerging or well-established careers, work identities have begun to replace personal identities, leaving fewer and fewer opportunities to express the varied aspects of one's private/personal self even to potential partners. The segmented, over-ritualized, compartmentalized lives Americans now lead leave precious little time to "waste" in such superfluous activities as seeking and selecting potential partners. Americans are rushing headlong on life's treadmill striving desperately to get ahead and knowing that the competition out there is stiffer than ever before. Little do Americans realize that they have turned down a dead-end street.

After a long history of unsuccessful relationships, the fear of "getting burned again" has made singles wary. Add to this the proliferation of borderline personalities and other emotionally damaged singles within the context of the very real fear of AIDS, and dating turns into a potentially toxic activity. How can a person feel free to be themselves within such a dangerous environment? How can individuals risk sharing their innermost selves with another when they have little or no idea who that other actually is? Certainly, potential partners may present themselves in one way, but who are they really? Personal identities are increasingly fluid and situationally defined. This question cannot be fully answered without a longstanding social and familial context on which to base such an assessment.

Many people have taken to falling back on their "gut feeling" about others, but while the majority consider themselves to be an "excellent judge of character," few actually are. Such judgments require extensive self-knowledge, superior perceptual and assessment skills, a refined sense of subtle contextual meanings, and an in-depth understanding of the deeper personal and philosophical significance of character. Isn't this asking a little much of John Q. Public?

In their youth, the baby boomers had McDonald's or some other version of the local burger joint. In contrast, today's teenagers have any number of potential "hang-outs," but foremost among these are the shopping malls. In addition to shopping for material goods, teens can simultaneously shop for potential relationships, many of whom are dressed in the latest fashions purchased (not coincidentally) at these very malls. When they first appeared on the scene, these enclosed shopping malls were heralded as the "new community centers" where individuals would be able to find all their necessary goods under one roof. In addition, these malls would be the new community gathering places (apparently replacing the town barbershop of an earlier era). Musical and cultural events could be brought into the malls for the enrichment of all the people. Friends would gather in social harmony while enjoying the clean modern environment. However, at some level shopping malls may somehow symbolically represent how far astray American cultural values have drifted. It is all part of the "bigger and newer is better" mentality. With less and less time to do more and more things, the shopping malls were ostensibly packaged for one-stop shopping. Unfortunately, what Americans got was a place with stale air, bad lighting, artificial everything, and which pays any number of employees (often female) minimum wage to work long hours in dead-end jobs with little or no hope for advancement. (For those Americans who grew up in small towns and went to the local Western Auto for their first bicycle, this is a far cry indeed.)

Shopping malls are symptomatic of the unreality of interpersonal relationships in the 1990s. Authenticity and real value have been traded for choice and convenience. Consumers are dazzled by a sparkling array of goods ranging from designer clothes to outrageously expensive automobiles. Unfortunately, many are now choosing potential mates much the same way that one selects a new car. Shop around and see how they look. Compare the relative features. Compare the relative value. Decide on what you want, what it will give you and if you can afford it. But, despite your best efforts, you have absolutely no idea what you are actually getting until you get it home. Caveat emptor!

CONCLUSIONS

At their core, Americans are a consumer society. We indulge ourselves in a vast array of designer clothes, exotic foods, expensive electronics, etc. Unfortunately, this consumer mentality is increasingly being applied to our interpersonal relationships (especially prospective dating partners). Today, individuals enter relationships focusing on what they themselves can get out of it, not what they can give their partner. Moreover, if individuals' needs and expectations are not satisfied they either refuse to buy the "product" or attempt to return it. What happens when this product is one's dating partner? Does one just get rid of him or her and "trade up" much like a used automobile? How do we recognize when we are satisfied? How much is enough?

The very real threat of AIDS and the xenophobic context of

contemporary urban society in which many Americans live have thoroughly confused the very nature of modern morality as it applies to interpersonal relationships. Americans' professed moral values have lagged behind changes in their social and sexual behavior thereby widening the chasm between what they believe, what they espouse, and how they behave. No place is this more painfully apparent than in American sexual values, attitudes and behavior.

REFERENCES

Alcock, J. 1984. Animal behavior: An evolutionary approach. Sunderland, MA: Sinauer Associates.

Batten, M. 1992. *Sexual strategies: How females choose their mates.* New York: Putnam.

Brehm, S. 1992. *Intimate relationships.* New York: McGraw-Hill, Inc.

Cate, R. and Lloyd, S. 1992. *Courtship.* Newbury Park, CA: Sage Publications.

Critelli, J., Myers, E., Loos, V. 1986. The components of love: Romantic attraction and sex role orientation. *Journal of Personality,* 54(2):354-370.

Derlega, V.J. 1984. Self-disclosure and intimate relationships. In: Derlega, V. (Ed.) *Communication, intimacy and close relationships.* Orlando, FL: Academic Press, Inc.

Ellis, B. and Symons, D. 1990. Sex differences in sexual fantasy: An evolutionary psychological approach. *Journal of Sex Research,* 27:527-555.

Essock-Vitale, S. and McGuire, M. 1985. Women's lives viewed from an evolutionary perspective. I. Sexual histories, reproductive success, and demographic characteristics of a random sample of American women. *Ethology and Sociobiology,* 6:137-154.

Faludi, S. 1991. *Backlash: The undeclared war against American women.* New York: Doubleday.

Feingold, A. 1990. Gender differences in effects of physical attractiveness on romantic attraction: A comparison across five research paradigms. *Journal of Personality and Social Psychology,* 59:981-993.

Festinger, L. 1951. Architecture and group membership. *Journal of Social Issues,* 7:152-163.

Fromm, E. 1956. *The art of loving.* New York: Harper & Row.

Goldberg, H. 1983. *The new male-female relationship.* New York: Signet.

Hatfield, E. 1988. Passionate and companionate love. In R.J. Sternberg and M.L. Barnes (Eds.) The psychology of love (pp. 191-217). New Haven, CT: Yale University Press.

Jourard, S. 1971. *Self disclosure.* New York: Wiley-Interscience.

Jung, C. 1921/1970. Psychological types. In H. Read et al. (Eds.) *The collected works of C.J. Jung* (Vol. 6), Princeton, NJ: Princeton University Press.

Lasch, C. 1979. The culture of narcissism. New York: Warner Books.

Marwell, G., McKinney, K., Sprecher, S., Delamater, J., & Smith, S. 1982. Legitimizing factors in the initiation of heterosexual relationships. Paper presented at the First International Conference on Personal Relationships, Madison, Wisconsin.

Maslow, A. 1968. Toward a psychology of being. Princeton, NJ: Van Nostrand.

May, R. 1972. Power and innocence. New York: Norton.

Mullen, B. 1984. The mating trade. London: Routledge & Kegan Paul.

Murstein, B. 1972. Physical attractiveness and marital choice. *Journal of Personality and Social Psychology*, 22: 8-12.

Reik, T. 1944/1957. A psychologist looks at love. In: Reik, T. (Ed.), *Of love and lust*. New York: Farrar, Straus, and Cudahy, 1-194.

Rothman, E. 1984. *Hands and hearts: A history of courtship in America*. New York: Basic Books.

Roszak, B. and Roszak, T. (Eds.) 1969. *Masculine/feminine*. Evanston, IL: Harper & Row.

Rubin, L. 1983. *Intimate strangers: Men and women together*. New York: Harper & Row.

Salholz, E. 1986. Too late for Prince Charming? *Newsweek*, 107:54-57.

Sprecher, S. 1989. The importance to males and females of physical attractiveness, earning potential, and expressiveness in initial attraction. *Sex Roles*, 21:591-607.

Sprecher, S. and McKinney, K. 1987. Barriers in the initiation of intimate heterosexual relationships and strategies for intervention. *Journal of Social Work and Human Sexuality*, 5(2):97-109.

Tannen, D. 1990. *You just don't understand: Women and men in conversation*. New York: Ballantine Books.

Weaver, J. 1987. Shyness: An inhibitor to the development of intimacy. *Journal of Social Work and Human Sexuality*, 5(2):111-122.

Chapter 5

Sex versus Intimacy

Sex and intimacy are increasingly and erroneously perceived as synonymous in American society. Beyond just sexual intercourse, "sex" refers to the full range of verbal and non-verbal behaviors which communicate love and/or desire. Nowhere are the gender-lects more dramatically different in both expression and meaning than in male and female sexuality. Whatever else one may say about sex, it is at least as much a social and psychological phenomenon as a biological one. Even the gender differences in sexuality are profoundly influenced by the prescriptions and constraints of the culture. While estrogen and testosterone make some difference in how men and women experience sexual need and desire, the larger differences between us reside in our heads, not in our hormones. Thus, whether we accept the sexual commandments of our age, struggle against them, or vacillate somewhere between the two, the context is defined by the historical moment through which we are passing (Rubin, 1990).

Brehm (1992) points out that people born at different times have encountered radically different cultural norms about sexuality which have shaped their sexual attitudes and behaviors. Consider a person whose teenage years were spent in the conservative and conformist 1950s. Imagine how different that individual's sexual identity would be when compared to a teenager born in 1960, who turned eighteen at the height of the "sexual revolution" in 1978 and encountered far more permissive attitudes about sexual activity. Last, consider someone born in 1970, whose teenage years were spent during a time of more conservative political values and growing concern about the dangers of sexually transmitted diseases, particularly AIDS. With regard to sexuality, those who were 18 in

1958 lived in a very different world than did people who were 18 in 1978, while the sexual climate for teens in 1988 was vastly different from those of earlier eras.

During the 1950s, a girl's reputation was her most prized possession and was inextricably intertwined with her virginity. Her "good name," was her best ticket to a respectable marriage, family, and slice of the American dream. This so-called "rep" not only determined the kind of relationship a girl would have with boys in high school, it was her most important bargaining chip in her search for a proper husband (Rubin, 1990).

Traditionally, males have been conditioned to pursue women as "sexual prey"–to be captured and conquered. Women were socialized to elude and resist until they finally found "Mr. Right" who would love, cherish, and take care of them forever within the sacred domain of holy matrimony. Sex was the price they would have to pay for "true love and lasting happiness."

Unfortunately, this social arrangement was inherently flawed. Men of this era were frequently incapable of emotional intimacy. On the other hand, women of that era were so conflicted about sex that they frequently couldn't enjoy it without feeling guilty, anxious, or somehow demeaned. The old voices simply would not go away.

Women's sexuality had been openly acknowledged since the 1920s. However, until the 1960s, its socially accepted expression was confined to the marriage bed. During the 1940s and 1950s tedious social rituals were played out in order to get a "good girl" into bed. Such masquerades assumed that she did not really want to, but under the right conditions could be caught up and swept away by forces beyond her control.

The 1960s ushered in the sexual revolution. The widespread introduction of the Pill finally freed women from the fear of unwanted pregnancy and enabled them to enjoy sex for its own sake. Effectively separated from its procreative function, the very nature and meaning of sexuality was forever altered. Seduction became abbreviated, compressed, or sometimes by-passed altogether, as women reveled in their newfound liberation. Women finally began to enjoy the sexual freedom which had for so long been reserved for men only. Yet this newfound sexual freedom had its price. With the ever-increasing frequency and casualness of sexual interplay came a diminishing return on the moral and spiritual value of sex. Sex became a public commodity. The question no longer was whether a couple was going to have sex. Rather, it was when they were going to have sex and with which partners. The fact that a person did not know another particularly well did not preclude a sexual encounter. Sex was "beautiful" in its own right. It was no longer necessary to enshroud sex in elaborate and outdated rituals of deference. "Make love, not war" became a rationalization for frequent and uninhibited sexuality. These were the days of "Woodstock Nation" and the "Hippie Counterculture." Sex, drugs, and rock 'n' roll had attained the status of a social movement. Couched in anti-war, anti-establishment rhetoric, the "free love" generation acted out their libidinal late adolescent fantasies in ways which totally outraged and bewildered their parents' generation. Only later did the younger generation realize that they had succeeded in effectively trivializing sex.

During the late 1970s and early 1980s female orgasm had been elevated to the status of a mandatory peak experience. It was no longer enough for a man to achieve orgasm, then roll over and fall asleep. He had to be able to maintain his erection long enough to permit his partner to experience one or more orgasms and if not, to sexually satisfy her in some other equally adept fashion. For their part, women were expected to be easily capable of having an orgasm (or multiple orgasms), preferably during penetration. Females were also expected to be as open to the idea of orally stimulating males to orgasm. The standards of performance and expectations for both males and females rose almost beyond human capacity, despite little training or preparation in how to achieve these incredible feats. In addition, little was then known about the comparable struggles other men and women were having so as to assess one's own reality within the larger context. Sexual competence was supposed to spring into being as if by magic. Intimate and accurate knowledge of one's partner's needs was naively believed to be an automatic byproduct of true love. Any indication of lack of interest or skill constituted an admission of male inadequacy and female frigidity, or worse yet, of not being with it (Macklin, 1983).

Unfortunately, the stage was set for a dizzying array of performance anxieties, frustrations, and finger-pointing which unceremoniously blamed the sexual dysfunctions on the insensitivities and shortcomings of the opposite gender. Men were instructed to relax and become less genitally oriented. They were now encouraged to view the whole body as an organ of sensual pleasure and to focus more on the intimate experience of touch and less on the goal of penetration. Suddenly, sex was no longer an achievement or a conquest, but a mutually unfolding process.

For their part, women were encouraged to explore their bodies (as in *Our Bodies, Ourselves*) and to become joyfully acquainted with their own capacities for sexual response. They were told to take the pressure for performance off their partners and to become more actively involved in achieving their own sexual satisfaction; stop faking their orgasms; and risk expressing their physical and emotional needs (Macklin, 1983).

Sex became a public commodity. Yet despite the fact that many aspects of the sexual revolution were very appealing to women, relations between men and women during this period were characterized by a subtle coercion. That is, despite the lip service given to sexual equality, the early days of the sexual revolution were far from egalitarian.

Sexual liberation was rooted in a deeply entrenched patriarchal structure of roles and relationships that was inevitably destined to corrupt the very ideals on which it was founded. Women soon realized that "sexual freedom," while offering the appearance of gender parity, only reinforced male prerogatives while maintaining the fundamental subordination of women. As Rubin (1990:94) put it, "sex does not stand alone, an activity isolated from other social, cultural, and institutional forces in our lives. The inequality in gender relations permeates every aspect of life, influencing if not determining women's decisions about such disparate life situations as what kind of work they'll do and whether they'll enter into a sexual relationship."

Hence, sexual involvement had other social and personal implications as well. The sexual mores of the day played their part, to be sure. But these new standards unfolded within the context of the old inequalities in the social-sexual relations between women and men. Thus, while the sexual revolution did achieve a new distribution of sexual pleasure which included women more fully, it took the subsequent gender revolution to begin realigning the structure of power between men and women, both in bed and out (Rubin, 1990).

Nowhere is the so-called "battle of the sexes" more intensely apparent and conflictual today than in current male-female relationships. Unfortunately, the heightened sexual expectations for men and women have frequently proved counterproductive. Angry over years of male exploitation, female "sexual demands" have begun to mirror dysfunctional male "sexual demands." Moreover, once sexual communication reaches the juncture at which sex has to be demanded, then both partners have already missed the point. Ideally, sexual expression should automatically consider both partners' perceived and expressed sexual and emotional needs.

Sexual dysfunction and pathology are increasing at an alarming rate. If, as many sex therapists contend, "good sex equals good communication," then it is no wonder why couples are struggling. The ways sexual needs are expressed, valued, and negotiated (often in very subtle non-verbal ways) comprise the essence of sexual communication. Rather than being preoccupied with one's own pleasure and performance, perhaps the more important question is, "What can I do to best satisfy/excite/fulfill my partner?"

TOUCHING AND INTIMACY

Touch invariably communicates. The tricky part is interpreting precisely what the message is, since touch may communicate any one of a vast array of emotions whose interpretation exists within the context of the particular situation and relationship. Male-female touch is laden with a variety of subtle embedded messages. Touch may be affectionate, aggressive, insincere, or profound. For some people, touch is their way of being in and relating to the world. Some years ago, Desmond Morris (1971) offered an exhaustive anthropological analysis of sexual intimacy. He suggested that all animal courtship patterns (including the human love affair) are organized in a typical twelve-stage sequence: (1) eye to body; (2) eye to eye; (3) voice to voice; (4) hand to hand; (5) arm to shoulder; (6) arm to waist; (7) mouth to mouth; (8) hand to head; (9) hand to body; (10) mouth to breast; (11) hand to genitals and (12) genitals to genitals.

Most human beings do not merely copulate; they make love to a particular and special individual, within the context of a highly specific relationship. Thus, for our species, all stages of the sequence including copulation can serve to enhance the pair-bonding process. It is also the presumable reason that the female evolved an extended period of sexual receptivity, stretching far beyond the limits of the ovulation period. As Morris (1971:101) stated, "It could even be said that we now perform the mating act, not so much to fertilize the egg as to fertilize a relationship."

An ever-increasing number of "professional touchers" are being employed to compensate for the shortcomings of the amateur and amatory touchers who are failing to supply us with our much-needed quota of body intimacy. Who are these professional touchers? They are virtual strangers or semi-strangers, who under the pretext of providing us with some specialized service, are required to touch our bodies. Such a pretext is necessary because of course, we do not like to admit that we are insecure and need the comforting touch of another human body (Morris, 1971). Such professional touchers may include: the chiropractor, dentist, doctor, nurse, masseur, hair stylists, midwife, etc.

At all ages, the female appears to be very much more responsive to tactile stimuli than the male and more dependent upon touch for erotic arousal. The male, on the other hand, depends more upon visual stimuli. These differences seem to be partly genetic, but cultural differences also appear to play a significant role (Montagu, 1971).

Sadly, Americans are not particularly fluent in the language of touch. Innumerable studies have shown that America is a relatively stand-offish society from a purely kinesthetic point of view. Nevertheless, the necessity of human touch and physical nurturance for healthy human growth and development is undeniable. Within the context of intimate relationships "loving touch" enhances intimacy by offering a profound level of acceptance and affirmation; an essential expression of caring and support which can connect the individual not just with another human being, but to his/her essential humanity. Is it any wonder that a culture so illiterate in touch would be having such difficulties with intimate relationships?

SEX AND INTIMACY

A vast body of knowledge now exists which analyzes the physiology of sex ad infinitum. The annals of pop psychology are littered with an assortment of self-help books about sex and intimacy. Unfortunately, these books and articles are frequently written at a fairly pedestrian level and offer little in-depth analysis to the professional reader. An obvious exception to this trend is David Schnarch's penetrating analysis of sexual and marital intimacy entitled *Constructing The Sexual Crucible.*

Despite all these books and articles, most salient, deeply evocative aspects of our sexual lives still remain *terra incognita* to both laymen and therapists alike. Having approached sexuality as if the secrets of life could be discovered on the dissecting table, the study and treatment of sexual dysfunction has confused sexual performance with the inner experience of sexuality, overlooking considerations of eroticism, desire, and personal meaning (Schnarch, 1993).

Douglas and Atwell (1988) feel that the sharing of repeated and prolonged excitements of adoration coupled with the lesser emotions (such as playful enjoyment) potentiates the emotional bonding between partners and constitutes the basis for romantic love. When this bonding is pervasive, as it is when individuals achieve the peak of intimacy, then each respective self becomes an integral part of the "thou" in the state of being in love called "true love." "Through sex, we can encounter–though we usually repress it–the fear of not being loved and the terror of losing what we love, the dread of exposing everything within us–that which is vulnerable and helpless, inadequate and impoverished or ugly and hateful . . . " (Schnarch, 1993:42).

People have boring, monotonous sex because intense sex and intimacy are unbearably threatening and require more adult autonomy and ego strength than many can muster. Genuine sexual intimacy is not realized by mastering specific sexual skills, reducing performance anxiety, or having regular orgasms, but by the ability to allow oneself to deeply know and be deeply known by one's partner. So simple to articulate, so difficult to achieve (Schnarch, 1993).

Good sex requires good communication and a mutual willingness to work at improving the relationship. It is ironic that sex therapy often focuses on particular techniques aimed at reducing performance anxiety. Such an approach can actually lessen one's capacity for intimacy and sexual intensity (Schnarch, 1993).

Sustained eye contact is a central feature of human sexual arousal and intimacy. Not only is eye contact in sexual initiation common among primates, it appears to be a phylogenetic trait in human beings as well. For instance, flirtation is a type of sexual communication comprised mainly of reciprocal signals sent via the eyes (Schnarch, 1993).

The American pursuit of intimacy has busied the offices of countless psychotherapists and fostered a host of human-potential enterprises aimed at reducing alienation and personal isolation. Yet most of these fail to see the inherent paradox of intimacy, thus confusing intimacy with togetherness and closeness. It is the acute and often painful awareness of our fundamental loneliness and separateness from other human beings that motivates intensely intimate contact. To be intimate with another should not mean emotional fusion, since two people cannot share one mind, body, or personality. Rather, it is a process of knowing oneself in the presence of a partner while still recognizing the other's immutable separateness (Schnarch, 1993).

Many intimate relationships today are ambiguous, painful, and transient. They are ambiguous because one can never fully know another or fully dissolve one's lonely separateness in merger with another, and painful, because every sexual relationship that approaches the limits of sexual potential triggers a "bottomless pit of past disappointment about love not received" and a terrible fear of loving and needing much more intensely than does one's partner. The experience of an intensely intimate relationship is both wonderful and terrifying, and yet loss is inevitable. Every love is broken by illness, separation, or death. The exquisite nature of love is that it provides great joy while simultaneously being threatened by potential change and termination and by the fact that the loved one does not always feel, know, or understand (Schnarch, 1993).

Case Interview: Rebecca

During an argument, my ex-husband used to try to get to get me into bed with him in order resolve the conflict. He didn't understand that for women, having sex is not a solution to a disagreement. Female anger is not resolved through sex! In fact, this only ended up compounding the problem because then I was angry with myself for "giving in" and having sex with him when I was so mad.

I later realized that my situation was directly connected not only to the way women handle anger vis-à-vis men, but also to female self-esteem. If a woman has low self-esteem, then she looks at her male partner as a security blanket and would tend not to leave even if the relationship is a destructive one. Other women see sex as something they have to give in order to hold onto the relationship. They live vicariously through their male partner. In one sense, he is their ego. That's why so many women in abusive relationships continue to remain despite the abuse. It comes down to a choice between living with a known quantity (however problematic) and facing the terror of being alone.

In addition, the way women feel about their physical attractiveness has a great deal to do with whether they feel sexual or not. With society's ever-increasing pressure on women to look good (i.e., "be thin") it puts tremendous pressure on women today. Back in the sixties, who you were as a person was far more important. Nowadays, if you look good, no one really cares very much about what kind of person you are. They just assume that because you're attractive, you must be a worthwhile person–and unfortunately, vice versa. The prevalence of eating disorders today is partly a manifestation of a society obsessed with "thinness." Ironically, however, eating disorders such as anorexia dramatically diminish sexual drive. To compound matters further, eating disorders are often correlated with childhood sexual abuse. Think of what that does to your sexual identity. There are a lot of conflicting messages for women today, especially with respect to sexuality.

Intimacy is a tremendous emotional risk which requires courage, integrity, and a strong faith in one's own resources. This emotional risk stems from the very personal self-disclosures necessary in order to meld sex and intimacy. However, the rewards are well worth the price to those willing to accept life on its own terms. As Schnarch (1993) explains, once the dream of fusion is relinquished; the experience of the "oceanic" oneness with humankind is realized, and the integration of sexuality and spirituality is possible. Sexual intimacy within the context of a loving, mutually satisfying relationship enables partners to exist for a time in that pure state of being without expectations or judgments. The act of "making love" is a gradual unveiling in which layer after layer of custom and appearance are stripped away.

Rose-Colored Glasses

The early stages of love relationships are characterized by a selective attention to the endearing characteristics of one's partner and an obliviousness to his or her shortcomings. In other words, love may not always be blind, but it is most likely myopic. This is sometimes referred to as the "pink-lens effect." Anyone with much experience with the powerful emotions of love and sex are quite aware of what is commonsensically called the "pink-lens effect" and somewhat less aware of the "gray-lens effect" (the focus on undesirable characteristics) that sets in when love turns to hatred and sexual desire to repugnance.

Douglas and Atwell (1988) also believe that emotions and uncertainty potentiate (amplify) each other, just as certain emotions such as sexual lust and adoration love potentiate each other. As a result even moderate amounts of sex and love mixed with moderate doses of uncertainty about someone can enhance mythical thinking. Because most people today do not know that much about those for whom they first develop sexual feelings, uncertainty exists. This "newness" and uncertainty can potentiate sexual arousal and further confuse the issues of love and lust.

The ultimate romantic synthesis of love and lust is falling in love at first sight. This phenomenon is central to the "myth of romantic love." Much of the most compelling folklore of romantic love (*Romeo and Juliet, West Side Story,* etc.) invariably includes one crucial moment in which one of the lovers or both are "stricken with love" completely beyond all reason or rationality. The very sight of one's "vision of perfection" instantly creates a profound spiritual connection (typically when the couple's eyes first meet). The lover knows from that first enchanted moment that somehow, somewhere, this love must be fulfilled, regardless of what impossible obstacles stand in the way. Fate has struck like a thunderbolt and destiny must be served despite the apparent odds against it. In fact, it is this very conflict which produces the agonizing ambivalence that serves as self-tantalization for the romantic lovers in the early stages of love's buildup. The "love at first sight" phenomenon occurs due to pre-existing archetypes which heretofore laid dormant in the stricken lover's unconscious and are triggered by the sudden appearance of the person who closely approximates these archetypes (Douglas and Atwell, 1988). Clinically speaking, this would be termed a "transference reaction." From a purely romantic perspective, the irresistible myth of love at first sight possesses a powerful, magical, and fated quality. The most profound characteristic of any myth is the power which it gains over us, usually without our knowing. People's individual archetypes of love represent their individual myths of love. The more obscure, mysterious, and magical their origins, the more power they have to cast their romantic spell and propel lovers into the heights of romantic fantasy.

Douglas and Atwell (1988) suggest that most "loves at first sight" are seen more as sexy than classically beautiful. This notion in itself is a clue to the fact that most of these "loves" are in reality, intense lust with undertones of adoration love (assuming that sexy beauty is the most effective trigger of lust). However, classical beauty also operates at another level to trigger even more intense "true love" at first sight. Anyone who has been loved in the past (such as a mother or father) has been partially idealized so that one's memories of them are more beautiful than other people would remember. This idealization makes them more like any beautiful person one might later see in everyday life. Hence, a beautiful person is more likely than most to trigger one's earlier love feelings.

However, there is another crucial factor involved in this process. No one falls in love at first sight under just any circumstances.

Individuals do not, for example, fall in love at first sight when they are already in romantic love with someone else, even if they see someone new who fits their archetype. If individuals are not highly aroused sexually by the person they are already in love with, then someone representing their sexual archetypes might well trigger sexual feelings. When individuals are in love romantically with someone else, they do not fall in love with this new sex partner unless they go through unbonding from the earlier love. Being in love largely blocks the development of new romantic loves. In order to fall in love at first sight, it is necessary that the individual be open to the new love experience. That is, the typical instance of "love at first sight" is someone who is extremely lonely and sexually starved–craving love and sex.

SEX, AIDS, AND ADOLESCENCE

According to Gladwell (1992) the campaign to encourage Americans to practice safe sex is faltering despite massive public awareness campaigns. During the 1980s condom use increased by about 25 percent. Yet those who responded to this threat were generally those who had the least risk of coming into direct contact with the disease. The intermittent use of condoms is minimizing the potential advantage of so-called "safe sex."

According to World Health estimates, an estimated 40,000 new HIV infections will occur this year. Nowadays, no sexual activity is risk-free. Many Americans (especially men) still resist condom use. It also appears that the most sexually active people appear to be using condoms the least. "According to the most recent survey of adolescent sexual behavior, of those males between 15 and 19 who have only one sexual partner a year, 63 percent use a condom. The rate drops to 56 percent for those with two partners a year; 45 percent for those with three; and only 37 percent for the core risk group with more than four partners" (Gladwell, 1992).

It is interesting to note that condom use is even lower among adults. According to a recent study of heterosexual unmarried men between 18 and 45 with two or more sexual partners during the previous 12 months–the heterosexual group most at risk for sexually transmitted disease–between 6 and 12 percent use a condom all the time, while 40 percent never use one. In contrast, homosexual males have managed to achieve levels of consistent condom use as high as 70 percent.

The cross-cultural variations in sexual behavior patterns are also noteworthy. Black adolescent males are the least sexually active of all teenagers with the average sexually experienced black male aged 15-19 engaging in sexual intercourse an average of 2.32 times per month. By comparison, sexually active white males aged 15-19 have intercourse an average of 2.75 times a month, while Hispanic teens average 2.85 times a month.

Contrary to prevailing cultural stereotypes, black youths are the most frequent condom users. In 1988, 65.5 percent of sexually active black males aged 15-19 used a condom during their most recent intercourse, compared to 54.4 percent for white teens and 46.1 percent for Hispanics (Gladwell, 1992).

AIDS is growing most rapidly among heterosexual teens and women. Yet, unprotected sex is still the norm rather than the exception. Why? Numerous experts have debated the relative effectiveness of latex condoms (as opposed to lambskin, etc.) as inhibitors for a myriad of sexually transmitted diseases including chlamydia, syphilis, and HIV. The prevailing wisdom is that while "safe sex" will reduce one's chances of becoming infected, it is by no means assured. Overall, it appears that despite the fact that individuals are more conscious of AIDS, their actual sexual practices have not changed very much.

The use of contraceptives requires a sense of pre-planning, responsibility, and rational negotiation, which is somehow not entirely in keeping with the spontaneous, frequently irresponsible and irrational act of making love. Moreover, the use of contraceptives has different meanings for males and females. Young women tend to view their own part in contraception negatively, feeling that the need for them to take the responsibility means their male partners do not really care about them. Further, there is apparently some vague moral stigma involved in obtaining contraceptives. On the other hand, since males are commonly known to dislike condoms due to their interfering with the tactile pleasures of intercourse, the use of condoms demonstrates a level of unselfishness and empathy for the woman's needs.

If, however, the aim of sexual intercourse is pregnancy, then the meaning and purpose of coitus is quite different. Due in part to inherent biological differences and roles, men and women have very different feelings about pregnancy. Many men (especially those who are not fathers) fail to understand the psychic and emotional benefits women derive from being pregnant. For some women, being pregnant affirms their basic femaleness in ways that nothing else can. Being pregnant is at the core of the traditional definition of femininity. However, it is also one way of dealing with the new and sometimes frightening roles that society is now demanding of women. Some women feel that becoming a mother enhances their worth as persons and see pregnancy as a path to increased self-esteem. Others may take risks in order to find out if they are fertile, especially if they had some reason to believe they might not be. To these women, fertility is like money in the bank; it is nice to know it is there, even if there are no immediate plans to use it (Scanzoni and Scanzoni, 1988).

Some women anticipate rewards in their relationships with other people as a result of pregnancy. Creating a child together may be seen as a deeper level of emotional bonding. Sharing in the creation of a new life which is a very real part of both partners is potentially a deep and enduring intimate experience. Sometimes, a female may use pregnancy to force her male partner to define his commitment to the relationship and possibly marry her. Teens sometimes use pregnancy to punish their parents or as an attempt to gain recognition as independent adults. Other times, pregnancy signals a desperate bid for attention or seeks to provide someone to love when the young woman feels unloved and unlovable. For some, becoming pregnant is a way of crying out for help from the social welfare system. Last, the risk of pregnancy may be used to bring an excitement of its own to the sexual act and enliven an otherwise dull existence (Scanzoni and Scanzoni, 1988).

According to the Guttmacher Institute, 11 percent of unmarried teenage girls in the United States become pregnant each year. This means that over 1 million American girls, one every ninety seconds, finds herself pregnant. This figure is almost twice that of other Western countries, even though their rates of sexual activity and the ages at which they begin, match the U.S. Not unsurprisingly, teenage girls account for just over one-fourth of the 1.6 million abortions performed annually in the U.S. (Rubin, 1990).

Most adolescents will not openly discuss sex with any adult and especially not with their parents. The confusion and struggle for the adolescents' own incipient sexual identity is too emotionally charged. Moreover, this is a developmental stage of increasing separation and autonomy vis-à-vis one's parents. It is an irony well known to most parents that at this crucial developmental stage, when their adolescent children could most benefit from parental input and support, teens are generally least likely to discuss such matters with them.

Current childrearing patterns are fraught with contradictions. Teens chronically complain about boredom and what is wrong with their parents' generation. However, this too is ironic because while this particular generation of teens has been encouraged to be independent in thought and action from early childhood on, these teens have also been shielded from responsibility by parents who believed they were entitled to a worry-free childhood. As adolescence unfolds, teens begin to insist on their right to greater freedom and independence. Yet once they get it, they want little or nothing to do with it. "We're all bored, that's why we drink and do all that other stuff," said Derek, a 17-year-old from Augusta. "I think adults make a big mistake when they don't make sure kids have real responsibilities. I don't mean like cleaning our rooms and stuff like that, I mean real responsibilities and things we have to do, just like they have" (Rubin, 1990:86-87).

Who is to blame for this state of affairs? Clearly, parents must take some responsibility for having raised children who are bored and irresponsible. Yet how else will children turn out in a culture where adolescents have no role or function and where a sense of responsibility no longer exists?

As Rubin (1990) explains, this is a society where politics have failed to inspire commitment to the larger social issues of the day; where those in public life seem to value self-aggrandizement and the accumulation of personal wealth above all else; where the environment is being criminally exploited and decimated for the sake of monetary gain for those multinational corporations which least need the profit; and where the senseless and deadly games of war are playing fast and loose with the destinies of entire nations. There is a pervasive sense of powerlessness among today's youth. They exist in a relative moral and spiritual vacuum which has severely undermined hope for a better future.

This is the malaise which underlies our children's complaints about boredom and the absence of responsibility. These are the long-term issues America must contend with if we hope to see the generations yet to come abandon the kind of superficial thrill-seeking so pervasive today. Ultimately, our children are merely a reflection the times. It is an era of superficial interpersonal relationships characterized by impersonal sexual encounters. How can we blame our children for the world they now inhabit; a world which we ourselves have shaped?

BETWEEN PARENTS AND CHILDREN

Generally speaking, a person's values and attitudes are the best predictors of premarital sexual behavior. Teenagers who are sexually active at an early age place greater value on independence, express less concern about academic achievement, and are less religious. Developmentally speaking, most teenagers are influenced more by the opinions of their friends than by those of their family (Rubin, 1983). But what are their peers telling them about sex? And how does the current context of adolescence shape sexual behavior?

Rubin (1990) suggests that the effects of the sexual revolution are strikingly evident in teenagers' sense of entitlement to make their own choices about sex and in their tolerance of all kinds of sexual behaviors–so long as they fall within current peer norms. A 1986 Harris poll found that 57 percent of the nation's 17-year-olds, 46 percent of the 16-year-olds and 29 percent of the 15-year-olds have had sexual intercourse. In addition, a recent survey of eighth-grade students (14-year-olds) from three rural counties in Maryland revealed that 58 percent of the boys and 47 percent of the girls had experienced coitus.

Present-day adults who were among the culture of youth during the 1960s zealously believed that individuals had every right to "Do their own thing." However, who among them could have predicted the extent to which their children would later take that sentiment, let alone their own discomfort with it? Ironically, today's female acquiescence to males is rooted in the very countercultural values of the 1960s which repudiated the middle-class ethics of self-denial, orderliness, and respect for authority. Now, the middle-aged children of the "tune-in, turn-on, and drop-out" generation gaze helplessly at the violent, drug-laden world which their children now inhabit.

At the other extreme from this mostly liberal, middle-class cohort of parents is an aggressive and highly vocal movement of social conservatives, fueled by the religious right, who have launched a vigorous attack on moral permissiveness and the very real consequences of uncontrolled sexuality. They decry the epidemic of sexually transmitted diseases among adolescents; are morally outraged at the skyrocketing incidence of teenage pregnancy; and are terrified by the ever-present specter of AIDS. It is difficult for any responsible parent to quarrel with many of the things they are saying. However, upon closer scrutiny, their repressive tactics, evangelical moral prescriptions, and endless sermonizing are only backfiring with most of today's youth. Add to these already mixed messages the undeniable fact that sex sells in a mass consumer culture, and the result is a kind of postmodern ambiguity about the meaning and value of sexuality. This double message alternately confuses, enervates, and mollifies today's youth who are themselves desperately seeking to make sense of the seemingly senseless world we have bequeathed them.

What most separates the 1990s from the 1960s is that behavior once at the rebellious fringe of late adolescent radicalism now permeates the cultural mainstream of teenage America. While teenagers of the 1960s boldly experimented with sexuality, today's teens expect and anticipate it. Sex is taken for granted. No longer is the question "Should we have sex?" Rather, the question is "When should we have sex?" And the "when" is happening at younger and younger ages. According to Hersch (1993) by the spring of freshman year in high school, 40 percent of all students have experienced sexual intercourse. By the beginning of senior year, almost three-quarters are sexually active. By the end of senior year, 29 percent of all high school students will have had four or more sex partners. In addition, this accelerated sexual activity among teens is increasing faster in white, middle-class families than in poor, inner-city neighborhoods.

It is difficult not to be struck by the rootless quality of adolescent social life in the 1990s. No longer connected to the civic or community organizations and alienated from their families, today's youth are drifting. Frequently aimless, affluent, and irresponsible, teenagers rove around in restless hordes, forming temporary groups, separating, regrouping in ever-changing locations, though not infrequently at local shopping malls. In one sense, such drifting is an important developmental stage and part of the luxury of adolescence. Even though it does not feel like it to them, at no other time in their lives will these young people be so unfettered by adult responsibilities. This lack of organized social options also removes traditional safety nets. "Most of the time parents do not have a clue about what their kids are doing, whom they are with, where they are or what's really going on. Kids from every background and age group mix far more indiscriminately than did prior generations, gravitating en masse to "where it's happening," which is often "the Party"–a large, usually unplanned gathering at somebody's empty house, fueled by alcohol and often out of control" (Hersch, 1993:26).

Teens lying to their parents about their whereabouts and activities is nothing new. However, their behavior is increasingly extreme, not just in the case of sex, but in terms of alcohol consumption and abuse. During their own adolescence, many of today's parents no doubt sneaked into their parents' liquor cabinet now and then, but routine drinking (not to mention drugs and sex) were relatively rare. Today, drinking is the norm for kids. According to the CDC, the average adolescent starts drinking at 13, and by senior year more than 90 percent of all high school students drink fairly routinely. For bored teens, drinking and sex are recreation (i.e., something to do to escape the lack of meaning and direction in many of their lives).

Hersch's analysis suggests that we live in a culture in which the kids call the shots while the adults try desperately to catch up. Teenagers spend huge blocks of time either alone or with friends or taking care of siblings after school. Meanwhile, their working parents have erroneously concluded that they can handle anything. And yet, the proliferation of alcohol, drugs, and sex without well-established moral and ethical guidelines is a sure-fire formula for disaster.

Unfortunately, their adult counterparts do not seem to be doing much better. Very few adults seem to adequately understand the complex dynamics which underlie their sexual interactions, let alone have any control over them.

SEX AND POWER

Sex is a metaphor for the couple's relationship. That is, the particular manner and style in which a couple makes love is the overt expression of each partner's covert emotional needs as well as an expression of each partner's particular sexual history. Rubin (1990) asserts that when it comes to sex and power, more depends upon the symbolic meaning than any hard-and-fast reality. Beyond the mere expression of passion and lust, the sexual interchange is also a complex micro-political negotiation in which both analogic and digital communication function to define relative status and power. To what degree are each partner's needs given priority? Who is dominant and who is submissive during sexual interchanges and to what degree are these roles interchangeable?

For some women, the issues are power and control, penetration and submission, while for others this sexual connection is an inroad to interpersonal and spiritual communion which renews one's spirit and staves off one's existential solitude. Sex can be affirming at some very basic levels. One's essential "maleness" and "femaleness" can be enhanced by an emotionally intimate sexual experience. In this sense, sex can be empowering, putting one in touch with his or her essential self. Sex can also be liberating. The dredging up and release of unconscious anxiety can also purge the burdens of one's spirit in what amounts to a cathartic experience.

Historically, the giving and withholding of sexual access has been one of the major sources of power which women could exercise vis-à-vis men. Males exchanged their economic status and security for female sexual availability and domestic services. As a result, the bedroom often became the site for symbolically acting out conflicts in the relationship. However, as women gain more economic status and power, sex will no longer be used for its exchange value and can be enjoyed for it own sake (Macklin, 1983).

Despite the gains of feminism, men typically have more permissive attitudes and more sexual experience than do women. The male ability to introduce sexuality in non-sexual encounters with women is uncanny. Persistent yet self-defeating male socialization patterns coupled with an insatiable media which encourages men to seek out and sleep with as many beautiful women as utterly possible sometimes turn dating into a "search and destroy mission." Male competitiveness, coupled with their determination to successfully complete the mission for which they have been training all their lives, necessarily objectifies women and classifies them as sexual prey. It is this mentality which dehumanizes women and makes them vulnerable to male exploitation and victimization. And men still wonder why women are angry? The scary part is how pervasive this "search and destroy" mentality still is in men today. If a war between the sexes is declared, women should not in their wildest dreams expect men to surrender. Traditional males live to engage in the glory of battle and the "thrill of victory."

For their part, women are rightfully outraged. Deeply embittered by men's historical sexual dominance, women are fighting back. Andrea Dworkin's recent book entitled *Intercourse* offers a caustic analysis of the socio-political relationship between gender, sex, and power. She contends that the sexual possession of women by men is pedestrian. Women have been chattels to men as wives and prostitutes, as well as sexual and reproductive servants. Being owned and having intercourse are virtually synonymous experiences in the lives of women. Intercourse conveys the quality of the ownership and the male passion for dominance. According to Dworkin, he owns you inside out and requires access to every hidden inch. Owning everything around you, on you, and everything you are capable of doing as a worker, servant, or ornament is one thing, but getting inside you and owning your insides is a deeper more intimate possession than any other kind.

Dworkin further contends that through the act of intercourse, the male expresses the geography of his dominance. Her sex, her insides are part of his domain as a male. He can possess her as an individual and thus express the private right of ownership issuing from his gender. Most women are not distinct, private individuals to most men, and so intercourse tends toward the class assertion of dominance. Women reside in the reality of being owned by submitting to intercourse. Their bodies learn to respond to what male dominance offers as touch, as sex, as love.

> For women, being possessed is the sex that has to meet the need for love or tenderness or physical affection; therefore, it comes to mean, to show, the intensity of desire; and being erotically owned by a man who takes you and fucks you is a physically charged and meaningful affirmation of womanhood or femininity or being desired. (Dworkin, 1987:66)

Female Sexual Experience

American society provides a series of double level messages to women about sex. According to Kitzinger (1983), sex is much more than whether or not a woman is in a sexual relationship, or whether she is having orgasms. Her sexual identity has to do with the way she expresses herself through her body to her children, friends, and lovers. Such expression emanates from her feelings about her body as it passes through all the changes of puberty, the ovarian cycle, childbearing and menopause, through grieving and loss and into old age. All this is inextricably linked with the way she gives and receives love.

Kitzinger feels that genital sex is just one part of this rich sensual and emotional experience. Reducing sex to the mere physical aspects separates it from what makes female sexuality exciting and alive with longing, tenderness, passion, and strength. Is it now time to reassess widespread assumptions as to the overriding importance of genital sex in women's lives?

Case Interview: Laura

My experience of sexuality deepens me as a person. It runs the full range from vulnerability and being taken care of to being the one who takes. It's affirming at a very basic level in terms of who I am as a person and as a woman. It's a risk to open up oneself at such a basic level, but it's a metaphor for opening up at other levels. Yet with that "opening up" comes risk–risk of not being accepted; risk of losing someone you've grown to care about. It's a curious paradox, but I find strength and power in being open and vulnerable. In a way, it taps the inner resources within me and lets me know what I'm about. Usually, I feel strong enough to take that risk, but again so much depends upon the context of the intimate relationship.

Yet even nowadays, women don't really know their own bodies, let alone their own sexuality. What's more, women don't really talk about it, especially those of my generation. Why? Because if you start talking about it you have to come face to face with the reality that things in your relationship may not be that great and that somebody else might have it better than you do. And the typical female reaction would be to say "What's wrong with me?"

During the early years of my former marriage, my husband used to tell me both explicitly and implicitly not to talk or make noises during lovemaking. He once tried to tell me that it was because he was afraid that the neighbors might hear, but in reality he was just uncomfortable with my expressing myself in that way. That was also an issue in our marriage. I felt like I had to hold back stifling my emotions just so he wouldn't feel uncomfortable. Is it any wonder that sex always seemed to "misfire" between us?

Unfortunately, this sexual misfiring made me feel like there was something wrong with me. Despite my best efforts, I just couldn't make it work. As a woman, if something goes wrong in the relationship, then it's your fault. That really made me angry. Angry at myself, angry at my husband. And I'm also angry at a society which hasn't given women any good role models or tools for resolving these problems. I'm angry at being the one made to feel responsible, and I don't think that's really fair. Why is the woman the one who always has to be responsible? I felt hurt and frustrated. Intentionally or not, somehow my self-esteem got damaged.

To me, the bodily expression of sex is a kind of culmination of everything that has gone on before. There may be some times when you just feel lustful, but that must occur within the context of a meaningful relationship. The depth of sexual intimacy cannot be there without the communication, connection, and empathy. But to say that genital sex is not important . . . no, I can't say that.

As far as "good sex" is concerned, to me, it's the whole constellation of physical sensations and emotional reactions and it's that interchange between two people on a physical and emotional level that culminates in the physical release of orgasm. And in order for it to be really satisfying, yes, I need to have an orgasm. For me, it deepens and magnifies the experience. For some women, maybe it's not as important. Maybe it's because I didn't have good sex in my marriage for so many years. My orgasms are incredibly varied in intensity, location, etc., but they always involve a release of emotional and physical tension. There are different layers of thoughts, images, and sensations–sometimes fleeting, sometimes very intense. Orgasms are very "textured" emotionally and physically. Sometimes it feels like little shivers. Sometimes it's like a waterfall. Other times it's focused in one spot and feels like a sudden burst and then other times it's like a satisfying sigh. It's kind of hard to explain, but overall you might say it rearranges the pieces of the puzzle so that they finally fit together. You feel complete. Like all is right with the world at that particular time.

The fundamental differences in male (external) and female (internal) genitalia make sex a biologically inherent more intimate experience for women. Allowing another person to be physically inside you in the most private part of your body requires much more trust, safety, and emotional connection. This inherent biological difference is perhaps one of the reasons that sex can potentially be less personal for males.

MALE SEXUAL COMPULSION

Despite the fact that we live in a high-tech age of sexual fantasy, there are those who are still having sex the old-fashioned way. Unfortunately, some are taking sexual passion to the extreme. Depending on one's point of view, these sexual encounters may either be referred to as "romantic interludes" or clinically diagnosed as narcissistic personality disorders. This is the world of those men who live, not to love, but to "make love," and to do so as frequently as time and energy allow with as many beautiful and challenging conquests as humanly possible. For males, there are alluring romantic overtones to this particular lifestyle which, though superficially appealing, is ultimately self-destructive, exploitive and mutually dehumanizing.

It is possible for sexual passion alone to result in a sexual delirium and a transcendence beyond one's everyday sense of self. Such sexual passion can also engender a prolonged craving for a specific sexual partner. In France, these sexual obsessions have long been referred to as "grandes passions." However, it is often difficult to distinguish such grand passions from these pathological characterological states.

Outside the context of love, most sexual obsessions are fraught with intense conflict. Sexual preoccupation is one of the most selfish and aggressive drives. For many insecure men, the narcissistic overtones of this sexual drive closely correlate with the drive for dominance and success. As Trachtenberg (1988) puts it: For people within the normal range of security-insecurity, the dominance drive is triggered as an undertone of the sex drive. Those with more intense insecurities tend to have strong desires for dominance in their sexual relations, if for no other purpose than to "control" the person from whom they fear rejection. Their need to control others is indicative of the fear of feeling out-of-control themselves. Ultimately therefore, this need to control is a projection. According to Douglas and Atwell (1988) individuals who are highly insecure about their potential attractiveness are precisely the ones most apt to develop sexual relations without the accompanying emotional involvement. These are also individuals who are most apt to be acting dominant during their sexual activity. These are the Don Juans and Dona Juanitas who seek to conquer "Mount Everests"–the most beautiful, popular, richest, most famous status symbols.

Paradoxically, their own compulsion and its psychic concomitants give Casanovas a great deal of power over women–a persistence, an urgency, a persuasiveness and sexual authority that many women find overwhelming. These men are as adept at finding sexual partners as alcoholics are at finding a drink when the bars are closed, as skillful at seduction as drug addicts are at getting money for their next fix. (Trachtenberg, 1988:29)

We are living in an addictive society–drugs, alcohol, gambling, relationships, and inevitably sex. As Trachtenberg so eloquently explains, "at the center of every addiction, as at the center of every cyclone is a vacuum, a still point of emptiness that generates circles of frantic movement at its periphery." Women are the primary object of compulsion for Casanovas. They pursue women with an intense and focused urgency that renders ordinary courtship casual and desultory by comparison. There is also a reckless abandon of reason and rationality which frequently jeopardizes their marriages, careers, and health, and in this age of AIDS, their behavior has now become life-threatening.

While some family therapists dismiss the concern with addictions as a harmless but misguided fad, many sex therapists see a danger in this latest trend to label problematic sexual behaviors as "addictions." Some argue that the sex-addiction label is irresponsible and destructive since the implied message is that sex is bad or harmful. While some may make bad decisions when it comes to sex, sex is not a disease and therefore the disease model is completely inappropriate. Other critics are offended that rapists and child molesters are being given permission to avoid responsibility for the harm they have done to others by hiding behind their so-called addiction, insisting that they could not help themselves. As one client put it, "It wasn't me, it was my addiction" (Hersch, 1993).

Part of the problem lies in the broad use of the term "addiction." Sometimes it refers to an obsession or compulsion (as in "psychological addiction"), while other times it is meant in a purely physical sense such as a biochemical dependency. Some believe that it is impossible for a person to become physically addicted to sex since there is no increase-dose tolerance, as alcoholics or drug addicts experience, no physiological dependence, and no physical withdrawal. All human beings possess an innate, biologically based, evolution-created drive to have sex (Hersch, 1993).

Patrick Carnes (1983) offers a different point of view. He believes that people do have the capacity to become physically addicted to a state of sexual arousal. In support of his argument, the biochemical changes (such as the release of endorphins) engendered by intense sexual activity are a well-documented medical fact. Carnes further points out that professionals who study addictions have learned that an addictive obsession can develop from whatever generates significant mood alteration, whether it be the self-nurturing of food, the excitement of gambling, or the arousal of seduction. One of the most destructive aspects of sex addiction is that you literally carry your own source of supply.

However, the 12-step model is not the only, or even the best solution for people with sexual problems–or those with chemical dependencies. Only one out of 20 alcoholics actually stays in the AA program. Consequently, there are a lot of people falling through the net.

In his insightful book, *The Casanova Complex*, Peter Trachtenberg argues that regardless of their chronological age, the men who engage in thrill seeking are prototypes for the video generation. They cannot live without novelty and excitement, and are used to getting sexual pleasure from women as easily as one flicks the channel selector on a television.

Chronically bored and unable to sustain any genuine intimate relationships, Casanovas are always on the lookout for potential new partners (even if they are currently involved in a relationship). Trachtenberg (1988) recounts a middle-aged man who spent half his wedding ceremony scanning the church for potential mistresses.

If one treats love and lovemaking as a game, then it is a game characterized by the unlikely combination of playfulness and grim perfectionism. Desire, sex, and love are stripped of emotional value with marriage representing little more than an insurance policy for sex.

For the Casanova, moral and ethical standards are conveniently rationalized in order to justify anything from adultery to multiple partners. The bedroom becomes the main arena for performance and every seduction is reckoned toward a strict ratio of success. "Every relationship, no matter how casual, is a showdown where whoever walks out of the bedroom first wins and whoever is left behind is a humiliated loser" (Trachtenberg, 1988:61).

Yet there is a more serious side to these "games." Haunted by the fear of failure and compelled by the need to succeed and thus feed his tenuous self-esteem, this is "serious play" for the Casanova. Winning is not everything–it is the only thing. All those years of training on the sports field from Little League to College Athletics have prepared him psychologically and emotionally to engage in this ultimate contest. It is not about money; it is about the power he can hold over another human being. The use of force would be totally alien and out of character for the Casanova. His target for the day must voluntarily choose to be with him. He is a player, a "hitter" whose skills and game plan have been carefully developed over the years. He is very creative and uses his manipulative interpersonal skills to achieve his chosen mark. This is no longer a game for amateurs because too much is at stake. And the fact that so much is at stake merely adds to the thrill of the hunt.

The escape artist's promiscuity is not really the pursuit of pleasure, but rather a flight from pain and fear. Casanovas use sex to flee from intimacy. After all, intimacy entails seeing the other as she really is and allowing oneself to be seen in turn (to expose one's deepest vulnerabilities and entrust these to another while they do likewise). In general, Casanovas suffer from an occluded vision of others as well as a damaged and fragile sense of self. For such men, a one-night stand can seem like the perfect substitute for closeness. It is a way of touching without really being seen oneself. In the vernacular, this is sometimes referred to as "a hit and run." The Casanova is a hitter looking for a mark. To sustain a longer relationship with a single partner fills Casanovas with the dread of being found out–that is, of being revealed for the impostors they are. Like agents working behind enemy lines, they can afford only the briefest and most neutral contacts with the native populace (Trachtenberg, 1988).

The Casanova Complex is more than a way of acting; it is a style of life and a way of being. It is a narcissistic personality disorder characterized by the compulsive pursuit and abandonment of women or by symbolic flight through chronic infidelity or multiple relationships. Those men afflicted with it define their relations with women primarily in sexual terms and are totally preoccupied with sexual frequency, variety, and performance. They also often suffer from parallel addictions such as drugs, alcohol, work, food, or gambling. Emotionally, they exhibit diminished capacities for intimacy and commitment, which stem from deep-seated feelings of worthlessness and personal impotence (Trachtenberg, 1988).

Unfortunately, the Casanova Complex is reinforced by a society which is itself obsessed with the scintillating aspects of sexuality. The meta messages promulgated throughout the media encourage men to conquer and control women. At some levels, the modern day Casanova is in part the unfortunate by-product of a society so deeply confused and ambivalent about male sexuality.

THE FUTURE OF SEX?

If the world of sex seems confusing now, some predict that it will only get more confusing as our sophisticated technology is used to gain entry into the fantasy realm of sexual experience. For example, since most Americans own VCRs, this means that pornographic movies are now more or less accessible to all. Can any clear-thinking adult in the 1990s seriously believe that restricting adult video rentals to 18 and over is really going to stop our children from renting and watching whatever they desire? Besides, with HBO, Cinemax, and a host of other cable TV options, all kids need to do in order to view explicit sex (and violence) is to turn on the TV. So, instead of having to skulk into a triple-X-rated movie in the seedy part of town, everybody can watch these films from the privacy of their own bedrooms. If that were not enough (and apparently it is not), the telephone sex industry has become incredibly lucrative. In addition, Americans are now using their personal computers for sexual recreation as well. Anyone can download erotic material, including games in which the player ends up having sex with the character on the screen, complete with sound effects. Strangers in different parts of the country are now discussing, in great detail, their most intimate sexual fantasies (Hersch, 1993). This can all be done anonymously. It is this anonymity which ultimately presents one of the most serious threats to sex and intimacy in the 1990s. By making sexual encounters ever more impersonal, we are once again devaluing and dehumanizing sexuality. Dialing 1-900-HOT SEX in order to meet one's own erotic needs is pathetic. Having an anonymous computer pen pal (code name "Lolita") while superficially amusing, says something deeply disturbing about our ever-increasing inability to initiate and sustain intimate sexual contact.

Sex in the 1990s has moved full speed ahead into the non-infectable, no-risk realms of sexual fantasy. Not the least among these is the emerging high-tech industry of "virtual reality" (VR) which employs existing technology used in the flight simulators of pilot-training courses to create imaginary experiences indistinguishable from the real thing. According to journalist Johnny Dodd, writing in *Eastside Week*, we are fast approaching a time when we will be able to have computer-generated "virtual sex." Wearing a bodysuit literally brimming with tiny vibrators would enable individuals to intimately feel what they experience in their VR world. Data panties and penis sleeves will someday deliver realistic sensations to the genitals and elsewhere. According to Dodd, "Information would be wired directly into the brain and whatever fantasies you could dream of would be played out in pure, organic Technicolor" (Hersch, 1993:29).

CONCLUSIONS

Sexual expectations have heightened to the point where no sexual relationship among mere mortals can adequately fulfill such unrealistic sexual and emotional demands. The stage is set for sexual disappointment and disillusionment. Sex and emotional intimacy have become increasingly dissociated due to the devaluation of sexual relationships. Sex has become a commodity in a buyers' market fraught with overchoice and unrealistic expectations. Today, male and female sexual expectations and experience are increasingly at odds due to the vastly differing genderlects that men and women are speaking about sexuality. Unlike women, men continue to separate sexual and emotional needs whereas for women these are more often synonymous. This separation is what enables men to engage in sex without being intimate, whereas most women yearn for more touching, emotional expressiveness, and genuine intimacy.

Throughout American history the public sexual ideology has lived side by side with a private sexual reality which deviated substantially from espoused cultural norms. Frequently, such behavior was shrouded in secrecy and invisible to the public domain, and therefore no threat to the established codes of sexual conduct. Yet when suspicion or knowledge of such sexual deviance became known, it represented a very real threat not only to established codes of sexual conduct, but the very fabric of the social order. This often misguided public morality was so thoroughly interwoven into the sexual socialization patterns of men and women that it directly contradicted certain natural biological imperatives. For example, Victorian women often repressed and denied the sexual messages their own bodies sent in order to reconcile their internal emotional experience with the prevailing social and sexual mores of that era.

Such debate about private versus public morality and society's responsibility to restrict the intimate behavior of its citizens has continued in earnest in modern times as well. Perhaps nowhere is this struggle more apparent than the current day debate about gays in the military. For decades, the conservative ideologues who dictated military policy have systematically persecuted homosexuals by arguing that a soldier's sexual orientation somehow can make him or her unfit for military service. Up until fairly recently, this persecution has gone on with both the sanction and support of the federal government. Now this debate is being reframed as a private morality versus public behavior issue. The vehement resistance within both the military and the Congress is striking. Part of the explanation could be that it is these very private (personal) beliefs which, when made public, represent the more serious threat to the established social order. Because the American military is, on many levels, representative of and deeply intertwined with American society, this controversy cuts to the very essence of mainstream American cultural values. Another source of resistance stems from the fact that as a culture, Americans are extremely uncomfortable with anything related to sex or sexuality, let alone anything which could potentially be classified as sexual deviance. The prevailing public morality is blatantly paternalistic and homophobic. Therefore, replicating such morality to the extreme within the U.S. military only compounds and obfuscates the essential issues while simultaneously violating fundamental human rights.

This example highlights the deep-seated ambivalence Americans have, not only about public versus private morality, but about sexuality itself. Based on residuals from our puritanical past and the double-level message being offered in the media and elsewhere, sex has become something many Americans fear. On the one hand, society tells us that sex should be a transcendent religious experience with "the" opposite-sexed person you love occurring within the context of a legally sanctioned marriage. On the other hand, sex should be daring, incorporating risk and seduction; athletic to the extreme with multiple orgasms for both partners; occur with someone who looks like a fashion model or movie star; and be focused on the ultimate pleasure of both partners without regard for legal, religious, or community sanctions. Also, if at all possible, sex should occur in some exotic setting such as a Caribbean beach, in a secluded mountain chalet, or at the very least, in a Boeing 747 cruising at 33,000 feet with a virtual stranger whom you have only known since Seattle.

BIBLIOGRAPHY

Brehm, S. 1992. *Intimate relationships*. New York: McGraw-Hill, Inc.

Carnes, P. 1983. *Out of the shadows: Understanding sexual addiction*. Minneapolis, MN: CompCare Publishers.

Douglas, J. and Atwell, F. 1988. *Love, intimacy and sex*. Newbury Park, CA: Sage Publications Inc.

Dworkin, A. 1987. *Intercourse*. New York: The Free Press.

Gladwell, M. 1992. "Safe-sex campaign is not slowing AIDS epidemic." *The Times-Picayune*, May 24, 1992.

Hersch, P. 1993. Sex and the boomer's babies. *The Family Therapy Networker*, 17 (2):25-31.

Kitzinger, S. 1983. *A new approach to woman's experience of sex*. New York: Putnam.

Macklin, E. 1983. Effect of changing sex roles on the intimate relationships of men and women. In: Maddock, J., Neubeck, G., and Sussman, M. (Eds.), *Human sexuality and the family*. Binghamton, NY: The Haworth Press, 97-113.

Montagu, A. 1971. *Touching: The human significance of the skin*. New York: Columbia University Press.

Morris, D. 1971. *Intimate behavior*. New York: Random House.

Rubin, L. 1990. *Erotic wars*. New York: Harper & Row.

Rubin, L. 1983. *Intimate strangers*. New York: Harper & Row.

Trachtenberg, P. 1988. *The Casanova Complex*. New York: Poseidon Press.

Scanzoni, L. and Scanzoni, J. 1988. *Men, women and change*. New York: McGraw-Hill, Inc.

Schnarch, D. 1993. *Constructing the sexual crucible*. New York: Norton.

Chapter 6

Intimate Strangers:
The Loss of Intimacy in Marriage

Marriage is widely assumed to be the most intimate relationship two adults can have–but is it? According to Patton and Waring (1985:177): Marital intimacy is a combination of: "(1) conflict resolution–the ease with which differences of opinion are resolved; (2) affection–the degree to which feelings of emotional closeness are expressed by the couple; (3) cohesion–a commitment to the marriage; (4) sexuality–the degree to which sexual needs are communicated and fulfilled; (5) identity–the couple's level of self-confidence and self-esteem. (6) compatibility–the degree to which the couple is able to work and play together comfortably; (7) autonomy–the couple's degree of positive connectedness to family and friends; and (8) expressiveness–the degree to which thoughts, beliefs, attitudes and feelings are communicated within the marriage."

As an institution, marriage is more popular with Americans than ever before. Current statistics show that 95 percent of Americans marry at some time in their lives. More and more Americans today are getting married in religious rather than civil ceremonies, and despite the fact that non-traditional weddings (such as sky diving, scuba diving, and the like) are being hyped by the media, more and more Americans are opting for traditional ceremonies in churches and synagogues officiated by priests, ministers, and/or rabbis. What is changing nowadays is who pays for the wedding. In contrast to the time-honored tradition of the brides' parents (especially her mother) planning and financing the daughter's wedding, many brides and grooms are handling the details and costs themselves.

What is more, the wedding business is booming! But bridesmaids, groomsmen, elaborate catered receptions, and all the necessary accoutrements down to the last detail do not come cheap. Even so, couples are sparing no expense to create the "perfect" wedding day for the "happy couple," their families, and an average of 100 to 200 invited guests. Clearly, the size, cost, and complexity of the wedding and reception are somewhat contingent on one's social and economic class. Nonetheless, even among working-class couples, the cost of getting married frequently runs in the thousands. So how is it that a relationship that begins so full of hope and promise will as likely as not end up in divorce court?

Part of the answer lies in what could best be termed a "failure in intimacy." As the preceding chapters have detailed, intimacy is at best elusive and sporadic for most Americans. The prevailing cultural myth holds that marriage is the key to lifelong happiness (sometimes referred to as "wedded bliss"). This permanent euphoria is supposed to occur magically and immediately upon reaching the blessed state of holy matrimony, and is supposedly intended to last a lifetime (". . . till death do us part").

The myth of the ideal marriage is central to fulfilling the "American Dream." It comes with a "guarantee" that each partner will always have companionship; will always be sexually and emotionally fulfilled; and will share his or her dreams and struggles with the other while growing old gracefully. What the myth fails to point out is, once infatuation wears off, such peak experiences in a marriage are fewer and farther between. Marriage, like any other important relationship, requires effective communication, role complementarity, mutual commitment, etc. But unlike other close relationships, marriage is shrouded in a romantic mystique normally reserved only for fairy tales. Moreover, people enter marriage with any number of material and emotional expectations derived from their personal developmental history, their early relationships in their family of origin, and from perceptions and interpretations of their parents' marriage.

Despite this so-called enlightened society, many of the values, attitudes, and beliefs about marriage have come from our own parents' role modeling. From childhood on, partners have watched their parents laugh, cry, fight, and make up over the years. These experiences have deeply influenced the ways they think about, interpret, and behave in their own marriages (though much of this imprinting is unconscious). By the same token, the parents' marriages were each the joint product of the imprinting derived from their parents' families of origin, just like their grandparents, great-grandparents, and so on. Hence, the legacy of marriage for particular couples is the combined product of generations of marriages before them, as each was played out within the social and cultural context of its era. Unfortunately, marital partners inherit the bad as well as the good traits (including for example, poor communication, lack of self-disclosure, inability to compromise, etc.).

Another piece of this marital puzzle can be found in each person's unique developmental history (as discussed in Chapter 2). One's childhood experiences in forming and maintaining intimate relationships with significant others powerfully influences one's predispositions and abilities to create a subsequent intimate relationship with one's spouse. Given that so many families today are dysfunctional, (abusive, violent, enmeshed, detached, or otherwise damaged), many adults have emerged with severely impaired abilities to form healthy intimate relationships.

Marital difficulties constitute one of the most common complaints presented to mental health professionals. Recent studies have found an inverse correlation between the degree of marital intimacy and the symptoms of emotional illness. (Or as a former psychology professor once put it, "Emotional isolation is the seedbed of neurosis.") According to Wamboldt and Reiss (1989) marital difficulties unequivocally increase the risk of physical and emotional disorders in married partners and their children. Neurosis is particularly associated with a paucity of close attachments and that the lack of close, confiding relationships can make women more vulnerable to depression. Happiness in marital and family life largely determines the degree to which people find life meaningful and gratifying. Given such unequivocal conclusions about the strong correlations between a successful marriage and physical/emotional well-being, it is obvious why understanding marital intimacy is so important.

INTIMACY IN A NARCISSISTIC CULTURE

During recent decades, values in marriage have changed radically. Today, people see marriage as being held together by the strength and significance of the couple's interpersonal relationship–a relationship based on love, mutual respect, affection, empathic understanding, and friendship. The myth of romantic love holds that "true love" is both the most legitimate basis for mate selection and the "glue" which holds the relationship together when all else fails. It is uncanny how pervasive this latter fantasy is among otherwise enlightened and well-educated people. Relying on the myth of romantic love to hold the relationship together lets people avoid taking responsibility for both the problems and solutions in their marriages.

The current narcissistic culture has also spawned numerous marital myths. Perhaps chief among these is the myth of entitlement. Americans believe their marriage should "have it all." Anything less is unacceptable. Should their marriage start to fall short, Americans appear increasingly apt to dispose of it and try their luck with new partners. The flaw in this approach is that individuals end up repeating their marital mistakes without taking responsibility for them and without improving their ability to build a successful marriage.

Because Americans strive for independence and equate dependence with weakness and immaturity, they have also created the myth of autonomy. Dependence is something to be feared and avoided at all costs. It is interpreted as a sign of immaturity and poor ego development. More recently, feminists have begun to see through this essentially patriarchal view of attachment and dependency and to offer fresh perspectives on the growth that occurs through significant interpersonal connections. Males and females grow up in very different social worlds, with very different interpersonal styles and values. However, nowhere are fundamental male and female socialization more at odds than in marriage. When two lives unfold in such close quarters, serious collisions in values, communication, and interpersonal styles are inevitable.

Another marital myth is that "the benefits of marriage are greater for women than for men." Traditionalists would have us believe that marriage fulfills the female's emotional needs: her needs for bearing and nurturing children as well as emotionally completing the female through her connection with her mate. While some of this is undoubtedly true for most women, the price females pay for such benefits frequently includes extreme self-sacrifice, loss of career opportunities, and sometimes even loss of individual identity.

Many feminists would have us believe that males benefit more through having a wife to care for the household, children, and husband–to sacrifice her individual identity and freedom of choice so as to cater to his every whim. In the radical feminist view, women are portrayed as powerless victims of a class struggle whose indentured servitude has been institutionally supported for generations. While the latter view is largely accurate given the historically patriarchal nature of marriage and society, women do indeed benefit from marriage both emotionally and economically. Men do sacrifice for the sake of their wives and families, but these sacrifices are typically instrumental (such as financial provider) rather than personal/emotional (such as caring for the children).

DEVELOPMENTAL INFLUENCES ON MARITAL INTIMACY

When a couple begins to live together, they establish an "emotional comfort zone." This automatically resurrects and reactivates conflicts with early significant figures. Though members of each partners' family of origin may no longer be physically present, they continue to live inside the person as introjects (internal representations). When the marital pair establishes an identity as a couple, they are simultaneously (thought unconsciously) recreating certain aspects of their separate inner worlds based on their early relationships with their parents (Solomon, 1989).

Getting married requires that the couple establish a system of mutually acceptable solutions to the various challenges of living together. This developmental task is compounded by the fact that each partner comes from a different family regulated by a different storehouse of possible solutions to the common problems of living (Solomon, 1989). It is not just the outcomes of developing compatible problem-solving styles which are important, it is also the process by which these outcomes are sought and achieved.

Marriage encompasses two individual subsystems which combine to form a single, new family system. Learning to live together requires that spouses devise a mutually satisfactory interdependent working system that allows them to function comfortably without completely sacrificing the values and ideals they brought into the marriage in the first place. Through the processes of interaction, accommodation, and acculturation, the marital system–with its own structure, roles, norms, and language–develops over time. The early stages of marital development are all important in establishing the relative power, positions, and roles of the partners. Partners are also influenced by other significant members of the extended family system. In a very real (and sometimes literal) sense, learning to negotiate with your spouse is tantamount to negotiating with your partner's family.

Distortions of reality based on early developmental experiences and the struggle for personal affirmation are so interwoven into the process of establishing an identity as a couple that they are only dimly visible (Solomon, 1989). The long-term outcomes in the relationship depend on what happens after the initial infatuation stage and how the partners deal with the fact that many of their expectations are unlikely to materialize. According to Solomon (1989) marriage can either foster growth and enhance individual functioning or it can become a repository for old conflicts and unmet needs. Yet it is possible that in many marriages, both processes–growth and stagnation–happen on different levels at the same time. To successfully sustain any functional relationship, a process of mutual accommodation and some level of personal growth must simultaneously occur. However, old conflicts and unmet needs are inevitably introduced into the marital equation (often unconsciously and unavoidably). This dynamic balance of individual growth and stagnation could also be viewed as the balance between change and constancy. Such a dynamic balance also exists in the marital relationship itself as the couple's identity struggles to emerge.

Berger et al. (1973) describe the process as two distinct biographies, subjectively apprehended by the two people who have lived them which are then overruled and reinterpreted during the course of their conversations. The couple thus construct not only present reality but reconstruct past reality as well, fabricating a common memory that integrates the recollections of the two individual pasts. A healthy marriage is a balance between these two, sometimes competing, forces.

Berger et al. (1973) further conclude that the segregated world of marriage and the family creates, stabilizes, and validates joint constructions of social reality. Though these subjectively constructed definitions may differ sharply from those of other families, within each family these assumptions are shared and acted upon, as each family member reaffirms the "truth" of the other members' realities. Couples begin to think alike, use similar words and expressions and create some level of common reality. Through this common reality, very subtle negotiations have taken place over the years which now pervade and unify each spouse's view of the world, its players, and the relative meaning of each.

Despite people's various difficulties in social functioning, Bowen (1966) noted that people tend to marry those who are at the same basic level of personality differentiation, but who have opposite patterns of defensive organization. When such an experience is reenacted, a person who experienced early rejection or abandonment may select a mate whose enmeshed family was engulfing. The former is seeking greater closeness in the relationship, while the latter struggles for more individuation and autonomy. These patterns are reenactments of familiar patterns originating in each partners' respective family of origin. Old patterns are repeated because the known, however unsatisfying, is more comfortable than the unknown, and is therefore less threatening. Some have noted that marital partners are chosen in the hope that they will erase old pains or pay off old scores. On a more pessimistic note, Napier (1978) hypothesized that people tend to marry their worst nightmares.

PERSONAL AND INTERPERSONAL BOUNDARIES

One major problem couples have in achieving intimacy grows out of setting and maintaining appropriate boundaries. There are boundaries within the self (intrapsychic process structures), boundaries between the two individuals (derived from differing developmental histories) and boundaries between the couple and their environment (sociocultural boundaries). Excessively rigid, impermeable boundaries inhibit growth, constrict, and devitalize both the self and the couple, whereas excessively flexible, diffuse boundaries create chaos and fear of dissolution. One of the main tasks of the marital relationship is to establish clear though permeable boundaries that maintain balance not only within the dyad but between the couple and the world (Solomon, 1989).

In a well-functioning marriage, partners retain their unique identities and understand, respect, and accept each other's separateness and individuality. At times, boundaries need to be solid enough to allow privacy and personal integrity. Yet at other times, they must be sufficiently permeable to allow free-flowing communication.

There are many high-functioning individuals today who are capable of intimate relationships, but remain emotionally isolated. Solomon (1989) believes that in some cases this is the result of the single-minded striving to develop independently at all costs. This is differentiation taken to its illogical extreme. Such people see any merging or blurring of boundaries as a regression to earlier, less functional types of relatedness. If maturity is seen solely as resulting from differentiation, then individuals lose the ability to use intimate relationships as a safe haven for regressing to dependent states in times of need or stress. Paradoxically, it is through this willingness to temporarily regress that many nonpathological needs may be met.

Solomon further observes that enmeshment is not necessarily pathological. Rather, it may be an attempt among intimate family members to temporarily remove the boundaries and merge for a time. Intimacy sometimes requires that regressive needs be met occasionally and reciprocally. When pathological family members use the open boundaries and vulnerabilities of others to feed their own excessive demands for attention and affirmation, dysfunctional relationships may develop. But the assumption that merging of boundaries between family members causes a pathological "undifferentiated family ego mass" must be reexamined in light of other developmental perspectives.

Lack of differentiation is a problem only when early development has yielded an inadequate and incomplete sense of self. In this case, the normal wish to relive the comfort of peaceful merger entangles with anxiety–or even dread–of loss of self within the boundaries of the other (engulfment). This internal conflict creates any number of problems in intimacy, including a misplaced longing for a "loving oneness" and a panic-driven withdrawal from the actual relationship. Love is mixed with a fear of closeness, feelings of loss of self, severe anxiety about any separation and a fantasy of ongoing merger with the loved one. These emotional circumstances create an "intimacy paradox" in which the desired other also represents a major source of anxiety and threat to the integrity of self. This "intimacy paradox" is readily apparent in the personality organization of many borderline personality disorders. On the one hand, borderline personalities deeply desire an intimate emotional connection. On the other hand, such a connection terrifies them. The defenses, created in response to early fears of incorporation or abandonment, may aim at isolating the individual from possible intimacy or at protecting the self from the dangers that may arise in loving or being loved.

Many narcissistically vulnerable individuals lack the ability to feel diverse emotions. They present a pseudo-sophistication to the world, but inside they experience emptiness, lethargy, or self-hate. Because they are exquisitely sensitive to failures, disappointments, and slights, they have learned to submerge feelings and put their emotional energy into developing relationships in which they can maintain an illusion of loving and being loved by others (Solomon, 1989).

Couples who have relationship problems, but do not have a history of severe narcissistic injury, may resolve differences through compromise, problem solving, better communication, and/or negotiation of basic differences. However, when there is a history of narcissistic vulnerability and failure of significant others to give needed emotional supplies, small arguments may cause fragmentation or emotional destruction–a loss of ability to think clearly and a reaction of either rage or total withdrawal (Solomon, 1989).

Sometimes the attempts to shore up a threatened self-image results in a distortion of the reality of the other as a separate person. The longing for a relationship combined with a narcissistic inability to tolerate "otherness" impedes the ability to experience life fully. Under such circumstances, relationships that appear objectively to be successful are experienced subjectively as empty and boring (Solomon, 1989). This could best be described as "pseudo-intimacy" in which the couple is living as "intimate strangers." They share all the external trappings of married life while feeling emotionally isolated and desperately unhappy.

Narcissistic Vulnerability and the Borderline Personality

The greater the vulnerability, the harder the defense system will work to resist change and nullify its effects. Pathological regression to earlier interactive patterns limits choices and threatens to open old needs and wounds. At the extremes of narcissistic vulnerability, there is a fear of fragmentation and disintegration coupled with a fear of inner emptiness and deadness.

Dysfunctional marital interactions are characterized by repeated failure to recognize one's partner's feelings and needs or by an inability to experience another as anything more than a provider of gratification. Depending on the type and depth of distortion, and the available internal resources, talents, and skills, narcissistic needs may be acted out in grandiose fantasies and expectations, or covertly expressed by filling such needs in others (Solomon, 1989).

One cannot trust and respect one's partner if one cannot trust and respect oneself. This is readily apparent in those with borderline personalities. Aspects of a core self have developed and there is an awareness of others, but object constancy has not been achieved and unstable boundaries predominate. The borderline experiences fluctuating states of joy and rage with little or no ability to control either.

Typical ego defenses utilized in their relationships include denial, isolation, undoing, splitting, projective identification, and extreme demandingness. Yet no matter how severe the disorder, there is a basic and desperate human need to be recognized for who one is as well as be accepted, affirmed, and secure in the feeling of being part of a loving relationship (Solomon, 1989). The borderline personality desperately needs a stable, loving, intimate relationship but feels severely threatened and out of control by being so close to another. It is this dilemma which renders the borderline personality so volatile.

This same paradox can be found with increasing frequency in so-called normal couples. Why? Perhaps it is because a parallel developmental dysfunction is happening between couples and society. The often violent and unstable social context in which most new couples grow and develop is by all accounts brutal and abusive. Like an abusive parent the tyranny of a violent and volatile society progressively erodes the possibility of a mutually satisfying intimate relationship. According to Teresa Adams (1992) respect is a prerequisite for intimacy, yet much about our culture is inherently disrespectful. Some areas in which this lack of respect is apparent include: (1) the way we conduct politics; (2) the way we educate our children; (3) the way we treat the poor; (4) the way we conduct business; (5) the way we treat criminals; and (6) the way we treat other cultures. Marriage does not exist in a vacuum. It is actively involved in a dynamic interactive relationship with an ever-widening socio-cultural context. Consequently, marital intimacy must always be assessed within the context and era in which it exists. For example, marital intimacy was quite different in Freud's Vienna than it is in urban America today.

Love, Marriage, and Intimacy

In many ways a new love resembles the very earliest object relationships. In the reflection of the other's gaze a lover finds a sense of being appreciated, affirmed, and uniquely loved. It is the "child" within the adult who tends to replay any traumas or chronic disappointments experienced in early life as part of his or her current intimate relationship. The "child" hopes, that a relationship with "that special someone" can repair past emotional damage and fulfill unmet personal needs. People often select partners based upon their ability to offer wished-for attributes lacking in themselves. Among more vulnerable narcissistic persons, the needed other becomes someone with whom they can strongly identify. Through such identification the vulnerable partner hopes to acquire the kind of power and strength that the other represents. Some wish to shine in the reflected glory of the "perfect" other.

The infatuation stage of the marriage is a time of passion, idealization, and unfettered optimism. Reason and rationality are utter strangers to "new love." It is also a time of regression to childhood innocence and unabashed joy. The childlike playfulness of "new lovers" is further evidenced by their communication patterns. They speak to one another with a deference and respect which will probably never be repeated with such ardor in later stages of the marital relationship.

Many well-functioning adults appear to carry an illusion of oneness; a memory of a sense of well-being in union with another; and a powerful wish to return to this benevolent state. Romantic love, so typical of the early stages of an intimate relationship, appears as a re-creation of this experience. Marked by a joyful coming together, a desire to avoid any separation, and a wish to share in everything with the other, it is reminiscent of a totally fused state of existence.

As a result, a deep pain arises from physical, emotional, or sexual separation (Solomon, 1989).

Lovers feel transformed by the energy that passes between them. Being with the loved one is experienced as a magical transformation of the self. This metamorphosis is more than mere illusion. When one observes someone newly in love, the joy, animation, and optimism are readily apparent. Two people in love share a common fantasy which is quite real to each at that moment in time. Each sees the other as the "special someone" to whom they will be totally devoted and who, in turn, will be totally devoted to them (Solomon, 1989). This idealization is of crucial importance to the long-term well-being of the marital relationship. It provides an essential cache of memories and experiences which bond the couple together both initially and over the long term. It is the beginning of their joint history and sets the tone for their later communication, perceptions of each other, roles, emotional needs, and so on. It offers that sense of "remembered perfection" when the relationship was all each wanted it to be, replete with passion, romance, and dreams yet to be lived. Those idyllic early days function not only to remind partners of who they are, but who they had hoped to become.

The desire for someone who functions as an unconditional mirror, the tendency to idealize and adore another, the need for an understanding and sympathetic alter-ego, and the wish for another to understand and assist with one's inner fears (however irrational) is a lot to expect of another person over a lifetime. The fact that one's partner expects the same only complicates matters. Such unrealistic expectations present a significant barrier to intimacy in marriage, especially when left unfulfilled.

In the intimacy of marriage or any serious relationship, difficulties arise over the long run when partners do not understand and accept undisclosed, thinly veiled aspects of the other. This sets the stage for a vicious cycle which is played out again and again. Because the human capacity for miscommunication and misunderstanding is unparalleled (especially in a marriage) and because marital communication is so complex and the average couple's listening and communication skills are frequently so poor, misunderstanding too often becomes the norm in marital interchanges.

As a result of feeling misunderstood, partners feel frustrated and angry (because each typically believes that he or she is communicating clearly while it is the partner who refuses to listen or understand). Over time, such perennial misunderstandings lead to feelings of resentment and bitterness. Such feelings then begin to color and interfere with future marital communication. This then leads to more miscommunication and misunderstanding, which results in a devaluing of the other (along with a further eroding of the marital relationship).

Over time, an adversarial relationship develops between marital partners in which so much resentment and bitterness exists (both conscious and unconscious) that even the most benign and innocuous interaction is severely contaminated. The telltale sign is when even the most innocuous request is greeted with a virtual maelstrom of anger or frustration. So, when such couples are confronted by any serious crisis, the potential for disaster is often realized.

THE HIDDEN DYNAMICS OF MARRIAGE

Frequently, one partner desperately wishes that the other would be responsive, but offers no overt sign of such needs. One of the myths of marriage at work here is that "If my partner really loved me, then he/she should be able to know what I need without my having to ask for it."

It has been said that we fall in love not with a person, but with our vision of that person. This is a variation of the "love at first sight" phenomenon, in which we are captivated by our own projections. Falling in love over time has many of the same dynamics. From a purely psychodynamic point of view, all love involves transference from aspects of early object relationships. So individuals symbolically seek in their marital partners the unrealized emotional rewards (real or imagined) from those early relationships.

Herein lies the paradox. Since our adult partners can never adequately fulfill our idealized memories from the past, disappointment and frustration are inevitable. This disappointment is narcissistic (not unlike a child who very much wants something, does not get it, then throws a temper tantrum). In the adult version of this scenario, one partner seeks admiration and appreciation and when it is not forthcoming, that partner feels empty and deflated. The other partner likewise seeks understanding and acceptance and when it is not forthcoming, reacts with frustration and anger. According to Solomon (1989), such narcissistic collusive patterns underlie numerous issues such as money, work, children's problems and/or sexual dysfunction. At first blush these issues appear to be the source of the marital problems. However, upon closer scrutiny, such narcissistic disappointments can be traced to unresolved developmental struggles. Through projective defenses it is possible to split off internalized, unacceptable impulses and feelings and hand them over to a mate who is more or less willing to accept them.

Accordingly, healthy differentiation from one's family of origin is a crucial step toward developing the mature ability to form intimate relationships. But it makes little sense to just work toward separation and differentiation exclusively when the whole purpose of an intimate relationship is mutuality and interdependence. Perhaps the central issue is one of balance. Given the dynamic interplay between two individuals, each with their own unique developmental histories and existing within a particular socio-cultural context, the major challenge of the marital relationship is to balance one's needs with the needs of one's partner. This entails a series of subtle and often complex micropolitical negotiations wherein relative role, status, and position are constantly defined and redefined vis-à-vis one another.

Another hidden dynamic in the marital relationship is how much one sees one's partner as the partner sees him or herself. Such congruence potentially reduces marital tension, miscommunication, and conflict. With projections and transference playing such important parts in marital relationships, couples' therapy seeks to help partners understand and let go of the projections and perceive each other more as they actually are.

Individual perceptions and expectations of one's partner are also influenced by sensational media images of contemporary marriage. Couples constantly compare their own marriage to the much-publicized and wholly unrealistic views portrayed in movies, TV, romance novels, popular magazines, etc. All these tend to depict marriage as far more exciting and intriguing than the mundane realities of most couples' day-to-day existence. An insatiable print and photojournalism media sensationalize the lurid details of romantic intrigue in England's House of Windsor, not to mention the lives of American celebrities whose earnings and lifestyles set them substantially apart from the average American couple. Nevertheless, these celebrities are held up as role models to be emulated as they are thought to be fully living the American Dream. Yet, for most Americans such dreams are largely unattainable. The most tragic aspect of this cruel hoax is the remarkable ability of average Americans to suspend disbelief and actually believe that such perfect marital bliss is attainable in their lifetime.

Intimacy and Self-Disclosure

According to Perlmutter and Hatfield (1980), the most profound way in which intimate and nonintimate relationships differ is in the depth and breadth of information exchange. In casual encounters, acquaintances reveal only limited, stereotyped information about themselves. Bankers pretend to be solid, responsible citizens when they are dealing with clients. Children pretend to be scholars when talking to their teachers, just as politicians pretend to have answers when talking to voters.

Intimate relations differ substantially. Within intimate relationships, people feel freer to expose more aspects of themselves. As a consequence, intimates share profound information about one another's histories, values, strengths and weaknesses, idiosyncracies, hopes and fears. In fact, one's willingness to disclose personal feelings and information is an important indicator of that person's desire for an intimate relationship. During dating and courtship couples who are serious about one another often cannot wait to learn all about the other.

The ideology of intimacy limits intimate self-disclosures to the marital relationship and makes one's spouse the sole confidant for one's innermost thoughts, feelings, and desires (Fitzpatrick, 1988). Unfortunately, this puts tremendous pressure on each spouse to act as father/mother confessor, therapist, chief confidant, and best friend in the midst of maintaining his/her other marital responsibilities.

However, not all husbands or wives consider their spouse to be their best friend and chief confidant. For example, in a national survey, 72 percent of married men said that they talked about their worries only with their spouse. Only 58 percent of married women said the same. (Veroff et al., 1981). While most men do consider their wife to be their best friend and chief confidant, only 46 percent of white women and only 20 percent of black women surveyed considered their husbands to be their best friend and chief confidant. The Boston Couples Study (Rubin, Hill, Peplau, and Dunke-Schetter, 1980), reported that married men and women differ greatly in self-disclosure. Women tended to disclose material that was personal or feeling oriented while males disclosed more readily when the information was factual and relatively neutral or positive in tone.

Another recent study found that a quantitative measure of self-disclosure accounts for half of the variance of the qualitative level of rated intimacy in couples, even though the two constructs are not identical. The couples studied also considered expression of affection, compatibility, cohesion, identity, and the ability to resolve conflict to be important aspects of intimacy. Sexual satisfaction was found to be less important than previous definitions of intimacy suggested (Fitzpatrick, 1988).

Meaningful interpersonal communication is basic to one's sense of well-being and affirms one's presence in the world. Self-disclosure is an integral component of such communication. Jourard (1964) observed that a self-alienated person (one who does not disclose himself truthfully and fully) can never love or be loved by another person. Genuine loving requires actual knowledge of another. One cannot love a person whom one does not know and vice versa.

Honest communication facilitates understanding oneself and others. Self-disclosure adds excitement and vitality to a relationship. When intimate partners complain that their spouse is boring, it usually means that either or both are afraid to take a risk. Revealing one's inner self to another in an intimate relationship requires conditions of trust, emotional safety, mutual respect, and substantial personal investment in the relationship. Ambivalence thwarts the development of intimacy by limiting both one's personal investment and willingness to risk.

In a healthy marriage, intimacy is not a luxury, it is a necessity. Epidemiologists have accumulated considerable evidence supporting the notion that intimate self-disclosure helps people maintain their mental and physical health. People with a confidant are less susceptible to mental illness, especially in times of intense stress (Hatfield, 1982). Male and female styles differ widely in handling stress. In general, women more often use talking to a confidant as a means of mediating or reducing stress (and as Tannen pointed out, ventilation is frequently an end in itself for women; whereas men want to move right into the problem-solving/solution-focused mode). Men are frequently more resistant to such personal self-disclosures due to the restrictive nature of traditional male socialization. From early childhood on, most males have not been schooled in the language of feelings nor have they been encouraged to talk through personal problems to help resolve those feelings.

Perlmutter and Hatfield (1980) analyzed casual versus intimate communication and found that intimates communicated more than casuals do on three different levels: (1) via linear communication–literal messages by word and gesture; (2) via process metacommunications–what does this statement say about our relationship? and (3) via intentional metacommunication–indirect though intended messages about the relationship.

A metacommunication accompanies every linear message, consciously or unconsciously, by means of often subtle paralinguistic and kinesic signals–which include changes of facial expression, hesitations, shifts in tempo of speech or movement, overtones of the voice, irregularities of respiration, and so forth. Individuals both prescribe and proscribe the limits of their relationship. Such process metacommunications are typically unmonitored between or among intimates.

Sometimes, however, people transcend ordinary communication processes. Instead of consciously communicating at the literal level plus unconsciously metacommunicating (engaging in process metacommunication), they begin to metacommunicate intentionally. For example, one's spouse may observe: "Your tone was a little sharp there. Were you trying to tell me something?" In such an instance, partners have begun to talk consciously about the relational context of their messages. Thus, the metamessage becomes the literal message.

Passionate versus Companionate Love

Passionate relationships are filled with both pleasure and pain. The hope or experience of fulfillment is inextricably mixed with the threat of loss. In fact, the original meaning of passion was "agony," as in "Christ's passion." Hatfield and Walster (1978) suggest that under the right conditions, both joy and anguish have the potential for deepening passion. In a related study, Dutton and Aron (1974) demonstrated that there is sometimes a close link between fear and sexual attraction.

As the term is used here, passion refers mainly to emotional intensity within the relationship. It may be manifested as sexual passion, but it is more broadly defined as a style of loving and type of relationship. In a marriage, passionate love is usually most apparent during the initial infatuation. Emotions run high and idealization of one's partner is at its peak. Over the ensuing years, this early passion fades and settles into a companionate love based on a shared history of important experiences which bind the couple together. It is this love which has mellowed over time and has settled like the taste of a fine red wine. Within our youth-oriented society, passionate love remains the ideal. Couples are expected to have an ongoing love affair all their lives. This is yet another myth of marriage because love will wax and wane over the years. At times, you will not like your spouse very much, nor will he or she always like you.

Research on couples who are content with their relationships points to the importance of companionship as a key to both the day-to-day satisfaction and the long-term maintenance of the relationship. Labeling this as a skill does not necessarily suggest that the partners need to be competent in the same companionate activities. Instead, this skill involves continuing to find pleasurable events and mutual interests that enrich the couple's relationship by introducing enjoyment and novelty. For most couples, this process evolves naturally during the early stages of a relationship when the partners are first exposed to the various dimensions of one another's life–including their work, friends, family, and hobbies. The ease of obtaining companionship benefits may dwindle as certain activities become routine, as partners develop different interests, or as they assume child-rearing or work-related responsibilities that compete for mutual time. Another important factor in marital satisfaction is whether a couple brings new interests into their relationship or whether their interactions become so routine that there is an erosive trend toward tedium, indifference, or obtaining gratification outside the relationship (Margolin, 1982).

An old friend and colleague once described her marriage as "not bad enough to leave, not good enough to stay." This description raises an intriguing question. Just how bad should a marriage be before giving up on it? How much should one try to fix and for how long? Clearly, there are no hard and fast answers to such questions. Individuals must decide for themselves what they are willing to live with and what they are not. Having a successful marriage requires that both partners actively invest in the relationship and show a willingness to accommodate the essential needs of the other.

The Role of Commitment

Mutual commitment is integral to establishing and maintaining any meaningful relationship. In this case, commitment refers simply to the strength of one's intentions to continue the relationship. Commitment can arise out of: (1) a sense of loyalty to one's partner (fidelity), (2) a religious, legal, or moral belief in the sanctity of marriage; (3) a continued optimism about the potential future rewards (emotional, financial, sexual, or otherwise); and/or (4) strong emotional attachment, dependence, and bonding (i.e., love). Different factors produce commitment in different relationships. Brehm (1992) suggests that the more freely, frequently, and publicly one acts, the more one becomes committed to the action itself and to the attitudes it implies.

The importance of commitment has been demonstrated repeatedly in research on dating couples. As one might expect, commitment is higher among those who say they are "in love" than among those who do not report being in love (Hendrick et al., 1988). Women report greater commitment to their present relationship than do men.

One reason commitment has such powerful effects is that it freezes one's thoughts and actions. Once individuals have privately committed themselves, they may no longer feel as free to change. But once one has made a strong, public commitment, change is even more difficult and much less likely. One risks public embarrassment and a loss of credibility. When individuals commit to a relationship, their interest in other possible partners declines. Should others try to convince them that they are wrong in their commitment, they resist. Commitment can also affect the ways that partners respond to one another. If committed to a relationship with that person, individuals are more likely to agree with their partner and less likely to react against the partner's attempts to influence them. In one sense, commitment tends to wed one to a relationship.

There are many positive aspects of commitment (including affection, attachment, loyalty, faithfulness, etc.), but commitment is not always a positive experience. Commitment to dysfunctional or abusive relationships can act like an addiction which painfully binds intimates to each other. In such cases, commitment is a crushing burden of obligation, entrapment, and limited options. When individuals are committed to a healthy relationship, each partner looks forward to staying together (Brehm, 1992).

POWER AND MARITAL INTIMACY

The law's assumption that a wife "owes" her domestic services to her husband undermines the economic value of the wife's work in the home (Weitzman et al., 1978). English common law has directly influenced numerous marriage laws and customs in the United States, including the idea that within the marriage a wife's legal identity was merged into and subsumed by that of her husband. An important corollary was that her labor belonged to him and was considered his legal right. A person's power over another person depends on the needed resources he or she controls, the degree of dependence the "other" person has on these resources and whether or not the other person can obtain these resources elsewhere.

At the dawn of the nineteenth century, a woman had few options open to her outside of marriage. If she wanted to be provided for, she needed a husband. This gave men tremendous power over women. Utterly dependent on a man for economic resources, the woman became his property through marriage. As employment opportunities increased for women, females learned to provide for their own needs. By the close of the nineteenth century, almost half (46 percent) of all single women were employed (Scanzoni and Scanzoni, 1988) while only 6 percent of married women worked outside the home. Moreover, married women's rates of employment increased more slowly than those of single women.

The availability of employment made a significant impact on even those wives who did not choose to enter the labor force. For the first time in American history, women began to have economic options (however limited). The possibility of a wife becoming a wage earner very gradually became part of the role and rights of the wife-mother. This placed married women in a position where they could bargain instead of merely yielding to their husbands' wishes. Women were no longer bound to unquestioning obedience out of a sense of helpless dependence on male economic support (Scanzoni and Scanzoni, 1988).

The word power derives from the Latin "potere," which means "to be able." In the context of this chapter power refers to the ability to control or influence one's partner and/or create outcomes in the relationship. Power in a marriage comes from one of four interrelated sources: personal, relational, institutional, and societal. Personal power is almost existential in nature and derives from the essence of one's own being. Relational power is the power granted within the particular coupled relationship. While this is based on the respective partner's personal power, it occurs within an institutional and social context. Depending on the type of marriage one has (traditional or egalitarian for example), and the respective views of the marital partners, power can vary dramatically. Institutional power stems from the power inherent in the institution of marriage itself. Marriage is a time-honored tradition in American culture and with it comes certain prerogatives which are frequently gender based (such as jurisdiction over children, home, etc.). Finally, power may derive from the ever-changing sociocultural context in which the marriage exists. For example, women's power in the marital relationship has changed dramatically in recent decades. As our society moves toward more egalitarian male-female relationships and forever relinquishes the notion of women as property with very strict roles and responsibilities, women have greater freedom to assert equal or dominant roles.

The Distancer and the Pursuer

When partners are first establishing an intimate relationship, they are already attached and committed to many others, such as family of origin, ex-partners, children, and friends. Each of these previous attachments say much about the preferred style, distance, and role of the individual. Finding out about such relational predispositions offers a glimpse into this person's future tendencies in marriage. However, the new couple relationship forces a change in these previously important attachments. For some couples this is no problem. For others, intense feelings are evoked in all parties. Fear of loss, jealousy, guilt about distancing, and fears about the new partner being accepted or rejected all collide in the partner's unconscious. As a result, the couple has intense conflict as they try to stabilize their commitment to each other while altering their previous attachments and loyalties (James, 1989).

The initial context of a relationship may involve circumstances which obscure the levels of attachment or commitment between the partners. For example, if either partner feels that they "have to get married" or that "deep down" the other really did not want the relationship, then the fear of commitment grows. The more committed partner feels exposed and vulnerable. On the one hand, this fear may be based on an accurate perception of the other's ambivalence. On the other hand, the perception may be inaccurate, because the other's actual attachment and commitment may be far greater than it appears. (James, 1989).

According to Harper and Elliot (1988) couples who perceived relatively little intimacy in their marriage but also expected little intimacy were as happy as couples whose intimacy scores were much higher. The amount of intimacy a couple perceived in their marriage does not seem as important in determining the extent of marital satisfaction as was the discrepancy between the desired and perceived amount of intimacy in the relationship. Consequently, it seems that the "ideal" level of intimacy varies from couple to couple.

James (1989) asserted that the movement of one partner toward a third party is usually brought on by tension or conflict between the couple. Frequently, this conflict originates because one person wants more closeness than the other. So either party may move toward a third person and thus create the triangle. In this pattern, the pursuer wants more intimacy while the distancer wants more separation and autonomy. In the ensuing dance, the pursuer demands closeness, causing the distancer to withdraw. This in turn, causes the pursuer to chase the distancer all the more.

The pursuing partner ends up feeling lonely, abandoned, and rejected, while the distancing partner feels emotionally cut off, angry, trapped, and guilty. James (1989) offers the following sequence: A pursues, B withdraws: A withdraws, B withdraws more; A attacks (either criticizing or demanding), B defends and/or criticizes. The end result of such a dance is anger, frustration, and possible withdrawal by either or both partners. Ironically, both partners fear that the other's commitment to the relationship is less than their own. Such fears only serve to reinforce the dysfunctional pattern. Under such circumstances, both partners often get defensive and move to protect their own emotional vulnerabilities. In the alternate scenario, couples may, after risking the expression of their deeper feelings, come closer and build a more solid foundation which minimizes their tendency to distance or anxiously pursue.

Commitment to a relationship involves both attachment and bonding. It demonstrates these through a material and emotional investment in the relationship. Though one partner may experience attachment, his/her partner may or may not perceive this attachment or even share the same level of attachment or emotional investment. This is an important indicator of relative power within the relationship. The partner who is less dependent, attached, and/or invested in either the other or the relationship is usually deemed to have greater power due to diminished vulnerability vis à vis his/her partner. Intimate relationships potentially create feelings of vulnerability to rejection or abandonment. When one partner reassures the other of his/her own feelings of commitment and attachment, he/she usually mitigates a partner's fears of abandonment by making the relationship feel secure and safe.

The distancer/pursuer pattern may underlie a number of other, more obvious patterns. Symmetrical patterns (where partners mirror each other's behavior) or complementary patterns (where partners elicit opposite behavior from one another) can be seen as components of an underlying distancer/pursuer pattern. Patterns of escalating symmetrical conflict are often maintained by an underlying distancer-pursuer pattern. One person attacks the other when feeling abandoned or rejected, which in turn spawns a defensive counterattack. In yet another dance, couples appear to mutually with-draw in a symmetrical manner. However, the distancer may have turned to someone else while the pursuer has changed his or her "tack" and also turned to someone else (often in the hope of getting the partner back). Unfortunately, this scenario frequently ends up mutually distancing the partners.

Both males and females can pursue or distance. However, the specific ways they do so often reflects differences in gender development and socialization. For many men the dominant theme is the conflict between the need to be nurtured (expressing vulnerability) and the desire to appear masculine (remaining emotionally remote). Because males are far more apt to separate sex and love, men are much more likely to distance emotionally, yet still pursue sexually.

Women who pursue emotionally often have deeper fears that their needs for intimacy and dependency are excessive. For many women, the fear of being emotionally and/or financially dependent on a man is deeply disturbing on several levels. First, it devalues the non-monetary contribution women make to home and family. Second, it defines self-worth exclusively in economic terms. Third, it taps into long-standing doubts about emotional autonomy derived from both family and cultural socialization. Yet such human dependency needs exist in both genders. As a result, women sometimes act out their ambivalence about dependence in unusual ways. This ambivalence can appear as anger at her partner (for her feeling dependent on him); withdrawal from the relationship (based on a fear of being too dependent) or "acting out" in other ways (which asserts her independence and differentiation). Part of this very difficult emotional array originates in the socio-historical legacy of a woman's role and her identity being subsumed within her husband's. Society's predisposition to grant an adult woman status and recognition based on her marital status has fueled justifiable anger, resentment, and ambivalence about dependency on one's spouse.

James (1989) asserts that women sometimes adopt a caretaking, mothering role with their partner in hopes that they will get by giving. If this does not occur, they feel abandoned and angry. A female pursuer demands greater emotional closeness through verbal expression and may become critical and demanding in response to her partner's withdrawal. So she may reject him sexually and distance herself.

A woman who withdraws emotionally usually does so as a result of feeling that her needs have not been met, either in this relationship or in the past. She sometimes withdraws sexually and turns to her child for emotional contact. If her husband pursues, she may see his demand for sex and attention as an attempt to control her. In extreme cases, some men become physically violent in efforts to control their partner. While this is by no means justifiable, these are often men who feel powerless and out of control themselves at many levels. They may see themselves as having no other options. In other cases, they believe that male dominance is their birthright. However, these are also men who lack the basic skills for identifying and coping with their own emotions (especially anger), let alone adequate skills in marital problem solving. Sadly, our patriarchal culture sanctions men's option of force, and by institutionalizing male dominance, it allows the possibility for men to deal with their emotional turmoil by using violence.

Guerin et al. (1987) asserts that it is often useful to think of individuals as having a preferred style of relating that fits with distancing or pursuing behaviors. A lifetime distancer is a person who has frequently been in the same distancing position in previous relationships as well as with his or her family of origin (James, 1989). The distancer and pursuer are reenacting family scripts about how intimate relationships are formed and conducted. Nevertheless, some changes in distancer/pursuer patterns evolve based on time and experience in the relationship. In couples' therapy, current patterns of closeness, distance, and triangulation can be understood and put into perspective by exploring the evolution of the couple's relationship. For example, during their courtship and early years who enacted which roles? How have these roles changed over time? What do these say about the relative emotional investment of each partner?

Extramarital Affairs

From society's point of view, marital infidelity is a betrayal of trust and intimacy in a sacred, committed relationship with one's spouse. It represents a threat not only to one's partner but to the very fabric of American social structure. Long-standing social prohibitions to extramarital activity have been designated to bind the family together and preserve the myth of the American family. Strict religious and moral injunctions have been prescribed to prevent extramarital involvement.

However, according to Glass and Wright (1990:7) "although 75%-90% of those surveyed report disapproving attitudes toward extramarital relationships, the actual incidence of extramarital involvement ranges from 30-60% of the men, and from 20-50% of the women." Lawson (1988) found that over 90 percent of women and 80 percent of men in her survey expected sexual exclusivity at the beginning of their first marriage. But during the course of marriage they became more tolerant and less insistent on sexual fidelity. Important steps for women becoming involved in their first EMS (extramarital sex) included knowing someone who had engaged in EMS, talking to that person, and thinking about EMS for an extended period of time after becoming aware of an opportunity. Glass and Wright further distinguish between three types of extramarital involvement: (1) emotional involvement; (2) sexual involvement; and (3) combined-type involvement (sexual intercourse and deep emotional involvement).

The real threat in extramarital affairs (both sexual and nonsexual) is the threat represented by another having emotional access to the most intimate aspects of one's lifemate. This is the deepest level of betrayal of intimacy and trust.

It is not uncommon for the betrayed partner to feel personally violated, rejected, and devalued. "How could you share something so personal with someone else?" Any extramarital affair is a reflection on the marital relationship. Some have argued that extramarital affairs are a dysfunctional attempt to solve problems which exist in the marriage. Others suggest that such affairs are motivated by anger at one's spouse, disappointment in one's marriage, unmet needs in the relationship, narcissistic disorders, male gender conditioning, a cry for attention or help, a need for sexual and personal affirmation, a misplaced attempt at obtaining love, and/or unmitigated hedonism. Glass and Wright (1990) found that sex, romantic love, and emotional intimacy appear to characterize the major justifications for different aspects of extramarital relationships. The sexual factor was further defined to include sexual excitement, sexual curiosity, novelty or variety, and sexual enjoyment. Love as an independent justification for extramarital relationships is not surprising since romantic love is a significant motivation for many extramarital involvements. However, the importance of emotional intimacy has not been given serious consideration in the extramarital literature. While men and women identified very similar factors, it is interesting to note that the first factor to emerge for women was the "emotional intimacy" justification, and the first factor to emerge for men was the "sexual" justification. This finding is consistent with traditional gender role socialization patterns discussed in earlier chapters. Males tend to sexualize relationships with women whereas females tend to focus far more on the emotional aspects of the relationship.

According to Glass and Wright, gender differences reported in premarital and extramarital behaviors suggest that men and women may also differ in attitudes toward extramarital involvement and in the link between attitudes and behavior. The literature has historically reflected a male bias by using extramarital sexual intercourse as the criterion for extramarital behavior instead of considering a full range of extramarital sexual and emotional involvement.

Glass and Wright (1990) found men are more likely than women to believe that EMS is justified and report less guilt about EMS. Atwater (1979) notes that a "justification" is associated with a stronger tendency to continue extramarital sexual involvement because it allows one to maintain a positive self-image, to legitimate an activity, and to assume responsibility without negative connotations. On the other hand, persons who offer "excuses" feel more guilt and have more negative emotional reactions. It appears that the "justifiers" attitudes match their behavior while the "excusers" may have an attitude/behavior discrepancy.

Thompson (1984) concludes that women are more likely than men to perceive all types of extramarital involvement as damaging the quality of the primary relationship. Also, women are more disapproving of EMS without love and are less likely to pursue such relationships. Generally speaking, women are more likely than men to believe that an extramarital involvement is related to an unhappy marriage. Reiss et al. (1980), propose that women's affairs are more likely to be "love-oriented," whereas men's extramarital involvement tends to be "pleasure-oriented."

Petersen (1983) found that women who are sexually satisfied in their marriages are less likely to engage in EMS, while men engage in EMS despite the quality of marital sex. As the depth of emotional involvement in a relationship increases, motivations shift from a self-centered focus to a relationship-centered one. So women's extramarital involvement may be associated with relational aspects such as needs for emotional intimacy that are not being satisfied in the marriage while men's extramarital involvement may be associated more with individualistic aspects such as desire for exciting sex, opportunity, and permissive moral attitudes.

Men are also much more likely than women to have EMS without emotional involvement whereas women tend to be more likely than men to be emotionally involved without EMS. Among those who had sex outside marriage, 44 percent of the men, compared with 11 percent of the women, report slight or no emotional involvement. Among subjects who have had moderate to extremely deep extramarital emotional involvement, 42 percent of the women, compared to 24 percent of the men, have not engaged in EMS (Glass and Wright, 1985).

Managing Marital Conflict

The sociological literature on marriage from the 1960s as well as the more recent behavioral literature identify two predominant domains of relationship: the affectionate and the instrumental. While the association between the affectionate domain and intimacy is more obvious, the instrumental aspects of a relationship are also important. Marriages function as socioeconomic units concerned with the variety of tasks related to maintaining a household; raising the children; handling finances and obtaining necessary resources from the community at large. While most individuals do not enter a relationship planning to accomplish all these tasks, incompetence in any or all of these areas can have a strong negative impact on overall marital satisfaction. This is likely to prove detrimental to the affectionate domain as well (Margolin, 1982).

The ability to manage interpersonal conflict and its accompanying negative affect is vital to relationship success. Without this ability, the many conflicts that arise in any relationship remain unresolved and the level of negative affect increases generating a toxic burden that erodes the level of satisfaction in the marriage (perhaps particularly so for wives). This suggests an important normative gender difference. Women, as "relationship specialists," appear more finely attuned to the subtleties of communication within their intimate relationships and tend to persist in their attempts to resolve areas of relationship conflict. Men (at least those in distressed relationships) are more likely to withdraw in the face of high intensity and/or persistent conflict (Wamboldt and Reiss, 1989).

Reaching agreement and resolving conflict are not identical constructs. Some married couples not only agree to disagree, but also revel in their disagreement as a sign of their individual autonomy within the relationship. However, the ability to reach agreement and build consensus is an important barometer of how well couples construct the two sides of their identity as a couple.

Wamboldt and Reiss (1989) also found that the more emotionally expressive the woman's family of origin, the greater the consensus reached by the couple about their own relationship. Further, women reporting greater perceived conflict in their origin families showed less agreement with their partners about the interpersonal characteristics of their own families.

These connections suggest that family of origin experience may influence current relationship satisfaction because prior family experience influences the consensus-building processes in the new relationship. However, the effect of origin family experience may be mediated by aspects of the couple's current interactional process. This latter point offers an important justification for marital therapy. Altering the couple's current interactional process can begin to shift any current basis for pathogenic relating and create greater role congruence and harmony within the relationship.

For many individuals, the primary attraction to the partner is the strong emotional response elicited by the presence, or mere thought of the other person. During the course of the marital relationship, this initial infatuation is gradually replaced by an emotional involvement based on closeness, supportiveness, and understanding.

One crucial aspect of communication in intimate relationships relates to how couples handle conflict. Due to the inevitable disagreements in all long-term relationships, couples must find some way of responding to conflict. Couples who successfully resolve conflicts generally develop a pattern of dealing openly and directly about differences of opinion and making necessary accommodations and compromises. Resolving problems depends not only on being able to discuss the issue, but also on taking specific actions that result in desired behavioral change (Margolin, 1982). This entails developing mutually acceptable methods of conflict resolution.

Over time, virtually all couples develop and adhere to well-choreographed sequences which lead them into and out of arguments. These patterns are so consistent over time that couples frequently report feeling like they are having the same argument over and over through the years. While the specific literal content may vary, the process and interactive sequence is often remarkably similar.

During marital therapy sessions, couples are asked to describe the "process" which gets them into arguments (as in "What does he do?" then "What do you do?" etc.). This forces partners to step back and look at their own interaction in a new way. When later asked, "And how do you get back together again after you've had a major argument?", couples again describe a remarkably consistent pattern. These are the dances couples do. Each couple has their own particular dance and favorite steps which they repeat throughout the years. One key therapeutic goal with couples is to assist partners in decoding and rechoreographing their dance into more functional sequences.

DISTRESSED VERSUS NONDISTRESSED COUPLES: A COGNITIVE-BEHAVIORAL PERSPECTIVE

The most consistent distinction between distressed and nondistressed couples is their reward/cost ratio in behavior exchanges. Partners of successful marriages tend to work to maximize mutual rewards while minimizing individual costs. In unsuccessful marriages, partners tend to work to minimize individual costs with little expectation of rewards. The point is that distressed couples engage in fewer rewarding (verbal) exchanges and more punishing exchanges than nondistressed couples, as evidenced in the couples' verbal communications (Margolin, 1982).

Another process which sets distressed couples apart from nondistressed couples is the way in which they resolve problems. Distressed couples rely on aversive tactics such as threats, blame, and withdrawal as a means of eliciting attention or compliance from their partner (Margolin, 1982). Based on interaction patterns displayed during problem-solving discussions, distressed couples display more negative and fewer positive behaviors and verbalize fewer constructive problem-solving statements. Distressed couples were also less effective problem-solvers in their ratio of agreements to disagreements.

However, the full explanation of couples' problem-solving difficulties portrays a generalized coercive process. Here partners learn to rely on aversive rather than positive stimuli to influence one another's behavior. This coercion happens more often and more intensely over time, until it becomes a reciprocal process with spouses shifting roles as aggressor and victim.

The third difference between distressed and nondistressed couples is reciprocity. This focuses on three basic questions about the pattern of the relationship: (1) To what degree is the partner's prior behavior influencing the mates' perception of current behavior? (2) Do partners keep a day-to-day account of the relative rewards and disappointments in the relationship? and (3) What is the balance of each partner's respective rewards and disappointments over time? Beyond these questions, how do the respective partners feel about the pattern of these interchanges over time? How does this affect each person's perceptions of his or her partner? How do these perceptions affect the marital relationship?

Distressed and nondistressed couples hold differential cognitive sets for interpreting behavior. According to Margolin (1982) distressed couples are more prone to selectively noticing and attending to negative behavior (negative tracking) while nondistressed partners tend to selectively notice and attend to positive behaviors (positive tracking).

The behavioral expression of intimacy depends on the developmental stage of the relationship, (i.e., the length of time the couple has been together and/or their progression through the cycle of family development). Studies report a curvilinear relationship between family life cycle and marital satisfaction. Marital satisfaction is highest among young couples. It declines after the birth of the first child, and remains depressed until the child grows up and leaves home.

A primary objective in a cognitive-behavioral approach to marital therapy is finding out what spouses are currently doing with and for each other as well as what they are thinking and feeling about each other. Hence, assessing intimate relationships entails: (1) identifying behavioral exchanges that are occurring too fast or too slow; (2) evaluating the couple's competence in specific relationship-maintaining skills; (3) exploring the partners' current and potential reinforcement value for one another; and (4) obtaining partners' subjective impressions and appraisals as to the strengths and weaknesses of the relationship (Margolin, 1982). Rather than being static, these four dimensions are in constant flux. From a social learning point of view, it is important to identify which environmental conditions control the shifts that occur in each of these domains. Under what stimulus conditions does the couple's exchange become more or less rewarding?

In general, all behaviorally oriented marital therapy can be viewed as helping partners to obtain more benefits from their relationship by increasing the frequency of desired behaviors. However, one must distinguish between behaviors that have been the source of intense emotional conflict versus behaviors that partners can and are willing to emit, but have simply overlooked. Behaviors which foster intense emotional conflict often lead to complex stalemates and require a more involved series of interventions, some of which are outlined in the next chapter. The cognitive-behavioral strategies described in this chapter apply to the second category of behavior. They seek to increase marital satisfaction by changing communication patterns and increasing the frequency of desired behaviors. These interventions directly address the problem of devaluation of reinforcers in a distressed relationship. They also enable the couple to experience fairly immediate gains from therapy without major costs, thereby priming them for more difficult (second order) relationship changes.

There is no single sure-fire method which enhances marital satisfaction. On the contrary, unless interventions are tailored to meet the specific requirements of each particular couple, the potential for increased disappointment is substantial. However, one beginning strategy for accelerating a couple's positive exchange is to allow the partners to define and articulate for themselves what they can do to please one another (Margolin, 1982).

A useful addition to this method is "rewriting the marital contract." In this approach, couples are asked to define two or three specific behavioral changes they desire in the relationship. A quid pro quo is created by the marital therapist who is acting as a mediator. During the therapy session a mutually acceptable agreement is negotiated, drawn up, and signed by each of the partners as well as the therapist. This contract accomplishes three things. It explicitly defines what each partner wants from the other. It begins to effectively contain the dysfunctional behaviors. Finally, it potentially provides a fairly immediate reduction in marital stress which encourages the couple to continue working on improving the relationship. In the event that the contract is unsuccessful, then that also provides an important indicator to both couple and therapist about the relative investment in the therapeutic process and the prognosis for successful problem resolution.

CONCLUSIONS

Two variables influence the course of all intimate relationships. On the one hand, there is a sense of separateness and autonomy. On the other hand, there is the universal desire for an occasional regression to a state of "symbiotic fusion"–perfect understanding by a loving other. Finding an acceptable balance between these two desires is the dilemma of love relationships (Solomon, 1989).

Today's couples are expecting more and more, not only from their partner, but from the marriage itself. Due to the narrowing of the emotional field because of the growing social barriers to intimacy, spouses are now forced to depend on their partners to meet a much broader and deeper range of emotional and interpersonal needs. Marriage has become a refuge from an otherwise brutal and uncaring world. People depend on it as an essential source of emotional support, personal affirmation, and mind-bending sexual fulfillment. Despite American society's flirtations with the sexual revolution some two short decades ago, in some ways we have fallen back into our Victorian past, especially in regard to our romanticized views of marriage. While sex before marriage is increasing and extramarital sex is also on the rise, the only "legitimate" fully sanctioned context for sexual expression among civilized Americans is within the context of legal matrimony.

Sexuality plays a unique role in marital relationships. Beyond its potential for physical gratification, a satisfying sexual relationship also enhances emotional closeness. Feeling attracted to and valued by the other person is an important source of emotional bonding. In contrast, a troubled sexual relationship tends to raise doubts about one's appeal and worth and raise serious concerns about overall compatibility with one's mate. There is a strong correlation between a satisfying sexual relationship and the overall relationship in general. Some sex therapists believe that a couple's sexual relationship is a metaphor for the marital relationship as a whole. Since the full range of communication, negotiation, empathy, respect, need fulfillment, love, and tenderness are all embodied in sexual interaction, sex provides a useful barometer for the relative health and/or dysfunction in the marital relationship. That being the case, the high prevalence of couples with sexual dissatisfaction is cause for concern. Recent data indicate that more than 50 percent of nonclinical couples report either specific sexual dysfunctions or sexual difficulties such as lack of interest or attraction (Margolin, 1982).

While couples enter couples' therapy for many reasons, describing a myriad of different problems, the underlying issue is often a lack of intimacy. The presenting problem often involves some kind of difficulty in the couple's sexual relationship. Some 38 million Americans reportedly complain of low sexual desire. Couples frequently differ in their relative levels of sexual desire. But if sex is indeed a metaphor for the relationship, then the therapeutic process is a means through which couples are able to look beyond the obvious struggles in their relationship and uncover the deeper search for intimacy.

REFERENCES

Adams, T. (1993). Intimacy workshop. New Orleans, LA. 10/29/92.

Atwater, L. 1979. Getting involved: Women's transition to first extramarital sex. *Alternative Lifestyles*, 1(2):33-68.

Berger, P., Berger, B. and Kellner, H. (1973). *The homeless mind.* New York: Random House.

Bowen, M. (1966). The use of family theory in clinical practice. *Comparative Psychiatry*, 7:345-374.

Brehm, S. 1992. *Intimate relationships*. New York: McGraw-Hill, Inc.

Dutton, D. and Aron, A. 1974. Some evidence for heightened sexual attraction under conditions of high anxiety. *Journal of Personality and Social Psychology*, 30:510-517.

Fitzpatrick, M. 1988. *Between husbands and wives*. Newbury Park, CA: Sage Publications, Inc.

Guerin, P., Fay, F., Burden, S., Kautto, J. 1987. *The evaluation and treatment of marital conflict*, New York: Basic Books.

Glass, S. and Wright, T. 1985. Sex differences in type of extramarital involvement and marital dissatisfaction. *Sex Roles*, 12(9):9-10.

Glass, S. and Wright, T. 1990. Justifications for extramarital relationships: The association between attitudes, behaviors, and gender. Unpublished Paper.

Harper, J. and Elliott, M. 1988. Can there be too much of a good thing? The relationship between desired level of intimacy and marital adjustment. *The American Journal of Family Therapy*, 16(4):351-360.

Hatfield, E. 1982. Passionate love, companionate love and intimacy. In M. Fisher and G. Stricter (Eds.). *Intimacy*. New York: Plenum, 267-291.

Hatfield, E. and Walster, G. 1978. *A new look at love*. Reading, MA: Addison-Wesley.

Hendrick, S., Hendrick, C., and Adler, N. 1988. Romantic relationships: Love, satisfaction and staying together. *Journal of Personality and Social Psychology*, 54:980-988.

James, K. 1989. Distancer-Pursuer Patterns. *Australian and New Zealand Journal of Family Therapy*, 10(3):179-186.

Jourard, S. 1964. *The transparent self*. New York: Van Nostrand.

Lawson, A. 1988. Adultery: An analysis of love and betrayal. New York: Basic Books.

Margolin, G. 1982. A social learning approach to intimacy. In Fisher, G. and Stricter, M. (Eds.) *Intimacy*. New York: Plenum Press.

Napier, A. 1978. The rejection-intrusion pattern: A central family dynamic. *Journal of Marriage and Family Counseling*, 4:5-12.

Patton, D. and Waring, E. 1985. Sex and marital intimacy. *Journal of Sex and Marital Therapy*, 11(3):176-184.

Perlmutter, M. and Hatfield, E. 1980. Intimacy, intentional metacommunication and second order change. *The American Journal of Family Therapy*, 8(1):17-23.

Petersen, J. 1983. The Playboy readers' sex survey. *Playboy*, 30(3):90ff.

Reiss, I., Anderson, R. and Sponaugle, G. 1980. A multivariate model of the determinants of extramarital sexual permissiveness. *Journal of Marriage and the Family*, 42(2):395-411.

Rubin, Z., Hill, C., Peplau, L., and Dunke-Schetter, C. 1980. Self-disclosure in dating couples: Sex roles and the ethics of openness. *Journal of Marriage and the Family*, 42:305-317.

Scanzoni, L. and Scanzoni, J. 1988. *Men, women and change*. New York: McGraw-Hill, Inc.

Solomon, M. 1989. *Narcissism and intimacy*. New York: Norton.

Thompson, A. 1984. Emotional and sexual components of extramarital relations. *Journal of Marriage and the Family*, 46(1):35-42.

Veroff, J., Douvan, E. and Kulka, R. 1981. *The inner American*. New York: Basic Books.

Wamboldt, F. and Reiss, D. 1989. Defining a family heritage and a new relationship identity: Two central tasks in the making of a marriage. *Family Process*, 28(3):317-335.

Weitzman, L., Dixon, C., Bird, J., McGuinn, N., and Robertson, D. 1978. Contracts for intimate relationships: A study of contracts before, within, and in lieu of legal marriage, *Alternate Lifestyles*, 1:303-378.

Chapter 7

Couples in Therapy

Lynn Finnegan
Philip M. Brown

Frequently, the task of the couples' therapist is to find ways to enable the partners to lower and/or overcome their barriers to intimacy. Many couples enter therapy with a very specific presenting problem and are surprised to learn that their "process" in therapy and eventual problem resolution will invariably involve enhancing their capacities and skills for creating intimacy. Several authors, (e.g., Karpal [1976], Givelber [1990] and Schnarch [1991]) note that barriers to intimacy underlie symptoms of dysfunction in couple relationships. "The symptoms are myriad: fighting, avoidance, difficulties in communication, interactional patterns, sexual problems–particularly disorders of sexual desire. The clinician is alerted to problems in intimacy by these behavioral manifestations of the conflicts" (Givelber 1990:178). Though symptoms often function defensively to reduce fears of intimacy, they ironically end up perpetuating destructive interactive patterns.

In assisting partners to lower their barriers to intimacy, the therapist employs a variety of strategies and techniques. Despite one's theoretical predilections, certain general principles are useful in guiding the therapeutic process. First, the therapist must create a safe environment in which the couple can explore and experiment with taking the emotional risks required to enhance intimacy. Previous chapters have detailed the sources of anxiety in individuals' early personal and familial histories which interfere with them taking the risks that intimacy requires. The couple's therapist acknowledges this anxiety and, when appropriate, explores its origins. This empowers individuals to establish the necessary preconditions for their own sense of emotional safety.

As both partners are present throughout this examination, each gains a deeper and more intimate understanding of him or herself and the other. With this understanding, the partners gain awareness of what they can do to make the environment safer. Schnarch speaks of the latter as self-validated intimacy and describes its importance in long-term couple relationships. "When the response of the partner is acceptance and reciprocal disclosure, intimacy is experienced as loving and validating" (1991:121-122). When this does not concur, there is a threat to one's sense of self. In the absence of "other-validation," self-validation is necessary. Such self-validation depends on the ability of the risk taker to self-soothe and thereby reduce his or her anxiety about risk taking. Within this therapeutic environment, the risk of destructive responses and reactions can be minimized by the structure the therapist provides through limit setting, judicious siding, and predicting the pain and disappointment that comes with the downside of intimacy. The therapist can also highlight the potential benefits for the relationship.

The recognition that intimacy is painful is the second general principle. While working with the couple to foster intimacy, the therapist likewise acknowledges the risks the partners are taking in letting the other truly see and know them. The therapist uses the couple's anxiety about such risks to prepare them for any negativity that may arise during the stage when a partner's response to greater honesty and deeper sharing is painful. Later, this anxiety can turn into relief and help to heal the barriers in the relationship as the partners become more comfortable meeting at deeper and more honest levels. As David Treadway wisely cautions his clients: "Being intimate frequently doesn't feel good and it doesn't feel safe" (1993:38).

Third, the therapist validates the couple's need to be open and to interact in close emotional proximity, while still allowing them space to be separate and private. By respecting each individual's right to privacy the therapist allows for more fulfilling togetherness and greater self-disclosure in the relationship. This therapeutic validation of the need for separateness is crucial because it addresses the major challenge to intimate relationships previously described—the balancing of one's own needs with the needs of one's partner.

This intervention is particularly important for enmeshed and disengaged couples. For disengaged partners it begins to allay fears of engulfment or loss of self. For enmeshed or fused couples, it enables them to learn that separateness and individuality are necessary components of intimacy.

Fourth, couples' therapy must either directly or indirectly motivate the partners to disclose some aspect of themselves that they have not previously been willing to share. This self-disclosure may involve a feeling, desire, fact, etc. As discussed in Chapter 4, conversations, exchange of information, and self-disclosure are the tools of intimacy. Research has shown that half the quality of intimacy is directly related to the amount of self-disclosure in the relationship (Waring, 1984). In order to motivate the partner, the therapy needs to demonstrate how this self-disclosure relates to the couple's presenting problem. Thus, a fuller understanding of the context in which the presenting problem occurs is the fourth step in decreasing a couple's barriers to intimacy.

Fifth, having recognized the risks involved and the anxiety surrounding lowering the barriers in the relationship, the therapist supports the now motivated couple in taking that initial step toward a greater intimacy. At times, the response to greater self-revelation between the partners is painful for one or both of them. However, closeness, acceptance, relief, freedom, and/or comfort will eventually emerge in the relationship as the conflicts and feelings generated by this openness are successfully worked through. The partners can then experience the benefits of the risks taken. After successful initial forays, the anxiety around taking such risks gradually decreases for many partners. Partners begin to sense their strength and start to realize that their relationship can withstand the ugly as well as the beautiful, the unpleasant as well as the pleasant, the bad as well as the good. Employing these five principles in the early stages of therapy re-educates the couple to the realities and the challenges of intimate relationships.

Intimacy requires a safe environment. In reality, however, intimacy is unsafe. Intimacy requires closeness as well as distance, connection as well as separateness. Stating that all couples are intimate, Frankel (1982) developed the notion of functional versus dysfunctional intimacy.

Mate selection is based on two unconscious principles: (1) the potential for the partners to jointly work through similar developmental conflicts and (2) a joint collusion to resist working through these developmental conflicts. The latter leads to dysfunctional intimacy in which the couple maintains a frustrating homeostasis. They remain embroiled in repetitive patterns which require the partners to deny, repress, project, and/or give up certain aspects of themselves. On the other hand, functionally intimate relationships are characterized by self-disclosure, empathy and support, the ability to resolve conflicts, mutual confirmation of lovability, enjoyable physical contact (from affection to sexuality), a unique sense of "we-ness" as a couple, an acceptance of each other's differences and identities as individuals, mutual assurance of availability during crisis, congruity between role expectations and behavior.

Waring et al. (1981) identify intimacy as the interpersonal dimension which most influences healthy marital adjustment. Schaefer and Olson (1981) describe five types of intimacy: emotional intimacy, social intimacy, sexual intimacy, intellectual intimacy, and recreational intimacy. Clinebell and Clinebell (1970) also use these five types of intimacy and add spiritual, aesthetic, creative, work, crisis, conflictual, and commitment intimacy to comprise their twelve parameters of intimacy. These twelve parameters, along with the eight additional aspects identified by Waring et al., provide the clinician with twenty potential dimensions along which to assess intimacy in couples who enter therapy. Since no couple is intimate in all areas, couples need to determine the areas in which they desire intimacy (Hof and Treat, 1989). Treatment needs to be grounded in appreciating the couple's contract around intimacy rather than the therapist's ideal model (Givelber, 1990)

The assessment of intimacy with the couple can provide a useful road map for the couples' therapist, charting territory that the therapy must travel to arrive at the couple's destination. Jay Haley (1976) points out that the family therapist can work with any problem the family chooses to present in therapy because the work of therapy concerns how the family is organized and how it organizes itself around the problem. Similarly, when the couple in therapy is dysfunctionally intimate, the content of the couple's therapy will revolve around the problem the couple presents. However, the process through which the therapist helps the couple solve their problem(s) can simultaneously develop the intimate aspects of their relationship.

Barriers to intimacy may assume many forms in couple relationships. While the forms may be as varied as the couples themselves, therapists working with these couples observe certain consistent patterns. The following case examples illustrate the impact of these barriers on couples' relationships as well as the therapeutic process necessary for overcoming these barriers and the consequent impact on the couple's relationship.

THE CONFLICT-AVOIDING COUPLE

During the course of therapy many individuals find that they have not been revealing essential aspects of themselves to their partners. They are not letting their partner know their genuine feelings, thoughts, desires, or dreams. In this hiddenness, problems, resentments, and distance can develop in the relationship. The self may be hidden from the partner because the person does not trust the strength of the relationship. Both know the relationship is not meeting the early hopes and dreams each of them had. If they reveal who they really are, they fear their partner will no longer like them. It could create conflict, and they do not trust that the relationship is strong enough to withstand such dissonance, let alone be improved by it. Worse yet, they fear that such conflict will cause their partner to depart, leaving them abandoned and lonely. Such is the profile of the Conflict-Avoiding Couple.

The Conflict-Avoiding Couple resides in a paradox. They avoid the honest self-disclosure and open communication so essential to intimacy. In order to maintain what they perceive as closeness in the relationship, these couples end up creating a "pseudo intimacy." Like cancer that goes untreated, this choice to close off a part to themselves often grows and festers, and eventually deadens the relationship, either in whole or in part.

Typically, as children they were not taught how to confront problems constructively, handle each others' differences and/or work through conflicts. Often, their parents did not deal with disagreements openly or addressed conflicts so ineffectively that their children would not want to emulate them.

In working with Conflict-Avoiding Couples, the therapeutic task is four-fold: (1) to create an environment which is safe and supportive enough for the partners to risk communicating more openly and more intimately with each other, (2) to give the couple a realistic, rather than idealized, picture of what healthy relationships look like, (3) to facilitate each partner accepting his or her own and the other's differences and the inevitable disagreements and disappointments of intimate relationships, and (4) to guide the couple in developing their own unique ways of dealing with these inevitabilities.

Case Example: Bill and Linda

In some cases, the Conflict-Avoiding Couple comes into therapy in such crisis that little time needs to be spent building a safe and secure environment for them. Linda and Bill were such a couple. An attractive, professional couple, they entered therapy when Linda discovered that Bill was having an affair. Both had perceived their marriage as ideal (as did many of their friends). Unlike many couples who manage to avoid conflict, but carry the unspoken, unresolved tension around with them, this couple had mastered the art of conflict-avoidance. They always appeared so caring and considerate of one another. They rarely disagreed and never argued. Childless by choice, they devoted most of their time and attention to each other. Bill appeared almost as mystified as Linda by the affair.

Linda's hurt and anger over the affair opened up a whole area of emotional expression of negative feelings that had never come out in their marriage. It quickly became clear that this "perfect couple" had been far too careful with each other throughout their eight years of marriage. It turns out that each had kept secrets, some large and some small, from the other. Although Linda knew that Bill had been married previously, Bill had neglected to tell her that he had, in fact, been married twice before. He rationalized his omission because both he and his first wife were nineteen and the marriage had lasted only six months. Underneath this rationalization Bill did not accept himself for having made such an impetuous decision when he was young and feared that Linda would not accept him because of it. On a day-to-day basis, neither of them bothered to share the little annoyances each had with the other. In their silence, an invisible barrier was unknowingly constructed between them. Bill's affair was the symptom of their mutual isolation.

Couple Therapy with the Conflict-Avoiding Couple

A primary goal of therapy was to help Bill and Linda see that their marriage did not need to be perfect to be happy. They could be caring without being so careful with each other in the relationship. Techniques of education and normalization were used extensively in therapy to challenge the romantic myth of the ideal marriage which they pursued with such dedication.

Indeed, ideal marriages might be characterized by long-lasting, deep romantic love, continual sexual and emotional fulfillment, shared dreams and struggles, absence of conflict, and constant acceptance and approval of each other. The therapist, however, emphasized the fact that such marriages do not exist. Real marriages, on the other hand, do exist. In a real marriage, romantic love grows into companionate love as partners learn and begin to appreciate each other's strengths and faults. Despite these weaknesses, the partners usually like and accept one another, but not 100 percent of the time. Conflict and differences are not avoided, but can be verbalized. At best, they can be worked through and resolved. At worst, they can be tolerated. Real marriages are expressive not only of positive thoughts, beliefs, attitudes, and feelings, as in their marriage, but of negative ones as well. The fact that Bill and Linda had failed to achieve an "ideal marriage" was normal and understandable. The therapist congratulated them for how hard and how long they had tried to achieve this "ideal marriage." They now needed to decide whether or not they wanted to have a "real marriage" together.

The couple separated for a short time and were each seen in individual therapy. During this time, Bill needed to decide whether or not to end the affair. Once he ended the affair, he needed a period of time to mourn its ending. For her part, Linda needed to work through her feelings of outrage, pain, and betrayal, and ultimately decide whether or not she wanted to forgive Bill. Both decided that their marriage, though no longer "perfect," was strong and important enough to continue.

At this point therapeutic goals included: (1) healing the relationship both as a result of the affair and in the areas that led to the affair, (2) facilitating greater self-disclosure and open expressions of differences between partners and (3) developing skills in resolving conflicts and differences as needed. The analysis and subsequent understanding of the role each played in contributing to the dynamics which led to Bill's affair played a significant role in healing the relationship. The energy with which both of them tackled the issue of self-disclosure in the negative as well as the positive aspects of the relationship further contributed to healing. It helped to build the trust that both really wanted from each other. Over time, their joint efforts helped to heal the scars from the affair. They were motivated to do what was necessary to have a successful "real marriage."

After several months, Bill risked telling Linda that she was, in fact, his third wife. Linda felt angry and betrayed. This was a deception which she found difficult to accept. This revelation evoked a confrontation which ultimately helped both to realize that they were strong enough to stand alone without the other's approval. Bill felt relieved because he no longer had to maintain this longstanding deception. Linda gradually began to feel better about Bill. The couple had been desensitized to disagreement by the conflict which resulted from Linda discovering her husband's affair. They were now able to tolerate and deal with the lesser marital conflicts and differences as they arose.

Linda and Bill have been back together for many years and conflict is now an acceptable part of their relationship. While they continue to do thoughtful things for each other, they do so more out of their own desire and less out of the pressure to meet some ideal.

Case Analysis

Like many couples, this couple had sought to achieve the cultural myth of the "ideal marriage" without conflict. Contrary to the prevailing cultural mythology, the frequency of marital conflict is not necessarily correlated with divorce. Bill and Linda were well on the path to developing a disengaged relationship as Bill was becoming more emotionally intimate within his extramarital relationship. Thus, he was more at risk for divorce had he not begun therapy.

It was very important for Bill and Linda to understand how the dynamics of their relationship contributed to Bill's affair. This understanding helped the couple to decide to continue their marriage despite the pain and confusion it caused. Ironically, this couple who had striven to maintain a relationship of enduring romantic love was ultimately bound together by their companionate love based on their shared history.

Communication is the primary means through which intimacy is achieved. Self-disclosure and conflict resolution are two essential aspects of communication which strongly affect the couple's quest for intimacy. Yet this couple scrupulously avoided conflicts. Self-disclosure was primarily positive and focused on aspects of the person or relationship that were congruent with the "idealized image" of the other.

This marriage was based on what Schnarch (1993) describes as mutual-validation pacts. In such relationships, partners implicitly promise emotional acceptance of the other in return for having their fundamental sense of identity and self-worth validated. These relationships occur when the partners lack a firmly grounded sense of personal identity. A negative reaction from the partner threatens to destroy one's carefully constructed facade. When people marry, they expect and even demand that their partners invariably respond to any self-disclosure with love, appreciation, warmth, and approval. When these expectations are not met, the partner either matures or concludes that "you don't love me." Along with these expectations, the partners are simultaneously afraid to self-disclose because they know that such total validation would be flattering but inauthentic and dishonest.

Bill was terrified that Linda would not accept him if she really knew him. As the oldest child in a poor, severely dysfunctional alcoholic family in which he was verbally abused, he was left with a very tenuous sense of self-worth. As a result, he didn't feel "good enough" for Linda. Linda's upper-middle-class family never openly argued with one another. Thus, she learned to equate conflict with the absence of love. In reality, self-disclosure does not always bring a loving, nurturing, or understanding response from the partner. As they revealed their secrets during the course of therapy, Bill and Linda learned that they could withstand these negative responses and accept each other's separateness and differences.

Schnarch (1991) describes two aspects of intimacy: caring and self-awareness. Conflict-Avoiding Couples can be very comfortable with the caring aspect of intimacy. They shelter each other from information, irritation, or anything that will be painful for their partner. In so doing, partners also shelter themselves from the pain of the other's hurt, anger, and disappointment when it is directed at them. Each partner's innermost self feels that: "If you really knew who I am, you would not be with me." By developing the self-awareness aspect of intimacy, the partners are more able to accurately see and express their actual selves to one another. Therapy can assist Conflict-Avoiding Couples in recognizing that this type of "caring" is doing as much lethal damage to their relationship as any fears of honest self-disclosure could. As Schnarch points out, when partners are well-differentiated and possess this firmly grounded sense of self-identity and self-acceptance, a negative response does not have the power to generate anxiety or depression. Only then is true intimacy possible.

THE ACHIEVING COUPLE

Many of today's couples find themselves so busy with work and children that they have little time for each other. In closely bonded or enmeshed families, such partners are often likely to be both exemplary employees and devoted parents. While they have a strong relationship as parents, such partners frequently have an undernurtured relationship as a couple. In more distant and disengaged families, these are exemplary employees who engage in numerous activities outside the home. In high-achieving couples, one or both partners may work 50 to 70+ hours per week. Those who have children are likewise raising high-achieving children who may be simultaneously involved in sports, music lessons, Scouts, church, and homework (not to mention playing with their friends). These high-achieving couples make time for work; time for their children; time for their children's activities; but cannot find time for each other and their own relationship.

Do these partners stay busy in order to avoid spending time together nurturing their own personal relationship? Or do the partners have the capacity to be emotionally connected but the stresses of modern life prevent them from developing an intimate relationship? For some couples, the former is more true; for others the latter applies. In many cases, however, it is the interaction of both these factors that contribute to the lack of intimacy in the couple's relationship.

Case Example: Sarah and Jim

Sarah and Jim had decided that she would not continue in her work as a social worker while they were raising their three young children. Since Jim's income as an attorney provided them with a comfortable living, they were free to make their children the priority. Unlike many in his profession, Jim rarely worked evenings or weekends. He had intentionally sought a position with an 8 to 5 workday. This enabled him to coach his daughter's soccer team, help the children with their homework and projects, and be a part of family activities evenings and weekends. Sarah was able to volunteer at her children's elementary school and occasionally helped teach her three year-old daughter's nursery school class. She helped her children with their music lessons and took the two older children to their weekly soccer or basketball practice. Being at home not only gave her time for the basics of parental nurturing, but also for the extras such as making the children's Halloween costumes or a special treat for them to take to school. These were the reasons she was not working outside the home. These were the aspects of the decision which she loved. Nonetheless, she disliked the day-to-day tasks of housecleaning, laundry, and meal preparation. Even so, Sarah saw these tasks as her responsibility and dutifully completed them.

As Sarah progressively lost interest in sex over the past four years, Jim had become increasingly enraged. Sarah's continued disinterest and Jim's growing rage were destroying their relationship. Strongly committed to their marriage, neither wanted a divorce.

Couple Therapy with the Achieving Couple

At the onset of therapy, Sarah expected Jim to accept her disinterest in intercourse without rage whereas Jim desperately wanted

Sarah to be more sexually attentive. The first step in therapy was to explore and better understand the context in which this shift in their relationship had occurred. Some therapists may have been tempted to move directly to the treatment of inhibited sexual desire through the use of sensate focus. However, in Sarah's eyes, such a move on the therapist's part would have allied a demanding therapist with her demanding husband. This would have sabotaged both partners' ability to actively embrace therapy. Inhibited sexual desire was the merely symptom of underlying issues in the couple system.

Sarah and Jim examined the origins of the loss of their once-enjoyable sexual relationship. The therapist was able to help them see that the choices they made and the circumstances they created left almost no time for their own relationship. Over a period of five years, Sarah gave birth to three children. Their sexual relationship remained mutually satisfying until shortly after the birth of their third child. At this time, a significant change in their lives occurred when they decided to move Jim's paternal grandmother to a nearby nursing home because she was seriously ill. They agreed that she could no longer live alone in her own home some 200 miles away. During the year prior to her death, Sarah regularly visited Jim's grandmother, three children in tow. Likewise, Jim visited his grandmother almost daily on his way home from work. Since his own parents had not been very nurturing, this was the something he could do for the one person who had cared for him so unselfishly during his childhood.

Shortly after Jim's grandmother died, Sarah's 6-year-old nephew was diagnosed with brain cancer. Since she was so close to her brother and his wife, she now became an important source of support to both of them and her nephew through the latter's many treatments and hospitalizations. Her nephew died three months after the couple began therapy.

Sarah's capacity for nurturing was being depleted by caring for her three children and two dying family members. What Sarah had once experienced as a mutually satisfying sexual relationship, she now experienced as her husband demanding that she take care of him too. Family-of-origin issues contributed heavily to the couple's expectations of themselves and each other, and in so doing, constructed serious barriers to intimacy. Having come from a dysfunctional family herself, Sarah worked hard at being the "perfect mother" for her children. With the added stresses of an infirmed grandmother-in-law and critically ill nephew, she was left with virtually no time to nurture herself. Her lone concession to meeting her own needs was allowing herself one hour nightly to read prior to going to sleep. Unfortunately, this was precisely the time that Jim looked forward to spending with her.

Jim had grown up with a needy mother, who expected others to take care of her. Consequently, she was unable to meet her children's emotional needs. Jim's father was emotionally distant and unexpressive. As a child, Jim had no choice but to put up with them. However, as a adult, he could not tolerate this kind of treatment from his wife. He felt emotionally exiled by Sarah and reacted with anger and resentment. Unfortunately, rather than solving the problem, Jim's anger pushed his wife further away. Jim's changing behavior and attitude only succeeded in reminding Sarah of her father's intense anger. As a result, the destructive cycle of "anger to withdrawal to anger" only compounded Jim and Sarah's marital discord.

Alienated and recoiling from her husband's anger, Sarah would not talk with him about what she did not like and what made her angry. When their life was less complicated, the problems between them were less complicated and more easily resolved. As more people were integrated into their life (namely their children and extended family members), discussing issues and resolving problems became increasingly complicated. The couple also began to take on certain characteristics of the Conflict-Avoiding Couple. Now the only issue about which they openly conflicted was their sexual relationship.

Helping the couple understand that they had become too busy for each other helped them begin to see the road to the solution. The next therapeutic goal was to help them reconnect in a positive rather than conflictual way. Tasks were assigned with consideration for the demands of parenting three children and the continuing commitment they had to their dying nephew and his family. The therapist was cognizant of preparing them to be supportive to each other through the painful process of their nephew's imminent death and the difficult grieving period that would inevitably follow.

The therapist worked with the couple to help Jim find ways to be more supportive of Sarah–ways that she would appreciate and not find demanding. Though he was always involved in caring for the children, Jim now took on more responsibility, sometimes taking a day off work, so that his wife could stay overnight and assist in the care of her dying nephew. During therapy they came to understand the sources of their unhappiness. As a result, their barriers to intimacy were lowered, and they became more motivated to spend time together. Though they were still busy with work and heavily taxed by the demands of this family tragedy, they did make time to go out together once every week or two. These "dates" were mutually enjoyable, and gave them an opportunity to support each other without distractions during this difficult time. Over time, these positive changes began to enhance and enrich their relationship.

Not all of the tasks assigned by the therapist were completed by this couple. Interestingly enough, they did not do the assignment to spend 10 minutes a day talking together about themselves as people. Rather, they continued to discuss children and schedules. However, their response to this assignment was diagnostically useful and aided in directing the next steps in therapy. It enabled the therapist to see how stilted their communication was and how uncomfortable they were with each other at home. Developing their ability to interact as spouses rather than simply as parents seemed less threatening outside their home than in it. Most likely, such time spent together at home would have led directly to the issue of sexuality in their marriage without first resolving the underlying emotional issues which were intertwined with their sexual problems.

One of the reasons their sexual relationship had stagnated was that Sarah was not being open with Jim about what she did not like, or what she wanted to be different in their overall relationship. Sarah and Jim began to recognize the circular causality in their relationship. Sarah found her life and her marriage going in directions she did not like, but said nothing out of fear that her husband would respond angrily, as her father had. Consequently, her interest in having sex with Jim steadily waned. Feeling unloved and rejected by his wife, Jim became angry and resentful. Motivated by their mutual unhappiness, yet invested enough to work on the relationship, Sarah tentatively began experimenting. As the therapeutic process unfolded, both Sarah and Jim began taking more risks. Increased understanding of Sarah's feelings helped Jim's anger to gradually abate. He started to recognize and better appreciate Sarah's anxieties around self-disclosure. He also began to express his anger with less vehemence. Over time, he was increasingly able to offer Sarah what she needed emotionally. This reassured Sarah because it made a strong statement about the importance of her needs and Jim's continuing commitment to improving the relationship. In this way, Jim joined the therapist in creating a safe environment for Sarah's self-expression.

As Sarah began talking about her wants and needs, the couple was then able to move forward into dealing with the business of their relationship. What had once been difficult for Sarah continued to be difficult. Her anxiety persisted, but with less severity. She had to make a conscious effort to bring up areas of dissatisfaction with their relationship, including bothersome differences between them or things she wanted from Jim. Sarah was finding that they could both be angry without having a destructive impact on their relationship. Unlike some Conflict-Avoiding Couples, Jim and Sarah did not need to develop skills in expressing and managing conflict before lowering the barriers to better communication. Jim's response to Sarah's expressed needs was rarely vehement. Occasionally, however, Jim's anger still got so intense that it made Sarah uncomfortable. However, she could now tell him how it made her feel. For the most part, Jim was then able to temper his response. Jim and Sarah agreed that they wanted Sarah to express herself without Jim's anger silencing her.

Once Sarah and Jim made progress in lowering their barriers to emotional intimacy, Sarah became more willing to address the barriers to intimacy in their sexual relationship. As they struggled with these obstacles, the couple maintained hard-fought gains in other aspects of their relationship.

At the outset of therapy, the couple was engaging in sexual intercourse at approximately three-week intervals. Like many couples with differing desires for sexual intercourse, little affection was expressed between them because of Sarah's fear that it would lead to sex. At this point in the therapeutic process, the couple was now ready to begin a very slow process of sensate focus.

It was necessary for the process of sensate focus to be gradual with this Achieving Couple for several reasons. First, they needed to prioritize their personal and sexual relationships and integrate these as regular parts of their lives alongside other priorities such as children, work, etc. Moving too quickly might temporarily improve their sexual relationship, but would not necessarily carry over into their ongoing relationship because they had not sustained the pattern long enough to integrate it into their day-to-day life. Second, after three children and a total change in life-style from the childless, working professional, Sarah was much different sexually than she had been when their sexual relationship had last been enjoyable. Therefore, both Sarah and Jim needed to discover who she is today, sexually speaking. Third, Sarah needed to be empowered both personally and sexually. For a time she resisted exploring their sexual relationship and experiencing her own sexuality. As she began to experience her personal power, she became more open to developing sexual intimacy in their marriage.

Just as sexual intimacy in a relationship involves negotiation, so the development of Sarah's and Jim's sexual intimacy through the use of sensate focus involved negotiation–between the couple and the therapist as well as each other. Negotiation between therapist and couple also increased the potential of developing styles of relating that could realistically fit their lifestyle. With the therapist's help, they had already negotiated several areas of social, emotional, and recreational intimacy. These included how they would talk to each other about areas of dissatisfaction in their relationship, as well as when they would spend time together and what they would do. Having practiced negotiation in these areas, they were now ready to explore their sexual relationship. The therapist asked the couple to set aside three times per week where they would spend 20 minutes together in enjoyable and physically close ways. The therapist knew that the time allotted was limited, but it was necessary to give this "busy" couple a task they were willing to perform. The initial phase of sensate focus involved kissing, holding, massage, and any kind of touch that did not include breast or genital touching. However, both partners had the right to request or refuse any type of touch at any time. The intervention was structured such that they could either receive for half the allotted time and give for half the time or they could alternate days as giver and receiver. Though they currently engaged in sexual intercourse approximately every three weeks, they were asked to cease intercourse during the first two stages of sensate focus. The couple did not progress to the second stage, which added breast and genital touching, until Sarah was willing.

The adaptation of sensate focus to this particular couple's needs took an unusual progression and yielded some interesting results. The first phase lasted almost seven weeks. Within several weeks of the initiation of sensate focus, the couple came to therapy reporting that they had extended their time to 45-60 minutes, since 20 minutes was insufficient for enjoying each other. Despite the initial instructions, they had also chosen to spend their time in this initial stage doing only massage. Once again, the therapist instructed them to include other forms of affectionate and caring touch (with the exception of breast and genital touching) during these "special times together." The therapist also encouraged them to show each other affection outside of the prescribed times. This allowed them to reclaim affection as a part of the relationship without affection always being a prelude to intercourse. Four weeks later, the couple was ready for the second phase of sensate focus which added breast and genital touching but still omitted sexual intercourse.

After another three weeks (some ten weeks after the initiation of sensate focus), the couple independently decided to add intercourse to their sexual activity. It is interesting to note that in the first phase of sensate focus, they had slowed the process. The therapist slowed down with them and adjusted the process accordingly. Interestingly, this enabled the couple to move faster. For the next six weeks the couple structured their time together as before (three times per week for 45-60 minutes), so that intercourse could become a regular part of their busy lives. Sarah found that she enjoyed their sexual relationship more now than ever before. She attributed this to being more comfortable with herself and learning how to better relax. The extended initial phase of sensate focus, particularly the extensive massage, enabled her to know her body better and to associate her husband's touch with relaxation and comfort.

The entire process of assisting the couple to develop their personal and sexual intimacy was very gradual. It required about 11 months to achieve and another six months to stabilize. The couple has maintained the gains they achieved for several years now. Sarah has successfully reconstructed her sexual feelings for Jim and periodically comments on the positive changes in their relationship.

Case Analysis

In the clinical setting, therapists often proceed through the stages of sensate focus too quickly. A therapist and a couple who move too rapidly through these stages may not uncover important nuances which may prove crucial to ensuring long-term improvements. In Sarah and Jim's case, both of them discovered and enjoyed new ways in which Sarah experienced her sexuality. For Sarah, learning to relax in a different way significantly enhanced her sexual enjoyment. Other couples, however, may need time to develop the other aspects of their sexual relationship. For example, some couples may need to develop a language for sexual communication, (i.e., for seduction, arousal, and sexual enhancement) which is mutually comfortable and understandable.

The work with Jim and Sarah did not follow the "bypass method" recommended by some sex therapists in which the dynamics that led to the symptom of inhibited sexual desire are bypassed. Sensate focus is employed at the onset of therapy to alleviate inhibited sexual desire. In contrast, this alternate approach focuses on issues of intimate communication. Sarah's inhibited sexual desire was, in fact, an unintentional, indirect metacommunication about her feelings about their overall relationship. The meaning of her message was more important than the literal message conveyed.

Therapy with Sarah and Jim illustrates the need for an integrative approach to couples' therapy, in order to enhance the couple's ability to overcome particular barriers to intimacy. A variety of clinical approaches including structural, strategic, family-of-origin, communications, and behavioral were integrated in the therapeutic work with this couple. Their story demonstrates how the lack of intimacy in one area of the relationship eventually permeates intimacy in other areas as well. While their commitment to their marriage was strong, Sarah and Jim's marital relationship was undernurtured because of the time they spent nurturing other commitments. They spent less time together as husband and wife and more time together as parents and members of an extended family. Little time and effort was spent protecting and nurturing their social, emotional, and recreational intimacy. Sarah's lack of expression of emotional intimacy (her disagreements, wants, needs and desires) eventually impaired her desire for sexual intimacy. As her desire for sexual intimacy decreased, she became less affectionate with Jim. Although there were times when she did feel affectionate toward her husband, she withheld her affection in order to avoid engaging sexually.

Whether this progression was caused by the aforementioned circumstances, by how very difficult intimacy is, by a more deep-seated lack of differentiation from their families of origin and each other, or by a combination of these factors cannot be precisely determined. However, Jim and Sarah's story does illustrate how family-of-origin experiences and expectations reappear in the new family that is created by coupling. Once the romantic phase of love segues into the business of daily living, developing and maintaining an intimate relationship becomes a challenging and treacherous journey.

Therapy with the Achieving Couple typifies the flexible, multi-level approach needed to rebalance the relationship between sexual desire and sexual intimacy (Schnarch, 1991). On the behavioral, intrapsychic, and interpersonal levels, therapy focused on risk-taking negotiation and intrapersonal conflict. Two distinct, yet parallel, isomorphic processes occurred in therapy: first, their process toward spending time together as husband and wife (social and recreational intimacy which led to emotional intimacy) and second, the development of sexual intimacy in their relationship.

Isomorphic transactions simultaneously occurred on multiple levels. The process and necessity of negotiation were validated as the therapist and couple negotiated the steps for modified sensate focus and time spent together. The therapist's patience and respect for each partner's difference set a tone for this negotiation as well as the couple's future negotiations. In addition, engaging in this process with the therapist helped hone the couple's negotiation skills. As negotiation was taking place between the therapist and the couple, the partners also needed to negotiate with each other about what each was willing to do. These negotiations revealed each partner's respective fears, concerns, and underlying resistances. In so doing, it also highlighted their separateness. As long-repressed fears and unconscious resistances were uncovered and confronted, the partners encountered themselves and each other at deeper levels. Such interactions are the substance of intimate relationships.

THE COMPLEMENTARY COUPLE

Some partners are capable of intimacy at different levels and in different ways. One may be more verbally disclosing, while the other may be more physically affectionate. This difference can be a source of frustration for each as they long for fulfillment in an intimate relationship where they feel comfortable and capable. It is not uncommon for this disparity to be the couple's presenting problem. Careful assessment may reveal that these strengths in intimacy are complementary. A lesbian couple who came for therapy offers an example of how complementary strengths in intimacy can be used to facilitate the therapeutic process.

Case Example: Kate and Leona

Kate and Leona have lived together in a committed relationship for three years. They entered therapy because Kate was interested in sex far less frequently than Leona and because Leona would not talk with Kate about matters that Kate would find unpleasant or upsetting. Assessing the intimacy in their relationship revealed that Kate was comfortable with emotional intimacy but avoided sexual intimacy. On the other hand, Leona was comfortable with sexual intimacy but feared emotional intimacy. However, intellectual and recreational intimacy were strengths in their relationship. They spent time together in mutually enjoyable activities and had lively discussions about politics, books, and mutual interests.

Couple Therapy with the Complementary Couple

An exploration of family-of-origin issues quickly revealed the roots of each partner's barriers to intimacy. As a child, Kate was physically abused by an unpredictable and volatile mother who at one minute would strike her daughter and the next minute would hug her. In contrast, Leona's enmeshed family rarely displayed anger. Disagreement created such discomfort for family members that they developed passive-aggressive means of getting their wants and needs met (such as acting secretively or "accidentally forgetting").

The therapist helped the partners appreciate their own and the other's strengths in intimacy. This realization also pointed the direction for therapy. Kate could teach Leona how to provide a safe environment for self-disclosure by accepting negative as well as positive communication. Leona could teach Kate about sexual intimacy by creating a safe atmosphere for physical touch. Kate wanted Leona to be more emotionally intimate as well as learn how her avoidance of sex was creating a barrier in their relationship. Leona's willingness also motivated Kate to work to overcome the fear of physical touch underlying her avoidance of sexual intimacy.

As Kate struggled to lower her barriers to sexual intimacy, Leona struggled with being more self-disclosing. Initially, Kate stated flatly that she did not like being touched. When the therapist gently asked if there was any type of touch which might feel safe or acceptable, she acknowledged that a gentle pat on her hand or a hug from behind could be mildly enjoyable. However, a face-to-face hug was too threatening as was any touch other than a gentle pat. Leona assured Kate that she would touch her only within her comfort range. Gradually, Kate learned to trust that Leona would not touch her in threatening or uncomfortable ways. Like many survivors of abuse, Kate was prone to out-of-body experiences when being touched and feeling threatened. With Leona's reassurances, Kate made a conscious effort to remain in her body and allow herself to experience Leona's touch.

The role of the partner can be very important in working through issues of abuse and Leona was an excellent partner. She did not push Kate and stayed within the boundaries of touch Kate had established. With such a trustworthy partner, Kate could begin to gradually lower the barriers to sexual intimacy established in response to those early years of abuse. She wanted to be comfortable with intimate physical contact and gradually opened more areas of acceptable touch, albeit within carefully delineated boundaries. Leona assured Kate that she would honor her wishes and thus prove her trustworthiness. Gradually, Kate was able to enjoy a wider range of physical touch. Her out-of-body experiences gradually diminished, though periodically recurred as an occasional warning of her discomfort.

Within the revised boundaries of their relationship, Kate began to reexperience the pleasure of her body and of being touched. Sexual intimacy in their relationship grew. During these stages of the healing process, there were times when even familiar, acceptable touches induced fear. However, Kate had learned that she could refuse any kind of touch and Leona would honor her wishes. Wanting Kate to be more sexually intimate motivated Leona to be more self-disclosing about negative aspects of herself as well as her feelings about the relationship. Nonetheless, her journey through this process was no less arduous that Kate's.

Case Analysis

Strengths in certain areas of intimacy affirmed Kate and Leona's capabilities for developing intimacy in other areas. These complementary strengths and weaknesses were used by the therapist to facilitate their progress in therapy. Leona's strengths in sexual intimacy provided Kate with hope that sexual closeness was a possibility for her. She looked to Leona as a guide as she strove to become more comfortable in their sexual relationship. Kate's strengths in emotional intimacy functioned as a concrete model and reminder of Leona's goal. Understanding that each was fearful and anxious about certain types of closeness helped this couple patiently support each other through the often slow journey toward greater emotional and sexual intimacy.

Intimacy in their relationship was impacted by the experiences in their respective families of origin as well as their unique developmental histories. Exploring and working through these past emotional issues helped each better understand herself, her partner, and their relationship. Kate and Leona's relationship demonstrates the impact of childhood abuse on intimacy in adult relationships. Their case also illustrates a therapeutic model for working with couples in which one partner is a survivor of childhood abuse.

Throughout the sometimes painful and difficult course of therapy, this couple displayed exceptional sensitivity, understanding, and caring. To an extent, this heightened sensitivity was due to the frame the therapist constructed from the complementary nature of their strengths and challenges. In addition, it was not necessary for the therapist to translate different genderlects because, unlike heterosexual couples, these two women spoke the same language. Qualities associated with intimacy are closely linked to characteristics normally attributed to femininity. Schwartz (1989) notes the high level of intimacy potential in women and believes that the highest level of intimacy was possible in lesbian relationships. These higher levels of intimacy in lesbian relationships may result from femininity, behavioral flexibility and freedom from rigid sex roles.

THE VIOLENT COUPLE

Issues of power and control in relationships take many forms. Whenever power and control are exercised in the couple's relationship, intimacy is eventually affected. Partners tend to respond to this disempowerment by becoming subversive. This partner will then become secretive, hiding and avoidant in one or more areas of the relationship. Like a cancer which has metastasized, this pattern pervades the relationship. Frequently, the person exercising the power has no understanding of the impact their use of power has on the relationship. This impact becomes a key therapeutic tool in working with these couples.

Nowhere is the raising and lowering of barriers to intimacy seen more clearly than in the cycle of physically abusive couples. In the cycle leading up to the abuse, the couple tends to be more distant from each other. Abusers frequently hide their vulnerability and true feelings, while survivors tend to be more secretive and avoid giving information about themselves and their activities which might anger abusers. As abuse continues in the relationship, abused partners reveal less and less about themselves over time. It is in the honeymoon-apology period following physical abuse that the couple once again experiences their greatest sense of closeness and connection. During that phase in the cycle of abuse, abusers are more willing to share their vulnerable feelings and insecurity and more willing to demonstrate consideration for their partner and verbalize their need for the relationship. Much of this may be motivated by guilt. For their part, the survivors are once again able to feel connected to and valued by their partner. It is the power of this connectedness during the honeymoon phase of the abusive cycle that binds the abused partner to the relationship.

Working with physically violent couples requires a multi-modal approach to treatment, including individual, group, and couples' therapy. With the understanding that the partners are each engaged in individual therapy and appropriate group therapy for abusers and survivors of abuse, much of the couple's work revolves specifically around issues related to intimacy.

Case Example: Bev and Tom

Throughout their ten years of marriage, violence had been an infrequent but haunting presence in Bev and Tom's relationship. Several years might pass without Tom pushing Bev, pulling her hair, slapping, or punching her. At other times, these violent outbursts would occur three to four times yearly.

This couple came into therapy shortly after Bev had given birth to their third child. Because of the demands of two young children and an infant, Bev was unable to perform the many tasks she had completed in order to please her husband and thus avoid his explosive anger. Tom felt their relationship was less loving now but did not connect this feeling with the fact that the family had expanded to integrate an additional member, thus straining available resources. This couple came into therapy not because of the violence, but to "get along better." Yet in reality, the incidences of violence were becoming more frequent and intense.

Tom's parents had no history of physical violence with each other even though as a child Tom had been physically abused by his father. Both parents had verbally abused him and his mother had failed to protect him from his father's anger. Bev's parent's had not been physically violent, but her father was very domineering both in his relationships with her and her mother. Bev's mother had meekly tried to please her husband. As is typical with many abusive relationships, Tom and Bev had been rigidly socialized into stereotypic gender roles in their families of origin. Therefore, both expected Bev to emulate the traditional feminine role model and Tom to emulate the traditional masculine role model.

Couple Therapy with Violent Couples

Couples' therapy with Violent Couples does not begin until each has participated in individual and group therapy to the extent that the couple is ready for conjoint sessions. Thus, once the violence in their relationship was revealed in therapy, Tom and Bev were seen individually. Throughout therapy a "no violence contract" was in effect whereby Tom had agreed to not become physically violent with Bev when angry. With the help of the therapist he had begun to identify other available means to handle and express his anger. Tom also participated in a group for men who abuse, while Bev joined a group for women who are abused. Both needed to better understand the cycle of abuse. Bev needed to be empowered, to begin to sense her own self-worth, power, and available options. Bev also needed to become sensitized to the broader implications of abuse for herself, the children, her husband, and the marital relationship. The women's group was effective in helping Bev achieve these goals.

Tom needed to understand his cycle of anger and its sources. He also needed to be motivated to handle his anger in the relationship without using physically or verbally aggressive means and to develop strategies and skills for doing so. In coming to understand the sources of his anger, Tom began to realize that his rigid understanding of manhood allowed him a limited range of emotions and few means of expressing these. In reality, his feelings were far more complex. With the support of the group of men who were engaged in similar struggles, Tom began the hard work of breaking through the denial. This could eventually lead to becoming more self-disclosing in his relationship with Bev which could potentially impact the cycle of anger manifested in their relationship.

With sufficient work in these areas accomplished in individual and group therapy, Bev and Tom resumed couples' therapy. Initially, their joint work would address the cycle of anger in their relationship. To do this effectively, they would need to infuse the individual work each had been doing into their marital relationship. Tom began by trying to integrate the non-physical means of expressing anger (that he had been exploring in his own therapy) into their relationship. He was now able to tell Bev how she could support him in not being physical with his anger. If she became less dependent on him, he could leave the house without her pleas that he stay even though he needed to go (e.g., when he felt he could not control his anger). Tom was asking Bev to see his separateness as non-threatening to their relationship.

More empowered by her work in group therapy, Bev no longer interpreted Tom's leaving as abandonment. She was also able to use this opportunity to help Tom see that her separateness was likewise not a threat to their relationship, (i.e., that she could spend time with a friend or family member and still see their marriage as her first priority).

As couples' therapy continued, Tom and Bev worked to develop their ability to resolve conflicts. With the aid of the therapist, they began to accurately hear what the other was communicating. Tom was surprised to learn how his aggression had silenced Bev. She had been neglecting to tell him what she thought because this might trigger his anger. In her silence, Bev was excluding Tom from her life and from the life of the family.

Tom was beginning to realize that he needed to become more flexible if their relationship was going to endure. He also found that he needed to confront his abuse as a child in order to quell the rage that dwelled within him. He realized that his anger at the father who abused him was the main source of his rage. However, he was surprised to discover his anger at his mother for failing to protect him. Therapy helped Tom realize that he was displacing his rage for his mother onto Bev. Understanding his own childhood abuse helped Tom develop more empathy for Bev and the abuse she had experienced. As Tom struggled to curb his violence, Bev struggled to overcome her anxiety and become more self-disclosing.

Building nonviolent means of conflict resolution involves multi-level interventions. At the same time a couple argues about an issue, they also convey important meta-messages. Differences and disagreement are to be expected in relationships. Moreover, anger is one way for couples to identify these areas. Tom and Bev also learned that not all differences and disagreements could or needed to be resolved. Some just need to be accepted.

Through the process of exploring new ways to express anger and resolve conflict, Tom and Bev began to differentiate from each other. Each could better see the other's separateness and they began to disclose how threatening this separateness was to each of them. Prior to these therapy sessions, the only time that Tom had allowed himself to be vulnerable to Bev was when he was remorseful for having abused her. He was now beginning to express his vulnerability without anger and within the safety of the therapy session. Bev realized that her image of "the strong male" had not given Tom room to be weak and vulnerable. Their self-disclosure was bringing them closer together without violence.

Case Analysis

Of all the varieties of couples, Violent Couples are among the most fused and undifferentiated. Their relationships are a caricature of a relationship lacking in intimacy. They are the extreme result of a relationship in which the lack of room for separateness and differences makes closeness and open disclosure impossible. While some Violent Couples extol the intimacy in their relationship (particularly during the "honeymoon" phase), they are often confusing intensity of emotion, even negative emotion, with intimacy.

Berman and Lief (1975) suggest that boundaries, power and intimacy are the three independent variables in interpersonal relationships. Violent couples, such as Bev and Tom, demonstrate the interrelationship between these variables. If power is used to violate boundaries (as in physical abuse), then intimacy in the relationship is impacted. The construction and maintenance of appropriate boundaries is an essential precondition for intimacy. Therefore, therapy must also focus on establishing clear, semi-permeable boundaries between the partners and between the couple and the world. In physically abusive relationships, these boundaries are consistently violated, thus disrupting a sense of mutual safety and inhibiting a healthy climate for intimacy.

Birtchnell (1986) identifies equality, separateness, flexibility, and closeness as requirements for sustaining marital intimacy. These factors provide a useful focus for therapy in working with Violent Couples who are lacking in all four of these areas. These partners are threatened by each other's separateness, adhere to rigid roles, and experience closeness only in response to their cycle of violence. For therapeutic gains to endure, couples' therapy must ultimately target second-order change by restructuring the ways the relationship is organized as well as how the couple relates to each other. Otherwise, abuse will recur.

Tom and Bev needed to see and accept each other as separate and different. Given their rigid, traditional views of male-female relationships, they each needed to develop a more flexible understanding of appropriate sex roles and acceptable feelings for men and for women. Both Bev and Tom needed to accept that Tom could be vulnerable. They both needed to accept that Bev could be strong and independent. Many of the strategies employed in working to assist this couple in eliminating physical violence from their relationship are the same as those used to lower barriers to intimacy.

CONCLUSIONS

Although their presenting problems differed, these four couples in therapy illustrate the relationship between the problems couples present in therapy and issues of intimacy in their relationship. They demonstrate how barriers to intimacy in one aspect of the relationship eventually impact intimacy in other areas as well. Intimacy is not without its risks. One vital role of the couples' therapist is to prepare the partners to take these risks.

Couples' therapy validates, rather than discounts, the essential self of each partner. Differentiation between partners is a necessary component of intimacy. The therapist must ensure that the partners can each maintain their separateness and individuality while still being intimately connected. Therapy works to maximize the ease with which the couple's relationship flows between times of closeness and separation.

Considerable debate is going on within professional circles as to what constitutes success in marital therapy. Some contend that unless the couple effectively resolves their conflicts and remains married, then therapy has been unsuccessful. Nevertheless, almost 60 percent of married couples experience some serious separation during the course of their marriage and nearly one out of every two new marriages will end in divorce.

Despite what some therapists believe, the goal of couples' therapy is not always to help the couple stay together. Sometimes the goal is to assist the partners to successfully uncouple. However, many couples' therapists lack a clear conceptual road map for this process. By better understanding the patterns and dynamics of marital separation and divorce, the therapist will be better able to guide individuals through this complex and painful process. Once it becomes clear that the partners are not going to continue as a couple, then the therapists' task is to facilitate adequate closure on the relationship.

REFERENCES

Berman, E. and Lief, H. 1975. Marital therapy from a psychiatric perspective: An overview. *American Journal of Psychiatry*, 132: 583-592.

Birtchnell, J. 1986. The imperfect attainment of intimacy: A key concept in marital therapy. *Journal of Family Therapy*, 8:153-172.

Clinebell, H. and Clinebell, C. 1970. *The intimate marriage*. New York: Harper & Row.

Frankel, B. 1982. Intimacy and conjoint marital therapy. In: Fisher, M. and Stricker, G. (Eds.) *Intimacy*. New York: Plenum.

Givelber, F. 1990. Object relations and the couple: Separation-individuation, intimacy and marriage. In: Chasin, R., Grunebaum, H., and Herzig, M. (Eds.) *One couple, four realities: Multiple perspectives on couple therapy*. New York: Guilford Press.

Haley, J. 1976. *Problem solving therapy: New strategies for effective family therapy*. San Francisco: Jossey-Bass.

Hof, L. and Treat, S. 1989. Marital assessment: Providing a framework for dyadic therapy. In Weeks, G. (Ed.) *Treating couples*. New York: Brunner/Mazel.

Karpal, M. 1976. Individuation: From fusion to dialogue. In: Gurman, A. (Ed.) *Casebook of marital therapy*. New York: Guilford Press.

Schaefer, M. and Olsen, D. 1981. Assessing intimacy: The PAIR inventory. *Journal of Marital and Family Therapy*, 7(1):47-60.

Schnarch, D. M. 1991. *Constructing the sexual crucible*. New York: Norton.

Schnarch, D. M. 1993. Inside the sexual crucible. In *The Family Therapy Networker*, 17(2):40-48.

Schwartz, V. 1989. Relational therapy with lesbian couples. In: Weeks, G. (Ed.) *Treating couples*. New York: Brunner/Mazel.

Treadway, D. 1993. In a world of their own. *The Family Therapy Networker*, 17(2):32-39.

Waring, E. 1984. The measurement of marital intimacy. *Journal of Marital and Family Therapy*, 10(2):185-192.

Waring, E. 1981. Facilitating marital intimacy through self-disclosure. *The American Journal of Family Therapy*, 9(4):33-42.

Chapter 8

After the Ball:
The Uncoupling Process

"Falling in love" is a widely romanticized notion in our society because free choice and affluence have made romantic love a common experience. Why then, is "falling out of love" not usually discussed or analyzed in any detail? According to Douglas and Atwell (1988) "falling in-love" normally involves an exhilarating emotional acceleration in which individuals inexorably pass a critical point of no return beyond which they have convinced themselves that they are undeniably and incurably "in-love." Some falling-out-of-love experiences follow the same path in precisely the opposite direction. The downward slopes of partnerships might better be termed "stumbling out of love" but are more commonly called "growing apart" or "growing away from each other." Yet rather than being swept off a cliff into an abyss of despair, most love partnerships go awry gradually, stumbling along from one crisis to another. The loving relationship must necessarily decay fairly severely before the former lovers begin to admit that the end is near. The experiences of "making up" and feeling "better than ever" can frequently hide the steady downward spiral.

ATTACHMENT OR SEPARATION?

Bowlby (1980) points out that as the individual emerges from adolescence and begins to establish an adult identity, attachment feelings direct themselves toward someone with whom later life may be shared. In early adolescence feelings of attachment and sexual strivings converge, so that the same person might be an object for both. In late adolescence and early adulthood it may also be important that a prospective attachment figure be someone compatible with the individual's newly developing identity. The prospective figure will have to be consistent not only with the individual's current views of him/herself, but also with perceptions of future selves. In a very real sense, the choice of an intimate partner may help to crystallize a particular identity.

During early adulthood, there may be two or more attachment figures. Yet, each time a significant emotional attachment is broken, no matter how sensible its ending may be, there will likely be feelings of desolation and self-questioning. With marriage, individuals assume that they are finally assured a permanently accessible attachment figure. This belief that marriage will ensure the accessibility of the attachment figure is perhaps one of the foremost attractions of marriage. Consequently, disappointment with this belief becomes an ongoing source of bitterness in separation (Bowlby, 1980).

Separation distress is a response to intolerable inaccessibility of the attachment figure. It is manifested in children through withdrawal of attention from other matters, tension, sadness, and sometimes tears. There may be longing for the lost figure, or angry or tearful demands for its return. The child may become diffusely apprehensive, worried by both stillness and noise. The child may resist falling asleep and may wake early. If the separation is protracted, the child may fall into despair (Bowlby, 1980).

In the same way that comfort and a sense of security tend to be associated with accessibility of an attachment figure, so distress tends to be associated with that figure's inaccessibility. Among infants, physical presence of the attachment figure is necessary to fend off distress. Once object permanence is achieved, physical presence becomes less necessary. However, it is uncanny how this process is reiterated in the early stages of adult love relationships. In the very beginning, partners absolutely crave the presence of their beloved. Being separated is intolerably painful. Then (once object permanence is achieved?) the partners are gradually able to be parted, but only for limited time periods. During the course of the marriage, partners (based upon their particular dependency needs and styles) may or may not function well without their spouse in close physical proximity. Contrast all this with impending marital separation in which the partners literally cannot wait to get the other out of their sight.

The symptoms of loneliness are like those of separation distress. Yet instead of longing for a particular figure, the individual longs for anyone who could love him/her and be loved in return. Instead of angrily or tearfully demanding the return of a particular figure, the individual laments the cold, uncaring world. The ending of a marriage produces separation distress, and later, as the other is relinquished as an object of attachment, loneliness (Weiss, 1980).

Throughout the separation process, the spouse and the troubled marriage occupy the separated individual's mind. Despite the anguish, it is common to long for the displaced spouse, though they may ruefully admit that they cannot understand why they should. Many want to hear about their former spouses and learn how they are doing. When they learn that the spouse is seeing someone new, they may feel jealous despite the fact that they know they should not. If they accidentally encounter the spouse, they may momentarily experience a fleeting flash of the old excitement. Should the spouse be among those at a party, or in the audience at a public event, even though some distance away, they can direct their attention to little else. This searching for the lost person is a natural and often involuntary aspect of the grieving process akin to learning to cope with the death of a relative. Separation also may produce episodes of deep sadness and regret for the lost chances for happiness.

This mourning for lost dreams runs very deep in the hearts and minds of separated partners. Over the years, each had consciously and unconsciously constructed a vision of what life together could and should be like. This vision was consistent with and integral to the overall life plan (complete with timelines, expected outcomes, and anticipated gratification). The disruption of the marriage is, at some levels, a narcissistic disappointment, because it effectively spoils one's overall life plan and thrusts the individual into chaos. Concomitant feelings of loss of control, direction, and meaning emerge in earnest. This psychic and emotional transition and reorientation constitutes a major source of separation distress. Although it is not entirely certain that separation and loss alone are responsible, severe depression is much more frequent among those who have recently been separated than among individuals of similar ages and socioeconomic status who have not (Weiss, 1975).

Another component of love is identification, the feeling that one's essential self is strongly associated with the other, so that when the other does well, one feels pleased for oneself, and when the other does badly, one suffers. If the other seems to need nurturance, then caring for the other and seeing the other happy can have the quality of caring for oneself, just as caring for one's children can gratify one's own dependent needs (Weiss, 1975).

There can be a sense of complementarity, in which the other is seen as having the capacities missing in the self, such as adeptness in social skills, or a strong sense of direction or purpose, etc. Thus, association with the other in some way completes the self. When some individuals talk about the loss of someone they love they often say, "I feel as though I had lost a part of myself." At another level, complementarity may act in another way. An individual may be reassured of his or her own worth because he or she is needed by the loved one. This provides an essential source of meaning and purpose for many partners.

Instead of giving rise to separation distress, sometimes the loss of the attachment figure produces a certain euphoria. Some separated partners report that for brief or extended time periods they felt just marvelous, as though they were walking on air. They acquired new self-confidence and higher self-esteem while feeling inspired by a world full of possibilities.

However, this tenuous sense of elation sometimes ended spontaneously, perhaps with the growing recognition that life without an intimate partner is ultimately unsatisfying. As a result, such euphoria often gives way to yet another level of separation distress and depression (Weiss, 1975).

ESCALATING CONFLICT

It is usually the protracted conflict of repeated confrontations which produces unbonding. Such bitter conflicts are obvious signs of falling out of love and divorcing. At a deeper level, the underlying purpose of these arguments is to progressively detach from one's former spouse.

The most serious emotional threat is experienced during those arguments in which the lover feels that the loved one intends to attack his or her basic sense of self. Such arguments deeply offend the individual's basic sense of trust, dignity, and selfhood.

The lover with whom you have communed deeply is the person who intuitively understands your deepest sense of security and insecurity and knows the secrets of your innermost self; the secrets of your security system of defenses; the secrets you hold most dear about your love partnership; and the secrets of your worldly affairs that can be used to undo you in your struggle with rivals and enemies (Douglas and Atwell, 1988). When your partner uses those secrets to attack you in the ways that can hurt the most–attacking the most personal and intimate parts of you–then this is experienced as a direct and vicious threat to your deepest and must vulnerable self.

Such attacks may be done as a provocation to goad one's partner into counterattacking, thereby "justifying" escalation of the love-war by counterattacking with even more deadly weapons, all the while drifting toward unbonding and divorce. Once the self feels sufficiently threatened, the counterattacks inevitably intensify. This emotional warfare soon escalates beyond all reason with the combatants launching massive personal attacks at the other's most vulnerable areas without regard for their own emotional safety or the long-term effects on their relationships (Douglas and Atwell, 1988).

Just as there appears to be a crucial point in the upward spiral of romantic love beyond which the lovers lose control, so there is a fatal zone in unbonding beyond which the accelerating downward spiral is very rapid and the partners cannot control it, regardless of their best intentions.

The "gray-lens effect" comes increasingly into play and mythifies the former partners. Each then seems far more threatening to the other than is actually the case. In the end, they are so concerned with protecting their own self-image and ego-integrity that they become very spiteful, striking out to destroy the other so the other cannot destroy them. That is when they spend hours arguing over who gets the blender in the divorce settlement. The actual value of the blender has nothing to do with the actual reason for the argument, whereas the protection of one's ego has everything to do with it. The relationship has gone from being a cooperative venture with shared outcomes, to a zero-sum game in which a victory by one automatically means a loss for the other.

CATASTROPHIC BREAKS

Just as one can suddenly fall in love, so one can just as suddenly fall into contempt. There are certain things one's partner can do or say to another which cannot and will not be forgiven. Such an incident can totally reorganize the partner's basic perceptions and feelings about the other. (As one woman put it "After he did that, I suddenly realized that he wasn't the person I always thought he was.")

Catastrophic breaks are frequently the result of one giant argument, though on occasion they are more the result of a misunderstanding of one's self and all the fate-laden meanings of unbonding and divorce (Douglas and Atwell, 1988). Usually such catastrophic breaks are initiated by only one of the partners. Frequently, this is one partner's way of beginning the unbonding process, as in the classic "Dear John" (Jill) letter in which the partner still in-love has been unaware that the other was unbonding and heading for termination. Though at some level the receiving partner may have been vaguely aware that something was "wrong," the sudden revelation and departure of the loved one comes as a tremendous surprise. Upon receipt of such a letter, the unwitting partner frequently reacts with shock and dismay. The "receiving" partner typically feels hurt, angry, and quite powerless because s/he had no voice in the decision to terminate the relationship. Such letters seldom arrive with room for negotiation or rebuttal.

Catastrophic breaks do not effectively unbond intimate partners because protracted conflict is necessary to "free" the sense of self from the fusion with the other. The mere passage of time (even decades) only leads to the love fusion falling into dormancy, lying there ready to spring into life. Moreover, it is quite possible that the "deserted" partner will tend to idealize the former lover over time. However, just as falling in love at first sight does not emotionally bond an individual with the other's sense of self, so suddenly falling out of love does not involve a true unbonding. Emotional unbonding occurs largely independent of the loss of adoration. Even when former lovers have "evolved" to "mutual hatred" they may still feel very "close" to one another and care for each other when either is endangered or hurt (Douglas and Atwell, 1988).

In an asymmetric catastrophic break, the victim often still suffers from the self-validating "pink-lens effect." Consequently, victims refuse to believe that the loved one no longer loves them, despite what the "leaver" may say. The remaining partner feels victimized and urges the former lover to reconsider. They dream obsessively both day and night of their erstwhile partner's return and often refuse to remove themselves from the site of last communion. They firmly believe deep down that their partner will come to his/her senses and return, at which point all will be forgiven. It is a time of tremendous psychic pain, excessive introspection, emotional desperation, and "magical thinking." While one's rational mind recognizes the reality of the end of the relationship, the emotional self is still unwilling and unable to accept it. The persistence of such unrealistic hope either demonstrates the importance of the now-departed partner or shows a significant lack of "reality orientation." It is ironic that the deserted partner (due perhaps to his/her own ambivalence or fear) sometimes confuses the former with the latter.

As the freshly parted pair spiral downward to mutual unbonding madness, the initiator is just as subject to this obsessive mythification process in reverse. For example, he/she may insist that: "No, we never loved each other–the whole thing was a mistake from the word go!" At other times the initiator often constructs the illusion of an idealized romantic lover waiting just beyond the magic portal of freedom. Initiators suffer both guilt and the underlying agony of unbonding. These seem to feed on each other and produce massive mythification alternating between pink hopes for deliverance and gray dreads of doom (Douglas and Atwell, 1988).

Rehearsing for Separation

Many couples in severe marital distress repeat the pattern of fighting, separation, and reconciliation over and over. Partners are caught in the throes of not being able to live with him/her, and not being able to live without him/her. Conflict may arise over the separation itself, with one partner wanting the marriage to continue, while the other wants to withdraw. This confounding emotional crucible has effects throughout their lives. While apart, partners obsess about the relationship, which only exacerbates their anger and anxiety. Because of the turmoil and embarrassment, they start cutting themselves off from friends and colleagues. Prior to the actual separation, they may almost totally isolate themselves, shut away from their former social world and suffering immensely. This process may go on for months even after separation.

Virtually all married couples bicker at times. During these interchanges, one spouse acts to dampen the anxiety or enthusiasm of the other by questioning or denying the partner's appraisal or view of the situation. The meta-message of such destructive interchanges may contain inferences intended to diminish or damage the spouse. These may be motivated by anger; a desire for revenge (conscious or unconscious); and/or a desire to neutralize the spouse's attacks. Because of each partner's intimate knowledge of the other's vulnerabilities, to one degree or another, these attacks usually find their mark. Angry spouses will tailor their respective indictments to the other's actual characteristics, and may draw support for them from confidences given in better times. Hence, such indictments are difficult to dismiss as they appear to be based on strong evidence; are made by the person in the best position to know; and are repeated at every opportunity.

The Erosion of Love

When the marriage is going badly, almost every aspect of the couple's early romantic love may come under attack. The veneer of idealization fades under the repeated exposure to the routines of daily life. Disappointment and betrayal erode trust. Feelings of identification give way to seeing the other as critic and antagonist. Instead of feeling reassured and enhanced by their relationship, severely conflicted partners begin to feel oppressed and diminished by it.

At the outset of the love relationship was the partner's sense that the other person is good, trustworthy, caring, and worthy of respect. According to Weiss (1975), the desire to vicariously obtain those traits which one lacks is probably very important to the choice to date and later marry this person. The prospective loss of that person also signifies the loss of these wished-for traits and their attendant psychic rewards. Such idealization undoubtedly involves projection onto the other of some aspect of one's wished-for self. Though there are different kinds of idealization, depending on what aspect of the wished-for self is projected, any of them may make one feel that association with the idealized figure is self-enhancing.

By the time a married couple separates, their fondness for each other has eroded considerably and is fast being replaced by many far less-flattering emotions and perceptions. The spouse's faults will often be much clearer than their virtues. Trust has given way to mistrust. Feelings of disappointment and betrayal have supplanted the romantic idealizations of earlier days. Although their love for one another has faded, ironically enough, the partners' sense of emotional attachment and bonding may well remain. They may squabble whenever they are in the same room. But after all that has happened, with all the bitterness they feel, with so much of their love now dissipated, former partners still feel deeply attached to one another. Why? They have shared so much important history together. However strife-ridden or unhappy, marital partners have jointly endured the pain and pleasure of sharing their lives.

For women who have been socialized to derive their status and self-worth through their husbands, the loss is likewise overwhelming. With so much of female identity still tied up with caretaking and nurturing their family, the loss of this role can be devastating. Despite the fact that women's roles are changing, it would perhaps be more accurate to say that women's roles have been expanding. In addition to all the traditional responsibilities with home and family, women have added job and profession to their ever-expanding list of "things to do today." On an emotional level, the vast majority of women still put their family's needs first–above their own and above their job. On the other hand, when push comes to shove, men will often say that the family comes first, but behave to the contrary.

One's marital identity is deeply connected to one's sense of self, beyond the obvious symbols such as wedding rings and joint checking accounts. Marriage is a vital part of who partners believe themselves to be. Some partners go beyond the more usual integration of the marriage into the self. Their sense of meaning and self-worth are directly linked to their spouses. When their marriages end, they feel that they have lost more than just the relationship, they feel they have lost themselves almost entirely (Weiss, 1975).

THE PAIN OF MARITAL SEPARATION

Marital separation means different things to different people. Often occurring after several major confrontations over a period of month or years, marital separation can sometimes be a last ditch effort to save the marriage. On the other hand, it may be an ominous prelude to divorce. Many couples work assiduously to "iron out" the difficulties in the marriage prior to resorting to leaving. Some couples attempt a "structured separation" (which may be initiated by a couples' therapist) with specific goals and parameters during the separation period. Other couples opt for a "trial separation," which offers each a chance to see what living apart feels like. Still others begin their marital separation by moving to separate bedrooms or different parts of the house. Regardless of these arrangements, marital separation typically creates sadness, confusion, and additional strife. It is a time of grave insecurity about one's future happiness or even survival. The grief consequent to the traumatic loss of one's lifemate invariably leads to depression and despair.

To cope with the trauma of marital separation, the separated spouses must necessarily come to terms with the progressive unraveling of their marriage. As Weiss (1975) put it, they develop a historical account, a history of the marital failure in which they mentally arrange significant events chronologically. They determine what each spouse did and did not do to contribute to the dissolution of the relationship. Then they affix and allocate blame. Once in order, this historical account enables individuals to begin coping with what probably will be one of the hardest transitions of their lives.

This account is of major psychological importance to the separated. Not only does it settle the issue of who was responsible for what, but it imposes a plot structure with a beginning, middle, and end on the confused marital events that preceded the separation. Thus, it organizes the events into a conceptually manageable entity. Once understood in this way, the events can be dealt with. They can be seen as outcomes of identifiable causes and eventually as part of the past, hence external to the individual's present self (Weiss, 1975).

This description is hardly an objective and impartial description. Moreover, the accounts of a failed marriage offered by a husband and by a wife are likely to disagree, not only in that they report different versions of the same events, but in that they also report different events. The uninitiated listener who first heard the husband's account and then heard the wife's might not realize that both stories described the same marriage.

In other instances, marital separation can be a relief. Not having to live with a spouse whom one no longer loves in a relationship one no longer believes in, can potentially lift a tremendous burden from one's shoulders. There is sometimes a sudden sense of enhanced freedom–freedom to start fresh and form a new identity or to establish a new and more satisfactory place in this world.

People who separate are often more reluctant to report the end of their marriages to their kin than to friends, neighbors, or, indeed, to anyone else, (with the possible exception of their children). The anticipated discomfort of telling family is sometimes sufficient to hold individuals in bad marriages long after they would otherwise have abandoned them.

Marital separation is a multidimensional process which drastically alters one's fundamental sense of family in new and often undesired ways. It is a major transition which realigns and reorganizes one's assumptions and perceptions of all intimate relationships. Virtually no one gets married expecting to end up separated or divorced. Despite overwhelming statistical evidence to the contrary, couples caught up in the unreality of romantic love effectively convince themselves that "divorce is something that happens to other people, not to me."

Many of these same couples later end up in the therapists' office in a state of shock, anger, protest, and despair. Their lives are falling apart before their eyes and an alarming percentage of them did not see it coming, especially the men. It would appear that men's ability for denial and self-deception is formidable indeed. Sometimes the couple enters the therapists' office and the wife says of the stunned husband, "I've been trying to tell him for years that things had to change, but he just wouldn't listen."

The harsh impact of separation is characteristic of the mid-separation period. As in early separation, the emotional distress is still felt. However, now it is compounded by the daily management tasks of living in two separate households. The beginning attempts at reorganization often highlight the importance of the absent spouse. The couple system now faces a deficit in structure. The person who has occupied a position in the system with attendant role responsibilities has left the system. Habituated roles had been negotiated and established early in the relationship with little thought required by the actors occupying the position. Suddenly, when these habitual ways of interacting are disrupted by the absence of an actor, thought is needed to realign both the tasks and relationships. This process of realignment passes through a series of transitions where there is much testing and experimenting (Ahrons and Rodgers, 1987).

THE DIVORCE PROCESS

Divorce always involves loss and grieving. In fact, descriptions of divorce in terms of loss and the recovery process as akin to mourning permeate the divorce literature. But while everyone experiences loss, some are less able to tolerate its pain.

Sometimes the spouse reexperiences a trauma associated with a specific loss in the past. This may be the loss of a child (through kidnapping, death, abortion, or adoption). Or it may be separation from one's own parents, sibling, or family (as a consequence of divorce, death, war, and forced migration). The loss of the spouse reawakens as-yet-unmastered losses, and the intense emotions that surround them. In this way, the earlier loss becomes more difficult to resolve because the psychic pain is compounded. Also, it is difficult to sort out past from current losses. According to Johnston and Campbell (1988), the second type derives from long-standing personal issues in separation and individuation of the spouse from his or her own parents or caregivers. Due to early, oft-repeated experiences of severe deprivation, abandonment, neglect, and abuse, or equally extreme indulgence and overprotectiveness, these individuals are excessively dependent or prone to fuse their identities with others. The present divorce, therefore, is experienced as yet another abandonment and a serious threat to their survival. The repeated disputes with the ex-spouses symbolically represent their often conflicted struggle to separate and exist as separate individuals.

The defensive use of custody and visitation disputes to ward off the painful loss, sadness, and loneliness of the divorce is common to both types–reactivated loss and separation-individuation. To varying degrees, such parents are unable to tolerate and accept the pain of the loss of separation from the spouse or child. As a result, they are unable to mourn, grieve, and let go of the child, spouse, or the marriage itself (Johnston and Campbell, 1988).

Some partners attempt to prevent the actual loss from occurring by prolonging or clinging to the marriage. They go to great lengths to set up roadblocks to ending the marriage, refusing to settle anything, including plans for their children. Others try to control the speed of the divorce and sometimes use mediation and counseling to put off the impending loss.

In an attempt to ward off the pain of loss, parents sometimes turn to their children as emotional replacements for the departed spouse. They become emotionally dependent and lean on their children to soften the pain and use the children as companions or confidantes. The intensity of their need for the child as surrogate parent or spouse increases in direct proportion to the stress of the divorce and the parent's own vulnerabilities.

Very often, spouses are not even aware that they are substituting the child for the recently departed spouse. For example, it is not uncommon for a woman to tell her son, "With Dad gone, you're the man of the house now." Some parents use their children as a means of staying connected to the ex-spouse. For example, they insist on increased visits or being present at the child's exchange to ensure their own (not the child's) contact with their ex-mate. Other parents over-identify to varying degrees with their children and project their intolerance of sadness and fears of being alone onto the children. They then seek to protect their children from distressful emotion and consciously view the custody suit as a means of doing so. In the end, the child's distress and their own loneliness is ameliorated in this flurry of protective activity (Johnston and Campbell, 1988).

The Reconstruction of Personal Identity

As Weiss states, with the end of their marriages, most divorced partners suffer the loss of some of the social scaffolding on which their self-definition had rested. They not only lose a partner but also the social definitions associated with marriage. They no longer have the same access to children, family, and friends. Partners may no longer feel themselves to be quite the same people they had been when they were married. In a very real sense partners lose a part of their personal history when uncoupling which can never be fully reclaimed. While the memories of times past may remain without the other to affirm and bear witness to their past, the memories lose a certain saliency and are more apt to fade. The obvious exception occurs when there are children who can also serve many of the same functions.

After divorce, individuals experience some loss of their former self-definitions, but have not yet gained new ones. They are caught in limbo between who they were and the person they have yet to become. While the former is typically well known, the latter is often virtually unknown. Such uncertainty about who one will now become further loosens the psychic moorings on the separated partners' sense of security.

It is interesting to observe individuals at this juncture of the divorce process tentatively experimenting with creating a new self. Changes in clothes, habits, rituals, etc., portend a shift in identity. Such experimentation sometimes produces what may have formerly been deemed unexpected behavior for that particular person. This is an important phase in rejecting the "old self" in favor of a "new, improved self." In particular, this "new improved self" should now possess the missing traits so fastidiously enumerated by one's former spouse which have allegedly contributed to the "failure of the marriage." As one former client put it, "My husband always claimed that I couldn't be spontaneous. So now, I'm flying to Cancun with a girlfriend tomorrow strictly on an impulse." Psychically, this woman is still fighting an old battle with her now-absent spouse in order to prove that he was "dead wrong about her alleged lack of spontaneity." In fact, she said, "He was dead wrong about a lot of things. Too bad. He had his chance and it's too late now."

Many spouses report a need to "try again" after being apart for a while. The daily stresses of living separately become intolerable, thus highlighting the positive aspects of the marriage and making it appear more acceptable. For many parents, children's pleas for Daddy to come home may be more painful than the parent can bear. Hence, another attempt to put the family back together again may commence (Ahrons and Rodgers, 1987).

MALE AND FEMALE INTERPRETATIONS OF DIVORCE

When asked why they divorced, former partners often refer to a "lack of communication." In so doing, they are trying to make sense of private experience by drawing on an ethic and vocabulary of love that is peculiar to contemporary American culture. This factor is identified more often by women than men. According to Reissman (1990), nearly two-thirds of women studied said they did not get the kind of "emotional intimacy" they expected from their husbands–inner connectedness, warmth, and sharing, and/or communicating deeply and closely. It is not uncommon for divorced men and women to later insist that they had "nothing in common" with their former spouse. The "gray-lens effect" may account for a part of this perception.

Joint activities and shared leisure are expected, because they solidify the marital bond. Looking back, many formerly married partners explain the dissolution of their marriages in terms of "problems with companionship and its corollary complaint–that the commitment to the marital tie was not primary enough" (Reissman, 1990). However, women interpret the relationship between primacy and companionship differently from men. Part of this may be explained by the contrasting ways in which men and women have been socialized to behave in intimate relationships (instrumental versus expressive).

Women and men have different ideas about how emotional intimacy, primacy, companionship, and sexual fulfillment ought to come about. For women, marriage flounders because husbands are not emotionally expressive and intimate in the ways wives expect them to be. This expressive, intimate quality is central to many women's vision of a "happy marriage." Men's explanations differ dramatically. To many of them, their marriage failed because other relationships (i.e., children, kin, and friends) were not subordinated to it. The marital relationship was not primary enough to the wife (or at least not primary in the ways that her husband wanted). For both husbands and wives there was a failure in companionship.

Moreover, fulfilling the essential requirements of the companionate marriage depends on equality between husbands and wives. Yet since institutionalized roles call for role differences, neither husbands nor wives have been socialized to be equals. As providers, men have diffuse power in the family and this automatically makes husbands and wives unequal. Wives, in turn, may encourage segregation of roles along traditional lines early in marriage, defining housework and children as their exclusive domain. Within this uneven context, women become victims and are subordinated within the marital relationship (Reissman, 1990).

When a marriage ends, differing vocabularies of emotion are available to women and men. Some men are functionally illiterate in articulating complex emotions and their attendant implications for themselves, their spouse, and the relationship. As Reissman points out, just as women and men interpret their marriage differently, they likewise interpret their divorce differently. How much these interpretations vary reveals just how socially constructed emotions are. Although they do not score high as a group on depression inventories, men are far from immune to the harmful emotional effects of marital dissolution. Men do not report the usual symptoms of depression, because such symptoms are not the culturally approved idioms for males. Expressing fear and insecurity for example, might well be viewed as a sign of weakness for traditional males, while for women, expressing such feelings remains far more socially acceptable. So the notion that men adjust to divorce differently than women needs to be empirically reexamined in light of their differing "genderlects."

Reissman also postulates that the psychological distress in divorce is socially produced for women in a very different way than it is for men. For men, the issues are also complex, and likewise rooted in the norms and traditions of North American culture. Masculinity is defined and institutionally situated in such a way that certain outcomes are more likely. At the same time that the culture provides for men's material advantage, it does not provide for their emotional development or expression. Thus, men are deprived of a language for their feelings. Talking about emotions remains the exclusive domain of women (Reissman, 1990).

For women, stress comes mainly from the sudden and significant drop in income and material well-being. Living and parenting with far fewer resources is a major source of distress for divorcing women. Interestingly, North American culture also supports the emotional demoralization of women by supplying them with a language for emotions while simultaneously failing to provide for the material distress that fosters many of those emotions.

Divorce demands that one break existing modes of thinking and reclaim aspects of the self that had been given over to the other to manage. Both men and women question how and if they can survive on their own. Each constructs accounts to "prove" that they can manage, but because men's and women's dependency in marriage is so different, so are men's and women's understandings of divorce.

In some ways, the cultural emphasis on individuality and finding oneself has made it easier for spouses to abandon their marital commitment under the heading of "finding oneself" or "seeking personal growth and fulfillment." Americans appear to view such a search as an almost inalienable right. Central to such an existential journey is the concept of "freedom." However, on closer scrutiny, men and women appear to mean very different things by "freedom." What's more, they appear to manifest it in very different ways (Reissman, 1990).

The concept of freedom is particularly important to women who have been physically abused by husbands, though women also value escape from subtler forms of male authority. As Bellah et al. (1985), state, the sharing and commitment in a love relationship sometimes seems to swallow up the person making her (more often than him) lose sight of her own interests, opinions, and desires. Divorced women frequently draw from these cultural themes and recall their marriages as being filled with constraint, subservience, and vulnerability to the authority of husbands. From this perspective, they see divorce as an opportunity to "take back their lives."

One unanticipated benefit of divorce is the forced opportunity to strengthen ties with kin, construct social networks that provide material and emotional aid, and generally intensify their relationships with others (Reissman, 1990). This process enables women to construct a new self after divorce through social relationships. Moreover, they measure their personal growth by contrasting the way they are now with the way they were during the marriage.

Many have argued that identity and intimacy are inextricably fused in women, with intimate relations playing a central role in women's sense of who they are. Because their married identities were fused with intimacy, being divorced means women are free to have their own separate identities. Yet this newfound freedom can be intimidating or even downright frightening to those who are not used to it. After spending years constricted by the needs of children and husband, some women have great difficulty adjusting to and enjoying their sudden autonomy. As one recently divorced woman put it, "I'm so used to checking with my husband and children before I do anything, that it feels a little strange to suddenly be on my own."

Reissman also found that as a group, men tend to interpret their divorces less positively than women do. Some 15 percent of these formerly married men saw no benefits to divorce whatsoever. Many men defined divorce as a personal failure.

Jobs often become the main arena in which divorced men find meaning. For middle-class males, careers have become a central preoccupation. Many divorced men speak of pouring energy into the job to fill time and evade loneliness. The loss of marriage and family thrusts men into a major crisis about the purpose, meaning, and direction of their lives. It also forces them to face those aspects of themselves which have been glazed over or handled by their wife during the marriage.

Unlike women, who tend to have a variety of confiding relationships, men begin to realize they have lost their primary confidante with divorce. Although sexual partners may be available, men soon see that a deeper bond is now missing from their lives. Men miss not having someone there to reconstitute family for them. In the absence of a close relationship, men rediscover the value of relationships. This explains why some divorced men find spending time alone so difficult. Their previous self-image as self-reliant has been cast into question. While many women become more autonomous through the crisis of divorce, it appears that some men actually become more relational.

Partners who divorce leave marriages that did not live up to their definition of what marriage should provide. Using culturally shared vocabularies and structures, partners construct narrative accounts to explain and persuade listeners that their definitions of the divorce are correct.

Members of a culture also interpret what goes on around them, assign motives, and develop shared understandings of social life. In the case of divorce, the collective definition is usually negative as reflected by the descriptive language. Divorce is termed a "social problem," as evidenced by the "broken families" (as opposed to "intact families"). "Whole families" have a husband and wife whereas those headed by single parents are "broken." Such value-laden cultural definitions clearly stigmatize so-called "non-traditional families," even though such families are now in the statistical majority (Hartman and Laird, 1983).

Men and women make sense of their divorces by comparing it to the so-called "ideal marriage" which supposedly provides intimacy, primacy, and companionship, as well as sex in great abundance. Although women and men are alike in noting these three aspects, they tend to define and value each somewhat differently. This suggests that women and men construct their perceptions of marriage quite differently. The ideology of the companionate marriage is, in fact, two ideologies–his and hers–with separate perceptions and beliefs forming the basis each gender uses to explain what went wrong.

Filing for Constructive Divorce

No partners endure the trauma of unbonding without winding up with emotional scar tissue in order to protect them from future traumas. Yet the price of such protection is not being able to fuse as quickly or deeply the next time. Once wounded in the wars of love, partners emerge less secure about their lovability and they carry the emotional scars as permanent reminders of their ill-fated journey.

According to Kressel and Deutsch (1981) the minimal criterion for a constructive divorce is the absence of strong, unrelenting feelings of failure and self-disparagement. "Successful divorce" also entails increased self-understanding, the ability to form satisfying new intimate relationships, and a heightened sense of personal competence. This personal and interpersonal growth results from achieving adequate closure on the relationship. The final indication of such growth is often seen as one's ability not to repeat the same mistakes made in the prior marriage.

The "same-mistake twice" syndrome can be avoided by gaining insight into one's unconscious conflicts and distortions and appreciating one's contribution to the dysfunctional behavior in the old marriage. One major obstacle to a constructive divorce is the turmoil of psychic divorce. Difficult divorces are more likely when one spouse is eager to end the marriage while the other is reluctant to do so. This uneven motivation is linked not only to a changing balance of affection but to a perceived imbalance in post-divorce prospects. For example, a divorced man of forty may just be reaching the peak of his professional and financial attainments. Moreover, the statistical odds for single men in his age group dating and remarrying are clearly in his favor. In short, his prospects appear very good. Not so for his homemaker wife with custody of their two minor children. She may have cause to suspect that her social and financial situation after divorce will be far less advantageous and satisfying.

Partners who wish to end the marriage often feel very guilty about abandoning their spouse. Kressel and Deutsch (1981) explain that this may inhibit a candid discussion between them because the "initiator" would rather avoid the issue. Once the initiator finally broaches the topic of divorce, guilt and a strong desire to leave the relationship may produce a dangerous mindset of "settlement at any cost." Not coincidentally, the settlement terms demanded by the spouse who wishes to keep the marriage may escalate. Such escalating and sometimes unreasonable demands may be motivated by feelings of anger, humiliation, and revenge coupled with anxiety at the prospects of a bleak and unchosen future. At another level, this may also be a strategy to prolong the marriage and ultimately prevent the marital breakup.

A constructive divorce is also hindered so long as partners are heavily invested in casting blame or in bringing up long past grievances. These "Virginia Woolf" couples are so intent on wounding one another that neither is able to rationally achieve closure on the relationship.

It also appears that for divorcing couples with minor children the potential for a destructive divorce is greatly increased. First, the disjointed couple must plan for the children's current and future welfare. Such planning is complex and difficult under the best of circumstances let alone during the separation/divorce process. Many parents also feel extremely guilty over the potentially devastating impact the divorce may have on their children's emotional development. Some of this damage may well be real, while some may be exaggerated. Children are often masterful at exploiting such circumstances for their own advantage. It is the age-old game of playing Mom against Dad with a new twist since they no longer live together. It is the fear of damaging one's children which engenders the most anguish for loving parents. At many levels, the children are aware of this, and deliberately or not, many do not hesitate to triangulate their parents. Guilt may also result in defensive anger at the mate, or uncritical acceptance of any childcare proposals, however ill-conceived. Children also provide an almost irresistible opportunity for both spouses to embellish their feelings of anger and bitterness toward one another. It may be difficult to deescalate such a conflict, because its true roots are not openly acknowledged.

Kressel and Deutsch (1981) also point out that criticism of divorce lawyers is a recurring theme amongst divorcing couples. Under the current legal system lawyers are under a professional obligation to defend their clients' interests and attack those of the spouse. This invariably creates an adversarial climate. From the therapeutic perspective, this is the least desirable posture imaginable. In addition, lawyers are largely untrained in marital or family therapy. As a result, they may unwittingly contribute to the marital dysfunction rather than assuaging it. Last, the lawyer's objectivity may be compromised by financial considerations, since his fee is contingent on the amount of time and energy required to produce a final settlement.

Case Example: Cassandra and Michael

Cassandra and Michael grew up in the same working-class neighborhood. Their families had been friends for years. When Michael first met Cassandra at a friend's party, he was fifteen years old and she was twelve. Since they were both so young and attended different schools, they did not really have much contact over the next several years. After Michael graduated from college eight years later, he inadvertently ran into her at a local bar near their hometown. For Michael, it was pretty much "love at first sight" (or "second sight," as it were). Although Cassandra's reaction was somewhat less enthusiastic, they started dating and were eventually married about two years later.

For the wedding, Michael stubbornly insisted on a small, simple civil ceremony to which only their parents were invited. He was intent on not turning their wedding into a "circus" and also wasn't particularly fond of all of Cassandra's relatives. Cassandra reluctantly agreed, even though she was deeply disappointed at being deprived of her "day in the sun." She had always envisioned a large Catholic wedding complete with bridesmaids, a huge wedding reception, and all the attendant hoopla. Clearly, this marriage had started off on the wrong foot.

At the outset of their marriage, Michael attended graduate school while Cassandra was completing her teaching degree. The first two years seemed happy enough. Each was in school living the carefree student life. However, after Cassandra's graduation, the only teaching job she could find was back in their hometown some 75 miles away. Since elementary teaching jobs were hard to find and they needed the money, Cassandra was obliged to accept the position. She would stay with her parents during the week and return home on weekends. This proved to be a fateful decision because over time this commuter arrangement began to weaken the bonds of the relationship. Intimacy waned. Cassandra not only got more and more involved with her job, but also got drawn back into her family of origin. Meanwhile, Michael got increasingly involved with his studies and classmates. Their lives began to drift in different directions. Upon graduation, Michael found a job near Cassandra's and moved back with her to their hometown. At least he and Cassandra would once again be living together full-time. However, Michael grew increasingly unhappy with his new job, not to mention living back in their hometown. This was not a place that he ever enjoyed and he began to remember all the reasons he had moved away in the first place.

The marriage was becoming increasingly unhappy for each. They argued more often and more angrily. Their sexual relationship progressively deteriorated. Michael then lost his job and was unemployed. As a reaction to his life and his marriage spinning out of control, Michael became even more controlling. Cassandra began to feel smothered and engulfed. Her bitterness and resentment grew and her love for Michael steadily eroded. Michael and Cassandra continued to drift apart. After months of intense arguing, Michael decided that he could no longer survive living in their hometown. He accepted a new job some 40 miles away (equidistant between their current apartment and his old college town). Finally he could stand it no longer, so on April 1st he moved back to the town where they had first lived in the early days of their marriage. Michael desperately hoped that Cassandra loved him enough to move back with him once her school year was over. However, this was not to be. She interpreted his "moving out" as the final straw for their troubled marriage. "You moved out on me," she stated flatly. This gave her the excuse she was looking for to finally escape what she viewed as a stifling and strife-ridden relationship. Besides, why should she leave a perfectly good job to pursue a marriage which was at best, deeply troubled and highly unstable?

Their separation and divorce went through the usual turmoil and mutually destructive process with plenty of bitterness, anger, and pain on both sides. Marital therapy had already been attempted, but to no avail. Cassandra was not particularly interested in analyzing and repairing the badly damaged marital relationship. Basically, she just wanted out. Sensing the inevitable, Michael reluctantly filed for divorce. After some additional bickering, a settlement was reached and some months later, it was over. Or was it?

When their marriage ended Cassandra insisted that she did not love Michael anymore. In fact, she honestly questioned whether she ever did. Michael was deeply wounded by this. Certainly, their life goals, values, and interpersonal styles were quite different. But he insisted that he still loved her and could not accept that she no longer loved him. Her anger and bitterness had eroded any positive feelings she once may have had and she had absolutely no interest in having any further contact with him–ever.

This was emotionally devastating for Michael who could not understand how she could feel the way she did. What Michael didn't realize at the time was how painful this all was for Cassandra. She was emotionally torn up about ending her marriage, but was utterly convinced that remaining with Michael would mean giving up too many of her essential life goals, including, she believed, having a family. In part, she was also afraid that her continued rejections would hurt Michael even more than she already had.

Ultimately, Cassandra decided to "close the door entirely" on the relationship. It was too painful for her to reopen such deep wounds. She decided that it was best to have no further contact whatsoever with Michael. For his part, Michael very much wanted to maintain some manner of friendly contact and saw her decision as immature and avoidant.

In her mind, she had suffered enough and it was time to move on with her life. For Michael, it left him feeling dazed, confused, powerless, and utterly dismayed. It was very much Michael's style to want to analyze the problems in the relationship and work them through. This trait ended up driving Cassandra crazy. She concluded that he and the marriage were the problem. By getting out, she would free herself to discover and become her own person (as opposed to the person that Michael wanted her to be). It would also allow her to find a more compatible partner whose values and life goals were more congruent with her own. She eventually did so and still teaches at the very same elementary school some 15 years later.

Case Analysis

Unfortunately, because of the abrupt and total emotional cut-off, Michael and Cassandra were not able to achieve adequate closure on their marital relationship. Each was left to live with the unresolved pain and mourning which accompanies such a mutually destructive ending.

As with the case example, most marital break-ups do not achieve adequate closure. They end abruptly and painfully, lacking resolution and leaving lasting emotional scars on both partners. These scars can significantly interfere with one's subsequent ability to initiate and sustain intimate relationships. Because individuals have been emotionally damaged, they go to great lengths to protect their vulnerabilities. This may manifest itself in a lack of trust, a lack of self-disclosure, and/or a reluctance to form future emotional dependencies.

By themselves, most couples are unable to achieve a constructive divorce. Couples' therapy aimed at gaining adequate closure on the relationship would be highly desirable. However, with the residual anger and bitterness which frequently characterize marital break-ups, partners (like Cassandra) are often unwilling to spend time resolving issues in a relationship that they are eager to leave.

THE BROADER IMPLICATIONS OF DIVORCE

Although Americans will usually deny the fact that "their" marriage has an almost even chance of ending in divorce, most people readily acknowledge that the rising rate of marital separation and divorce is a serious social problem and a possible threat to the prevailing cultural values. The larger political debate over the place of the family in today's turbulent society raises a variety of troubling questions for and about our society and collective future.

Given that so many people end marriages and that it is so easy to do, it is ironic that individuals must take pains to make sense of divorce–to interpret it to themselves and to others. Reissman (1990) points out that legally, divorce has become an administrative action and is no longer a moral or judicial action. Yet while statistically normal, divorce is not normative in a sociological sense. Marriage is more popular than ever. The rituals and symbolism that surround weddings are conspicuously absent with divorce. Such rituals carry powerful meanings about role expectations as well as perpetuate those cultural beliefs necessary to maintaining a particular social order. Elaborate wedding customs have persisted for generations. The language of the ceremony reflects the belief and cultural value that the union will be permanent–"until death do us part." Even in so-called non-traditional weddings or for couples who themselves were raised with divorce, the expectation of "forever" endures.

Although the belief in living happily ever after is being replaced by the notion that marriage is "work," commitment still plays a central role in marriage. Despite massive changes in other aspects of family life, marriage continues to be something that people take very seriously. Divorce challenges the prevailing cultural value. It is not surprising that in spite of all the rhetoric of liberalization, most divorcing partners still consider themselves somewhat deviant. They often feel as if they have failed. In particular, women who have been raised to believe that "fixing the relationship" was their responsibility feel tremendous guilt when it ends. Never mind that they may have tried in earnest to repair it for the last twenty years. The ideology of women's role and place has changed, but the myth of marriage-as-forever has remained more or less intact.

Divorce has become a public policy issue because of its devastating impact on the economic well-being of families. According to Reissman (1990), children of divorce, along with their mothers, are disproportionately poor, and depend more and more on the social welfare system. In 1983, 13 percent of the children in two-parent families lived below the poverty line, whereas the figure for female-headed households was 56 percent. The majority of these were made poor by divorce. Sixty-six percent of children living in single-parent families do so because of martial dissolution. Of these, some 27 percent are children whose parents never married. According to author/activist Michael Harrington:

> In point of fact, more than 50 percent of the women who receive Aid to Families with Dependent Children (AFDC) receive it for two years or less. Those women go on AFDC not

because they want to avoid working, but because a man dies, divorces them, or deserts them. Furthermore, they leave AFDC in two years or less by getting a job. And now we also know that the average family size of families on AFDC is two children. The concept that there is this huge population of lazy welfare mothers breeding children to make money off the state or of young women consciously deciding to have a baby in order to make money from the state simply does not wash. (Harrington, 1986, 6-7)

Divorce has created a national crisis for men, women, and children. The devastating economic impact for women and children is only the beginning. A myriad of physical and emotional problems have also arisen consequent to divorce. Without adequate national health care, women and children are suffering tremendously. Research has shown that divorce is associated with any number of physical and mental health problems in both men and women. Yet men get the worst of it.

Demographers at the University of Michigan's Institute for Social Research reviewed divorce statistics for three decades. Their 1984 study concluded that men suffer more psychological and emotional maladies after divorce than women. This includes everything from depression to admission to all types of hospitals (including psychiatric). Not surprisingly, men are often less anxious to divorce than women. Less than one-third of divorced men said they wanted a divorce, whereas between 55 to 66 percent of time it was the women who actively sought it. Women were also found to be happier than men subsequent to divorce (Faludi, 1991).

Still, divorced women were at greater risks than their (female) married counterparts to suffer from acute illness or depression. Understandably, the loss of husband and/or children, disruption of family life, and social and emotional isolation deprive women of essential intimate connections which nourish their well-being. For many men, work becomes a convenient surrogate for the loss of intimate connections. Men have long been socialized to define themselves through their work, so they often substitute professional achievement for emotional satisfaction.

CONCLUSIONS

Change can be frightening (especially when the changes are so deeply personal). Marital separation and divorce are likely to bring about changes in almost every aspect of the individual's life, from relatively minor alterations in the organization of time to major changes in the individual's interpersonal relationships. Subsequent to separation, an individual's work may continue to structure his or her day, as it did during the marriage, but the sense of loss and solitude will be a major adjustment. New rituals gradually replace old ones as the individual is forced to take responsibility for what had previously been the spouse's domain. Such disruption in one's basic rituals is deeply disturbing and disorienting. Add the grief of traumatic loss and it is readily understandable how emotionally damaging the rupture of a long-term intimate relationship can be. The problem is not that the new tasks are difficult so much as that they are out of keeping with what had been understood to be appropriate responsibilities, with what had been the self.

Suddenly single, individuals not only must alter fundamental patterns and rituals which held their life together, they must alter their basic sense of who and what they are. Certainly, they may still be parents, but now they are single parents. Recently divorced parents are forced to have continuing contact with their former spouse due to shared custody and/or visitation. This presents an often irresistible opportunity to express any residual anger as well as revisit many of the same dysfunctional communication patterns which caused the break-up in the first place. One of the more confounding ironies of uncoupling is that despite the fact that individuals may no longer love their ex-spouses, these persons are nonetheless important parts of their personal history. For a time, it may be necessary or even functional to deny their ex-partner's emotional significance. An important stage of the uncoupling process is distancing oneself from an ex-spouse in order to re-establish an independent, autonomous identity. However, working through these issues and achieving adequate closure on this important relationship potentially detoxifies the memories and submerged pain which can exist (repressed though intact) throughout the partners' respective lifetimes.

REFERENCES

Ahrons, C. and Rodgers, R. 1987. *Divorced families*. New York: Norton.

Bellah, R., Madsen, R., Sullivan, W., Swider, A., and Tipton, S. 1985. *Habits of the heart*. New York: Harper & Row.

Bowlby, J. 1980. Affectional bonds: Their nature and origin. In: R. Weiss, *Loneliness*. Cambridge, MA: MIT Press, 38-52.

Douglas, J. and Atwell, F. 1988. *Love, intimacy and sex*. Newbury Park, CA: Sage Publications, Inc.

Faludi, S. 1991. *Backlash*. New York: Doubleday.

Johnston, J. and Campbell, E. (1988). *Impasses of divorce*. New York: The Free Press.

Hartman, A. and Laird, J. 1983. *Family-centered social work practice*. New York: The Free Press.

Harrington, M. 1986. The current state of social justice in the U.S. In: Brown, P. (Ed.) *Social justice and the human services*. Kalamazoo, MI: 3-23.

Kressel, K. and Deutsch, M. 1981. Divorce therapy: An in-depth survey of therapists' views. In: Erickson, G. and Hogan, T. (Eds.) *Family therapy: An introduction to theory and technique*. Monterey, CA: Brooks/Cole.

Reissman, C. 1990. *Divorce talk*. New Brunswick, NJ: Rutgers University Press.

Weiss, R. 1975. *Marital separation*. New York: Basic Books.

Weiss, R. 1980. *Loneliness*. Cambridge, MA: MIT Press.

Chapter 9

Intimate Illusions

Americans are rapidly approaching a point where there is more change than continuity in their lives. What happens to individuals' sense of identity and relationships with others when they ultimately pass that point? No longer able to insulate themselves from the hammering impacts of massive change, the contemporary family (even in its varied forms) is finding it increasingly difficult to provide a "haven in a heartless world." As life moves faster, uncertainty and confusion grow. As social confusion increases, the individuals' need for certainty correspondingly increases. The more individual and psychic moorings are loosened, the greater the chances of dysfunctional coping and aberrant behavior.

Developmental anomalies occur in a desperate attempt to cope. The developmental deficits so apparent in most dysfunctional families socialize children to a host of deviant attitudes and behaviors. Arguably, many of these families are themselves victimized by poverty, racism, and an economic system that has created and maintained a permanent underclass. These are families who have been victimized over generations, who have been brutalized by a sense of despair, and who feel utterly powerless to do anything about it.

Unsurprisingly, many of these are families fraught with violence, drug abuse, child abuse, and any number of other maladaptations. The pervasive daily realities of frustration, powerlessness, and despair create ongoing pain and deep-seated anger. Typically, violent people have themselves been victimized by violence. In one sense, violence is their way of fighting back.

Sam Keen (1991) suggests that men are violent because of the systematic violence done to their bodies and spirits. Violence begets violence. Thus, they themselves later become the perpetrators. Male violence toward women is far less frequent than male violence against other males. For example, the FBI reported that of the estimated 21,500 murders in the United States in 1989, two-thirds of the victims were males. "What we have refused to acknowledge is that these outrages are a structural part of a warfare system that victimizes both men and women" (Keen, 1991:46).

If violence is the "fight response" to untenable circumstances, then drugs are the "flight response." Drugs represent an attempted escape from an unbearable social and emotional world. Like violence, drugs are also inherently destructive and may likewise be the direct result of living in a hostile world with little hope for the future.

Perhaps the reason that the recent anti-drug, anti-violence campaigns have been so unsuccessful is that they address the symptom and not the cause. Stanton Peele contends that "The response people have to a given drug is determined by their personalities, their cultural backgrounds, and their expectations and feelings about the drug. In other words, the sources of addiction lie within the person, not the drug" (1975:30).

WORK AS AN ADDICTION

Rooted loosely in the Protestant work ethic along with the prevailing cultural belief that those who work hard will get ahead, a great many Americans are spending more and more hours on their job. Workaholism is running rampant in fast track Silicon valley where many professionals routinely work 70 hours weekly. Not just in Silicon Valley, but all across the United States, increasing numbers of Americans are addicted to their jobs.

Schaef and Fassel (1988) take this analysis one step further by suggesting that like individual workers, organizational systems can also be addictive. Organizations seductively imply that if individuals live up to what the company expects, then they will be liked, accepted, and promoted. This promise of the "good life" keeps people actively focused on the future in the belief that even if things are not so good now, they will get better. Like the attitude of losers in a competitive contest, those who do not get ahead are seduced by the prospect, however unrealistic, of their someday becoming winners (i.e., successful). This effectively keeps them from disrupting the status quo which nonetheless continues to demand their best, but offers only empty promises in return. The future orientation of these promises also prevents individuals from looking at the present functioning in the system and seeing it for exactly what it is, addictive. People often feel stuck in organizations. Rather than acknowledging their feelings, they find it easier to look forward to the weekend, vacations, or retirement. By continuing to present employees with the promise, the organization remains central in their lives, in control of their present, and "hooks" them into an addictive relationship with the organization.

For many people, the workplace, job, and organization are the central foci of their lives. Because the organization has become so important and because people frequently become totally preoccupied with it, they begin to lose touch with other aspects of their lives and gradually give up what they know, feel, and believe.

The organization becomes an addictive substance when the employees get hooked on the promise of the mission and choose not to look at how the system is really operating. The organization also becomes an addictive substance when its actions are excused because it has a lofty mission. There is an inverse correlation between the loftiness of the mission and the congruence between stated and unstated goals. When this lack of congruence exists, it is more probable that the organization will enter into a rigid denial system with concomitant grandiosity (Schaef and Fassel, 1988).

In addictive organizations, the prohibition against revealing one's genuine self makes intimacy almost impossible. Addictive organizations try to counteract this reality by setting up planned encounters and workshops in which individuals tell one another what they like and dislike about the other and practice "communication skills." Yet regardless of how many communication workshops the organization sponsors, intimacy is not possible because the person and the system are part of the same disease. Maintaining this disease is dependent upon keeping out of touch personally and institutionally, and while a quick "communications fix" may bring temporary relief, it does not address the underlying problem (Schaef and Fassel, 1988).

INTERPERSONAL RELATIONSHIPS IN THE
ORGANIZATIONAL MILIEU

The Impacts of Competition

As Kohn (1986) explains, competition not only strains existing relationships, it actually prevents them from developing in the first place. Camaraderie and companionship, let alone intimacy, scarcely have a chance to take root among those who constantly compete outside the arenas of sport–namely, those who compete in their personal and professional relationships. For example, in the workplace, most people try to remain on reasonably cordial terms with their co-workers. Yet, among those who are highly competitive there is a certain guardedness, a part of the self held in reserve. Even when rivalries have momentarily subsided, one never knows who one will have to compete against next week.

The knowledge that competition damages self-esteem bodes poorly for effective interpersonal relationships. Winning is the premiere American cultural value and is inextricably intertwined with self-worth. Winners are lauded while losers are disdained.

In order to win, contestants must essentially deprive their adversaries of personalities, faces, and/or subjectivity. Some people do this more effectively than others, but this posture is demanded by the very structure of competition. While some may try to reassure themselves with talk about "friendly competition," the fact remains that seeing other persons as rivals and seeing them as partners or collaborators are fundamentally different mind sets. The fact that competition demands such depersonalization is a telling indictment indeed (Kohn, 1986).

Despite the widely accepted notion that winning is inherently virtuous, this assumption has two potentially damaging consequences: "(1) The losers' contempt for the winners is mixed with self-contempt, and (2) the losers will set about not to change the system (a move that would, in any case, be dismissed as 'sour grapes') but only to become a winner next time" (Kohn, 1986:42). As a result, no one presses for changing the game. Consequently, the contempt for losers begins to tear at the fabric of human relationships as well as reinforcing the competitive status quo.

The issues of trust and mistrust are also integral to the analysis of competition versus healthy intimate relationships. Love is based on trust, but to a lesser extent, so is one's ability to function in any social system. Even among mere acquaintances, one expects certain things from and is vulnerable to the other. However, setting up a system in which individuals must compete against one another creates a breeding ground for distrust. Why should one trust another if the former has every reason to see the latter fail? This distrust can spread rapidly and easily contaminate an entire group, system, or community. In an atmosphere of competition and mistrust, a vicious circle is generated. Disclosing oneself to others is a key element of psychological health and is also an important part of effective interpersonal relationships both personal and professional. In a zero-sum environment, whatever individuals disclose about themselves can and will be used against them. In a competitive culture, individuals necessarily objectify others; lose their ability for empathy; and become less inclined to help. As a result, a chasm opens up between people, leaving them distrustful, envious, and contemptuous (Kohn 1986).

Berman (1984) argues that based upon logical positivism, empiricism, and scientific method, many peoples' worldview is becoming entropic and eating itself up–thus destroying itself from within. He sees the scientific worldview as a non-participatory model based on making the self and the other and the world objects to be observed. Thus, the self is removed from participating with others and with the world in which we live. He further insists that people must develop some alternative to this objectifying process, so he proposes the development of what he terms a "participatory consciousness." At the institutional level, many organizations function under the myth of objectivity–a myth that seems to be inherited from the scientific worldview. Along with this belief in the supposed superiority of objectivity is the tendency to worship the logical and rational. The illusion of control also undergirds this worldview and falsely presumes that persons are no longer participants in their own experience or in the world around them. Such illusion and concomitant detachment are frequently found in organizations (Schaef and Fassel, 1988). Increasingly, people are estranged from themselves, their co-workers, and the world at large.

THERAPY AT WORK?

The relevance of therapy is enhanced by the fit of the therapeutic attitude of self-realization and empathic communication to the increasingly interpersonal nature of the work one does. Co-workers give each other therapy to cement teamwork. People who meet only on the job make use of intimacy as a method to become more effective as a working "unit." Their sensitive and caring conversation is not a break from the job, it's a part of the job. Conversely, therapy's fee-for-service exchange and its strict procedural regulation (in which being a few minutes early or late, missing appointments, or forgetting payments are deemed significant) tie it into the bureaucratic and economic structure of society. Therapy's emphasis on personal autonomy presupposes institutional conformity. The modern self's expressive freedom goes hand-in-hand with the modern world's instrumental control (Bellah et al., 1985).

Shames (1985) suggests that the career environment in the eighties fostered and even required disturbed interpersonal attitudes and relationships. Those attitudes included hyper-competitiveness, habitual mistrust of one's colleagues, and a willingness to suspend or even defy personal values in favor of the demands of the organization. Those were the demons that needed to be dealt with in the name of success, eighties style, and dealing with them took its toll. The side effects of "successful" adjustments included feelings of entrapment, guilt, and self-betrayal, which left the person feeling out of kilter, off-balance, and unfulfilled, despite his or her success.

According to Bellah et al. (1985) the therapeutic attitude shapes itself along the contours of both entrepreneurial and corporate work. In larger bureaucratic settings, the therapeutic sensibility strives to humanize the corporation and thus make it more productive.

However, unlike dilettantes who succeed by exploiting the language of therapy without the accompanying training and expertise, therapists offer a very different kind of substantive relationship. They promise self-fulfillment and a sense of self-worth to basically benign people in a well-coordinated, yet often lonely, social world (Bellah et al., 1985). In truth, therapists do not actually cure or heal anybody per se. This is not to suggest that psychotherapy is not useful, for indeed it can potentially prove exceedingly helpful and growth-inducing. But any gains derived from psychotherapy are attributable to the client's hard work, the relationship with the therapist, and the interactive process between the two within the context of the client's family and larger social, cultural, and institutional environment. Thus, both Bellah's and Kopp's characterization of the therapist as healer or guru is somewhat misguided. Nevertheless, what is useful about their arguments revolves around the individual's existential search for meaning in an uncertain world.

Increasingly, the boundaries between private and public life are blurring. By emphasizing interpersonal process as well as task completion, work has become a much more personal endeavor. And with Americans spending more and more time on the job, and diverting more and more energy into their careers, it is not surprising that nowadays, many of one's most significant interpersonal relationships are with co-workers. The vast proliferation of single working mothers and the dramatic rise of two-career families have altered the very nature of family life and family relationships.

Changing gender roles also contribute to the changing interpersonal flavor of today's organizational environment. Gilligan (1982) suggests that female development and socialization stresses forming and sustaining mutually satisfying interpersonal relationships and decision-making by consensus. Males more frequently adopt a narrower focus on task completion within the context of a hierarchical authority structure. While the specific origins of these differences are debatable, it is clear that many men and women have sharply contrasting managerial, decision-making, and interpersonal styles in the workplace. And as more women enter the business and professional spheres and have made inroads into management and administration, the rules of the game are beginning to shift.

People may search for friendship at work, free of manipulation, or they may play their work roles tongue-in-cheek, making tradeoffs there for the sake of authenticity in their personal lives. Such juggling of roles and relationships can leave them with the feeling that who they really are lies beyond any of these roles. Bellah et al. (1985) suggest that therapy helps individuals translate their social experience into personal meanings, which then reshape subsequent social experience. However, in its attempt to reunify the self, the therapeutic attitude distances people from particular social roles, relationships, and practices; and from their attendant measures of authority, duty, and virtue.

Therapy itself is a tightly regulated and carefully balanced relationship. If applied to social interactions it confuses a professional contracted relationship with real emotional intimacy. The apparent contradiction contained in this ostensibly intimate relationship is that it is simultaneously a business and professional relationship which is distinctly one-sided. While clients are encouraged to move beyond their normal defenses and reveal their innermost feelings, therapists, by and large, reveal little or nothing about themselves. As Bellah et al. (1985) point out, even with its genuine emotional content, closeness, and honesty of communication, the therapeutic relationship is peculiarly distanced, circumscribed, and asymmetrical. Most of the time, one person talks while the other listens. The therapeutic relationship is tightly regulated by business as well as professional protocols that set fees, delimit fifty-minute hours, and schedule meetings while precluding such mundane social conventions as eating lunch together.

The problem posed by therapy is not that intimacy is tyrannically taking over too much of public life. It is that the purely contractual structure of the economic and bureaucratic world is becoming an ideological model for personal life (Bellah et al. 1985).

Today, the business of psychotherapy has splintered into countless philosophical and therapeutic offshoots. Increasingly, clients have begun to apply a consumer mentality to the relative efficacy of the therapeutic process. Scores of books have emerged in recent years that advise and counsel wary consumers against the dangers of charlatanism and the need to protect oneself from "therapeutic exploitation." According to Barker (1983), psychotherapy is now being offered by a broad and sometimes dubious array of providers ranging from highly skilled professionals to spiritualists who specialize in the occult or metaphysical. Thus, unwitting clients may potentially end up with anyone from a caring and responsible professional to a malevolent charlatan.

FALSE FRIENDS

One particularly troubling manifestation of an attempt at therapeutic sensibility is evident in the proliferation of talk show programs that are now playing the role of therapist for the everyday viewer. Oprah, Donahue, and Geraldo are now pandering to this nation's insatiable appetite for voyeuristically peering into the intimate lives of others as recounted by the actual participants themselves. Meanwhile, the hosts, along with one or two invited experts, cast themselves in the role of TV therapists, seeking to promote healing, educate the general public, and put on a great show all in 60 minutes minus commercials.

Due in part to TV's unparalleled ability to stupefy, Americans are substituting television personalities for real-life personalities. It is much easier to project valued qualities onto one's favorite celebrities than having to deal with the vagaries of real-life relationships. The celebrity personas are portrayed in ways that make them remarkably consistent and predictable. They never argue or talk back unexpectedly. If we don't like what they are saying, we can either switch them off or turn the channel. And yet, this constant relationship-building with fantasy figures ultimately interferes with one's interpersonal skills in real life. Relating to real people requires a much different style of communication, listening, empathy, and interaction. Americans' relationships with celebrities is safely circumscribed with limited emotional risk for both parties. Obviously, the celebrity typically doesn't even know that the fan exists as a distinct and recognizable person per se. Therefore, there is no actual relationship–except in the broadest, most general sense. By definition, celebrities require a cadre of loyal fans who admire or adore their performance. Unfortunately, these same celebrities are sometimes seduced into believing that such adulation actually has something to do with them personally rather than the person or role they represent. They begin believing their own press releases and fan mail. On the other hand, the viewers believe that they are in total control of the relationship. One case in point occurred recently when the viewers of The Home Shopping Network were personally upset about the absence of a favorite host who was unexpectedly hospitalized. Cards and letters of sympathy literally poured in. No doubt the celebrity was touched by this emotional outpouring even though he did not personally know any of his fans. At that point, the fantasy created by television had begun to become real for him. His fans had touched him at last. And when he returned and gratefully acknowledged his fans' good wishes, he expressed his heartfelt gratitude at their "genuine concern" for his well-being (Schickel, 1985).

Part of television's power is derived from its ability to create the illusion of intimacy. It appears to break down the barriers that formerly existed between the well-known and the unknown. It brings famous personalities into one's living room in physically manageable size. Unlike a stage, lecture hall, or movie theater, television deliberately make the actors appear real. Docu-dramas such as "Cops" and "America's Most Wanted" thrive on what passes for uncontrived realism. These programs actually encourage viewer participation by repeatedly flashing an "800" number on the screen so that the audience can actively participate in the hunt.

Among the seemingly endless stream of interview programs, the close-ups, and the lack of a realistic, individuated setting are precisely what make their generic content more believable. Since these are not attached to any recognizable place, viewers are able to relocate them anywhere that suits the purpose of their fantasies.

One of the most striking "intimate illusions" in the 1990s concerns the relationships between celebrities and their fans. This relationship is based solely on an illusion of intimacy which has been made possible by a society that has elevated celebrities to the status of cultural heroes. This pseudo-relationship is insidiously subliminal in its workings. It manages to nullify "the traditional etiquette that formerly governed not merely relationships between the powerful and the powerless, the known and the unknown, but, at the simplest level, the politeness that formerly pertained between strangers" (Schickel, 1985:4).

Television brings these people directly into one's own living room or bedroom, seducing viewers into believing that they know these celebrities personally, much like an old friend. As Schickel (1985:4) explains, "To a greater or lesser degree, we have internalized them, unconsciously made them a part of our consciousness, just as if they were, in fact, friends."

Over a period of time, mavens are able to learn the celebrities' faces, habits, and idiosyncracies as if they were close friends or relatives. The secret thoughts and emotions performers appear to reveal through their unconscious gestures are often contrived informality for the very sake of ingratiating them to the audience.

Many fans refer to talk show hosts who relieve the isolation and boredom of their days on a casual, first-name basis–Phil, Oprah, and/or Geraldo. After a time, fans can turn into devotees who follow the lurid details (real or imagined) of their favorite celebrities' lives on the pages of those tabloids found mainly at the check-out lines in the local supermarket. Reading these is a way of keeping up with and staying close to their heroes while simultaneously satisfying their own salacious curiosity. It also enables fans to bask in the reflected glory and notoriety of their favorite stars. Naturally, these sensationalized and often outrageous portrayals highlight, satirize, and invent the most embarrassing and degrading aspects of the celebrities' private lives. This effectively serves to knock celebrities off their pedestal and say to the reader, "See, your life isn't all that bad, look what happened to so-and-so" (Schickel, 1985). These oft-contrived character defamations also serve to further minimize the distance readers perceive between their lives and the glamorous lives of their favorite stars. At another level, this mindless attachment and devotion lends meaning and a vicarious sense of fulfillment to the reader's otherwise unglamorous life.

Such gossip also heightens one's sense of false intimacy with celebrated people. Moreover, it further blurs the line between fantasy and reality, which is an essential distinction if individuals are to maintain their social and psychological bearings.

In most of their private and professional dealings with people that they don't actually know, most mature adults retain some sense of decorum and social distance which protects both themselves and the stranger from intrusion. But such shyness is often rendered curiously inoperative when one is dealing with celebrities.

When inadvertently confronted by the rich and famous in a restaurant or other public place, many people stare, but do not actually approach the celebrity. Others, however, walk right up and thoughtlessly invade the celebrity's privacy. For this latter group, some part of them feels that they have been in intimate contact with the well-known individual for years. Secrets, hopes, and dreams have not exactly been shared with the celebrity, but are somehow bound up in them. Another part of the approaching stranger's mind is aware that they are totally unknown to the celebrity. And they unconsciously resent that unyielding fact (Schickel, 1985).

These false intimacies have reached unprecedented proportions in recent years. Not only have these effects reached celebrity stalkers like John Hinkley, Jr., but average middle-class people as well. These celebrities have become an important part of many Americans' social and emotional worlds.

It is growing increasingly clear that we now live in an age rife with such falsities and self-creations. This projective identification has historically been deemed harmless, but when taken to extremes can turn into a real nightmare for celebrities trying to live some semblance of a "normal life." When Connie Chung recently asked Michael Jordan what he would do if he could do something and not be immediately recognized, Jordan said that he would take his children to an amusement park because at present he could not do this without subjecting his family to his fans' overwhelming demands.

There is another form of false intimacy that involves the ordinarily powerless person "recasting life itself as a film and placing himself in the role of director, violently taking charge of formless existence and shaping it to his liking–every man his own auteur, the multi-talented director-writer-star of his own drama" (Schickel, 1985:7).

According to Schickel (1985), murder is the most intimate of acts, which–like hijacking or kidnapping–involves a forced intimacy between perpetrator and victim. Again there is a desperate yet terrible clutching at connection, a connection that the media involvement helps such deranged zealots maintain–not only between themselves and their victims, but between themselves and a previously indifferent world.

Politics has always been a performance and attracts people whose egos ache for instant gratification and the balm of immediate applause. Until recently, there was a separation between the public and the private politician, with the assumption that what the politician did in private was pretty much his/her own business, so long as it did not directly affect the ability to do the job. Naturally, word leaked out (sometimes intentionally) about a president's personal habits and preferences. Today, however, the personal lives of politicians are generally considered public domain by reporters and photographers alike.

Like politicians, today's rock groups no longer perform in intimate surroundings. Rock and roll is big business and playing to a stadium of 60,000 screaming fans is not only more narcissistically rewarding, it simply makes more money from the enormous gate receipts. For the privilege of seeing their idols live, passionate fans may wait in line all night to obtain good seats and then pay handsomely for these. However, once at the concert it is virtually impossible to actually come close to their idols. The sound is deafening as well as distancing. Performer and audience are separated by a virtual wall of noise. Ironically, whatever drugs are brought into the stadium by the crowd also have a distancing effect. So in the end there is proximity, but no intimacy (Schickel, 1985). Ultimately, these occasions appear perversely designed to frustrate the very emotional connection that their anticipation seems to promise. No wonder these encounters sometimes turn deadly.

These distorted fantasy relationships are passing for intimacy in the 1990s. Americans often imagine that they know someone intimately just because they have watched them on TV for years. Meanwhile, they may not even know how to carry on an intimate conversation with their spouses.

People's interpersonal relationships, as well as their expectations of what relationships should be, are migrating further and further from reality. Many Americans have gotten to the point where they are expecting their spouses and significant others to behave and communicate just like their celebrity favorites (or at least their projected image of what they are). And when "her" husband does not display Phil Donahue's sensitivity, she is disappointed. And when "his" wife doesn't seduce him the way he imagines Susan Lucci would, he is disappointed. Television and other media continue to shape America's images of ideal partners and intimate relationships. It has now become a case of life imitating what passes for art. Is it any wonder that intimate relationships in this country are in deep trouble?

THE DEATH OF INTIMACY?

Due to the increasingly impersonal nature of American society, it has become vastly more difficult to initiate and sustain "authentic" intimate relationships. Instead, modern life is characterized by a series of "apparent relationships" borne of convenience and lacking in substance. This is not to suggest that physical intimacy is less prevalent. On the contrary, due perhaps to the scarcity of emotional intimacy, the incidence of sexual contact with any number or partners (despite the threat of AIDS) appears to be increasing.

For many Americans, the average number of intimate emotional relationships is rapidly approaching zero. Individuals are losing their individual and collective abilities to effectively initiate and sustain emotionally satisfying relationships with others and are consequently existing in a state of "relational depravation," in which basic human needs such as physical and emotional intimacy, personal affirmation, and long-term commitment are conspicuously absent. Emotional intimacy has become one of the most elusive commodities in contemporary American life.

Due to the increasing depersonalization of social interaction, Americans are confronted daily with a parade of virtual strangers with whom they work, lunch, socialize, and live. The unfortunate casualty of their current lifestyle is the absence of authentic emotional contact. Despite the fact that Americans are bombarded with alluring images from the media about what intimacy should be, there is an alarming paucity of emotionally satisfying relationships in most of their lives irrespective of social class, education, or occupation. People are left with a vague sense of longing for authentic emotional experience rather than superficial titillation. Their senses have been dulled by the kaleidoscope of external stimuli without an accompanying sense of real human connection (almost like a series of interesting though unrelated vignettes). They hunger for "real experience" and lap it up as fast as it is manufactured by the media and others.

It is striking to note how much interpersonal values and relationships have changed during the last three decades. Is it possible that the symbolic slaying of the sixties by the neo-conservative establishment ended up throwing out the baby with the bath water? Embodied within that naive sixties idealism was a collective hope and a vision for a different kind of relatedness, a more humane world characterized by peace and justice rather than "the art of the deal" and "instant celebrity." Has America sacrificed its essential sense of humanity and connectedness?

Eighty percent of Americans now live in cities or metropolitan areas. Over the years, these cities have deteriorated from neighborhoods in which people shared a common sense of purpose and identification to a splintered, chaotic world in which drugs and violence rule. How is meaningful relatedness possible in such an environment? No single individual holds the magic answer to this extraordinarily complex problem. However, it can be surmised that since the problem is systemic, the solution must likewise be systemic.

This country will not solve its struggle for intimacy so long as contemporary urban life continues as an essentially anonymous existence sorely lacking in quality of life and common human decency. Urban America has become a toxic environment where people no longer know how to live together. A solution is not possible so long as narcissistic individualism supersedes Americans' commitment to the collective good. What many fail to realize is that these economic, cultural, military, and interpersonal relationships are inextricably interwoven. Unless the manner in which we communicate, respect, and collaborate is altered substantially on both the interpersonal and global levels, the U.S. will be left out of the new world order which has absolutely no patience for American greed or ethnocentrism.

In short, Americans must rediscover their essential humanity and sense of justice. Rather than being irrelevant to it, global citizenry and global responsibility have profound personal, interpersonal, and political implications. Ultimately, a dramatic shift in America's consciousness about its place and role in this world can potentially begin to alter both the context and style of relating both interpersonally and internationally and begin to move us forward toward creating a better world for ourselves and the generations who will follow.

REFERENCES

Barker, R. L. 1983. Supply side economics in private psychotherapy practice: Some ominous and encouraging trends. *Psychotherapy in Private Practice,* 1, Spring, 71-81.

Bellah, R., Madsen, R., Sullivan, W., Swidler, A., and Tipton, S. 1985. *Habits of the heart.* New York: Harper & Row.

Berman, M. 1984. *The reenchantment of the world.* New York: Bantam.

Gilligan, C. 1982. *In a different voice.* Cambridge, MA: Harvard University Press.

Keen, S. 1991. *Fire in the belly.* New York: Bantam Books.

Kohn, A. 1986. *No contest.* Boston: Houghton-Mifflin Co.

Kopp, S. 1968. *If you meet the Buddha on the road, kill him.* New York: Bantam Books.

Peele, S. 1975. *Love and addiction.* New York: Taplinger Publishing Co.

Schaef, A. and Fassel, D. 1988. *The addictive organization.* New York: Harper Collins.

Schickel, R. 1985. *Intimate strangers.* New York: Doubleday.

Shames, L. 1985. *The hunger for more.* New York: Random House.

Index